www.guentherbischofberger.com

Published by Guenther Bischofberger
ISBN 978-9-083008-32-5
2nd edition

A text. is content.
But whatever we pro-vide becomes its con-text

Caiaphas

In the far distance the skies over the black-brown mountain ranges were slowly turning from a dark purple to a bright red. They had travelled for hours, leaving in the middle of this moonless night like a thief breaking into a house - except instead of entering one, they were leaving theirs for this journey to an unknown location they had never even heard of.

'Travel alone or in pairs, but never more than two!' one of the instructions had been - from whom it all came they had no idea, but it was said to be of the utmost urgency. 'The kingdom is at risk and about to be destroyed! Your immediate presence is required and of vital importance; do not be late and most certainly don't be absent - God himself will judge all your actions on this very day'.

They could see others making their way towards the cave, and entered themselves when the first rays of dawn broke through the clouds: right on time. The small cave opening hid a grand hall with an enormously high ceiling where three or even four could have stood on top of one another. Lit by flaming torches in the back of the room, food and drinks were set on a makeshift table made of two wooden planks, flanked by travel chairs - and about a dozen people, with in their midst Annas the High Priest. Sitting next to him was a figure easily recognised; dressed in his usual crimson double-layered cloak that somehow straightened his sagging shoulders: Caiaphas, his ill-tempered son-in-law

'Hurry', Annas spoke, and waited before continuing until all were seated. 'On this Sabbath, let's break fast' and he lifted up his cup of wine, ignoring some of the startled looks, and took a sip. 'Today is a day that marks a change in times, for grave and troubling days lie ahead.'

He looked around at the men present. 'Each of you here has been called because you are highly respected and valued leaders of our community who have shown great commitment to our ways. There is no time to waste: you all have heard the treacherous words of this false prophet Jesus, mocking us and the holy words of our Lord.

"If heaven is in the sky then birds precede us!" he claims, "Praying is lying!" he dares to say. "Become like children and you will enter the kingdom!" and more of such delusional nonsense. We Pharisees would withhold knowledge from our flock, and wouldn't know how to use said knowledge - lies, of course; foul and utter blasphemy it all is.

But this blasphemy and these lies are spreading like a disease, and even from as far as Capernaum we hear rumours of Temple visits dropping and people gathering in houses to discuss matters of religion. Last week a man questioned me about fasting. Me! The High Priest of Israel himself! It will only be a matter of time before such arrogance and disobedience will manifest itself in public, worse, it might even happen in our holy Temple itself - God forbid.'

He leaned forward, resting his hands on the table. 'We have searched high and low for this Jesus, yet while everyone seems to have seen him everywhere he is nowhere to be found; and people claiming to have seen him never know where he'll show up next. We must stop these heathens, and let me assure you that I have abundant funds at our disposal, a fair part of which has been bestowed upon us by my beloved son-in-law, Caiaphas'. He laid his right hand on Caiaphas' shoulder, who rose and spoke:

'Israel is at risk here, make no mistake. Our most holy and sacred rites are being undermined and sabotaged as we speak, making the filthy Romans little more than a nuisance compared to this very plague. Our laws demand stoning to death - but we must find this Jesus first. So tell us your ideas', and he sat down and tore off a piece of bread.

The corpulent man in front of him spoke, seemingly breathless - Matthias, the city's treasurer. 'Well spoken indeed, valued Caiaphas. I have set a steep price on information about his whereabouts and spread word among the servants, who seem particularly fond of him. Yet so far all they've come up with is secondary sightings; friends of acquaintances and such. Galilee appears a place frequently mentioned and I have sent spies there - also to no avail. All we can do is wait'.

The man on my left stood up, taller than any man in the room. 'I've also heard of this Jesus, and attended meetings about his teachings - accidentally, but I must admit that his words and ways are quite different from everything we're used to. Rather refreshing really, and not what one would expect'. 'Don't get me wrong', another responded, 'but what if he is the Messiah? Every prophecy tells us of hardship and destruction before his coming, and he is not here to preach the same that we have been hearing for so long'.

'What?! Are you siding with him, this traitor? What does that make you then?!' Annas interrupted Caiaphas, saying 'Let's not rush to conclusions; I understand everybody's interest here. I must agree with Cephas that this enemy is not to be taken lightly at all: it is underestimating him that has brought us here, and he must be brought to trial and questioned. Continue'.

Then the man next to me spoke again, and all eyes turned to him: 'But it's just a story! Told by people to other people. Written down by a certain Thomas, some say - but no one knows him either, he's like this Jesus in that way - they're certainly not from around here, and might not even exist as far as we know. How do you fight an enemy that doesn't exist? An enemy that isn't alive?'

A thunderous crash made them all turn, and some fell off their seats. Caiaphas had slammed his fist down on the table with so much force that it broke, sending dishes and cups in all directions. Seemingly unaware of this he stood up, his face a deep red with the veins on his forehead pulsing purple. Saliva spat at the rubble at his feet and those around him, as he pointed his finger at the man and roared:

'So then bring him to life! And then we will kill him!!!'

The Jesus of Thomas: feverously anti-religious

...and so it happened...

Absurd idea? Yes. Preposterous? Maybe. But I'll work my way through the four gospels comparing all their versions of logia from the Gospel of Thomas and show their gradual transformations, their incorporation into the story that the Church tells about their Jesus, and in the end you might be just as convinced as I am today that this is exactly what happened.

There never was a Jesus, the Gospel of Thomas was certainly not written from any Christian point of view, and it's not Gnostic either - but stands on its very own, and brought about a revolution in the religious world of the first century CE.

From a textual point of view, it is evident that the Gospel of Thomas was first and that Mark struggled to write and wrap his story around him, trying hard to find an angle in his creation of the Jesus of the Church. It is also evident from a textual point of view that next Luke and then Matthew came, corrected most of Mark's errors, supplemented his story, and more than doubled the logia that Mark copied from Thomas - while slapping on prophecies fulfilled when and where they could by the dozens. Then John topped it off and added a handful more logia - of the cryptic and mystic kind - while presenting a highly remarkable angle on Judas, Thomas, and Caiaphas

The history of the Gospel of Thomas

What is this Gospel of Thomas?

In 1896 an ancient garbage dump was excavated at Oxyrhynchus, the location of an ancient Egyptian city, and a large number of Greek papyrus fragments was found: the Oxyrhynchus Papyri, one fragment being from the Gospel of Thomas containing 7 logia. In 1903 two more of those were found, and these three fragments together formed the first pieces of the Gospel of Thomas and are known as P. Oxy 1, 654 and 655.

Where a mere 10% of Oxyrhynchus contained literary documents (the remainder being of every other kind such as bills, certificates and income tax forms: most of it was "paper" trash from government offices), in 1945 a 6-foot sealed jar was excavated at Nag Hammadi, also in Egypt, containing 52 spiritual and religious documents. One of those was a complete version of the Gospel of Thomas - and it was only then that the Oxyrhynchus fragments could be attributed to it, and became recognised as fragments of the Gospel of Thomas.

With the Nag Hammadi manuscript itself dating back to the 3rd or 4th century, a date as early as the 1st or 2nd century has been proposed for the lost Greek originals of Thomas - the papyri from Egypt where all written in Coptic, an Egyptian language that came into existence in the first century. While we're at it, the majority view on the canonical gospels holds that those were written in the 2nd half of the 1st century.

With regards to the nature and origin of the Gospel of Thomas, it has most often become labelled as a Gnostic text, largely due to its being part of the Nag Hammadi collection which contained mostly Gnostic and / or early Christian writings, which were not deemed part of the New Testament - "fictions of heretics" is what the Church labelled them. Gnosticism, in (very) short, is a religious idea that God created spirit beings, one of which is the Demiurge who created this physical world. Gnosticism has a firm base in Platonism and regards matter as evil and spirit as good - their key to liberation is gnosis: knowledge.

The Gospel of Thomas became labelled as such with its discovery at Nag Hammadi and has made a huge impact among biblical scholars ever since. For example, Amazon.com has over 2,000 (that's their maximum number of search results) books on the gospel of Thomas, academia.edu contains 70,000 papers on the gospel of Thomas. I'll refer to it as the text of Thomas

As stories go, some must have gotten the whole Tao-like thinking of Thomas' Jesus, the non-dualistic approach and focus, completely devoid of religion. Tao? Isn't Jesus all about Christianity? Loving your neighbour, repenting, being meek? No - most certainly not, Thomas' Jesus is spiritual at best but most definitely not religious. What he teaches is about perception and insight: we have become separated from ourselves in a world that we view but not perceive; it's a play consisting of many stages upon which we are its actors; playing different parts on every single occasion, reading different scripts, wearing different costumes, each and every time:

(21) Mary said to Jesus, 'Whom are your disciples like?' He said, 'They are like children who have settled in a field which is not theirs. When the owners of the field come, they will say, 'Let us have back our field.' They (will) undress in their presence in order to let them have back their field and to give it back to them. (...)'
(36) Jesus said, 'Do not be concerned from morning until evening and from evening until morning about what you will wear.'
(37) '(...) Jesus said, 'When you disrobe without being ashamed and take up your garments and place them under your feet like little children and tread on them, then will you see the son of the living one, and you will not be afraid'
(78) Jesus said, 'Why have you come out into the desert? To see a reed shaken by the wind? And to see a man clothed in fine garments like your kings and your great men? Upon them are the fine garments, and they are unable to discern the truth.'

Clothes and children. No one comes into this world without a destiny, without a few sets of clothes already made or bought, washed and ready and waiting for you. Many people had many plans with you before you were born, or maybe even before you were conceived. If you want to know someone's deepest dreams and desires, look at how they dress their infants.

Your future grandmother perhaps wished to become a grandmother, probably longing for a girl. Her husband maybe wanted to become a grandfather, probably longing for a girl as well. Or a boy - probably a boy, right? But who knows.

Your father had plans with you, wanting a son he could go fishing with in the morning. Your mother wanted a girl that could become the ballet dancer she never became - a way too large part of children's destinies is having them proxy out the unfulfilled wishes or failed grand attempts of their parents.

Your sister wanted a baby sister to play with, your brother wanted a baby girl to play with too, not liking the idea of a rival boy getting all or most of the attention.

All these people, they all had plans with you, even before they knew you. All of them had images in mind of how you would take shape - in their eyes.

All of them had identities in mind for you. I-dentities? They should be called them-dentities, images of others, projections by them, which you were about to fulfil; even before you were born. Because a large part of your destiny, like it or not, is playing out other people's wishes: you wear the clothes that other people "lay on your bed for you to wear" and your entire life you are playing in a field that's theirs but not yours. You wear different "clothes" on every occasion and on some occasion you try even harder: you wear your best set of clothes, your finest garments - and those are the occasions on which you spend all attention to others and none to yourself. Disrobe! Don't be ashamed - trample and trash all your sets of clothes and allow for yourself to shine on the scene(s)

So you dress up when you go church. Dress down when you go to see your friends. Cheer up for that party you're about to enter. Chill out for that fishing trip.

And you speak up in front of the teacher. Speak "down" in front of uncle Steven, who gets angry so quickly. Listen up when you're in the front row, listen "down" when you're at the very back.

At some point you take over the programming done by others, and become fully autonomous in programming yourself according to the rules you've been taught with. Thus, the least tainted form of man and woman is a child. A newborn. A babe. A blank slate:

(50) Jesus said, 'If they say to you, 'Where did you come from?', say to them, 'We came from the light, the place where the light came into being on its own accord and established itself and became manifest through their image.' If they say to you, 'Is it you?', say, 'We are its children, we are the elect of the living father.' (...)'

(79) (...) 'For there will be days when you will say, 'Blessed are the womb which has not conceived and the breasts which have not given milk.''

(19) Jesus said, 'Blessed is he who came into being before he came into being. (...)'

(22) Jesus saw infants being suckled. He said to his disciples, 'These infants being suckled are like those who enter the kingdom.' (...)'

(46) Jesus said, 'Among those born of women, from Adam until John the Baptist, there is no one so superior to John the Baptist that his eyes should not be lowered (before him). Yet I have said, whichever one of you comes to be a child will be acquainted with the kingdom and will become superior to John.'

Newborns are still whole, one - one with themselves, their environment, all. Oneness is what gets lost in life, where and when you come into being, get taught duality; and then the one becomes two: man and woman, male and female. Good and bad. Left and right. Body and soul. First and last, high and low, heaven and hell. Be(come) like a child, and the two will be made one again:

(4) Jesus said, 'The man old in days will not hesitate to ask a small child seven days old about the place of life, and he will live. For

many who are first will become last, and they will become one and the same.'

(11) Jesus said, 'This heaven will pass away, and the one above it will pass away. The dead are not alive, and the living will not die. In the days when you consumed what is dead, you made it what is alive. When you come to dwell in the light, what will you do? On the day when you were one you became two. But when you become two, what will you do?'

(47) Jesus said, 'It is impossible for a man to mount two horses or to stretch two bows. And it is impossible for a servant to serve two masters; otherwise, he will honor the one and treat the other contemptuously. No man drinks old wine and immediately desires to drink new wine. And new wine is not put into old wineskins, lest they burst; nor is old wine put into a new wineskin, lest it spoil it. An old patch is not sewn onto a new garment, because a tear would result.'

(89) Jesus said, 'Why do you wash the outside of the cup? Do you not realize that he who made the inside is the same one who made the outside?'

(106) Jesus said, 'When you make the two one, you will become the sons of man, and when you say, 'Mountain, move away,' it will move away.'

Make. The. Two. One!
Duality. If anything, it's the fundamental and most important doctrine of religion. Of anything Western really; philosophy has followed the same thought since centuries BCE. Egypt, Mesopotamia, Greece: religion and philosophy alike, most if not everything was dualistic. Even Gnosticism was dualistic to the bone. Thomas disagrees: we are all one. We are born as one, then we identify ourselves and separation occurs; duality kicks in and we become two. Only if we make the two one again do we get back to the starting point and then we'll leave the darkness, and live in the light:

(24) (...) There is light within a man of light, and he lights up the

whole world. If he does not shine, he is darkness."
(61) (...) "I am he who exists from the undivided. I was given some
of the things of my father." [...] "I am your disciple." [...] "Therefore
I say, if he is destroyed, he will be filled with light, but if he is
divided, he will be filled with darkness."

How has this come to be? Thomas has no text on that. Who keeps
this dualism in place? The Pharisees do, among others by
withholding knowledge. A clear, unveiled attack. They're the
proponents of the most important religion at that time in that
place, and as such get the full load. Thomas accuses them of
deliberately hiding the truth; they're not wholly ignorant of the
road to happiness, but are carefully disguising it. Impotent to walk it
themselves they have created a phantasm to control people and
lead them astray:

(3) Jesus said, 'If those who lead you say to you, 'See, the kingdom is
in the sky,' then the birds of the sky will precede you. If they say to
you, 'It is in the sea,' then the fish will precede you. Rather, the
kingdom is inside of you, and it is outside of you. (...)'
(6) His disciples questioned him and said to him, 'Do you want us to
fast? How shall we pray? Shall we give alms? What diet shall we
observe?' Jesus said, 'Do not tell lies, and do not do what you hate,
for all things are plain in the sight of heaven. (...)'
(14) Jesus said to them, 'If you fast, you will give rise to sin for
yourselves; and if you pray, you will be condemned; and if you give
alms, you will do harm to your spirits. When you go into any land
and walk about in the districts, if they receive you, eat what they
will set before you, and heal the sick among them. For what goes
into your mouth will not defile you, but that which issues from your
mouth - it is that which will defile you.'
(39) Jesus said, 'The Pharisees and the scribes have taken the keys
of knowledge (gnosis) and hidden them. They themselves have not
entered, nor have they allowed to enter those who wish to. (...)'
(104) They said to Jesus, 'Come, let us pray today and let us fast.'
Jesus said, 'What is the sin that I have committed, or wherein have I

been defeated? (...)'

And so on, and so forth. It is a continuous bashing of the Judaic theatre at that time, ridiculing its concepts, its rituals, the every-day habits of the common Jew. Thomas certainly was well aware of Judaism and its customs, referencing the Tanakh (the Hebrew bible, of which the Church shuffled around most books and labelled the result 'Old Testament', which as such is the legitimisation of their 'New Testament') in his logia.
Thomas tears down piece by piece the concept of heaven in itself, the concept of punishing yourself in order to deserve it, and the teacher-student paradigm in general, with extreme focus on the Judaic teachers:

(34) Jesus said, 'If a blind man leads a blind man, they will both fall into a pit.'
(43) (...) 'You do not realize who I am from what I say to you, but you have become like the Jews, for they (either) love the tree and hate its fruit (or) love the fruit and hate the tree.'
(102) Jesus said, 'Woe to the Pharisees, for they are like a dog sleeping in the manger of oxen, for neither does he eat nor does he let the oxen eat.'

Lies, is what they teach. Damned lies. The Jesus of Thomas despises their rules and regulations, meant to keep you busy and test your obedience:

(53) His disciples said to him, 'Is circumcision beneficial or not?' He said to them, 'If it were beneficial, their father would beget them already circumcised from their mother. Rather, the true circumcision in spirit has become completely profitable.'

With that single sharp one-liner, Thomas strikes at the entire religious system: priests and Pharisees numb you with their rules and laws, they kill your spirit, dulling that very sharp edge it has and should have - they are continuously circumcising your spirit indeed.

And they build and uphold their system of control with that, keeping people as cattle.

Spiritually dead, is what he calls them. That is what happens when you stay ignorant, let yourself be lulled into sleep by religious fanatics, orthodox rules, but also by everyday life, career, motherhood and fatherhood and every other paved road that's laid out for you and which you are mindlessly treading on, without ever having given it any real thought. If only you were to open your eyes and see (the world for what it really is), you'd witness death all around you. Spiritually dead people:

(56) Jesus said, 'Whoever has come to understand the world has found (only) a corpse, and whoever has found a corpse is superior to the world.'

(60) [they saw] a Samaritan carrying a lamb on his way to Judea. He said to his disciples, 'That man is round about the lamb.' They said to him, 'So that he may kill it and eat it.' He said to them, 'While it is alive, he will not eat it, but only when he has killed it and it has become a corpse.' They said to him, 'He cannot do so otherwise.' He said to them, 'You too, look for a place for yourself within repose, lest you become a corpse and be eaten.'

(111) Jesus said, 'The heavens and the earth will be rolled up in your presence. And the one who lives from the living one will not see death.' Does not Jesus say, 'Whoever finds himself is superior to the world?'

(1) And he said, 'Whoever finds the interpretation of these sayings will not experience death.'

This Jesus tells everyone to look inside for the truth. Self-investigation is all you need. Don't listen to what others tell you, just discover that you have been led astray, clothed in other people's clothes. Reject duality. Reject the Pharisees.

Reject the concept of afterlife, crawling and begging and meekly serving your life away in the idle hope of a mere fable or fairy tale, promised to you - without any guarantees, of course - by, in all fairness, just some people who miraculously have been put on a pedestal - by whom, actually? And why? What have they done to deserve your respect or admiration? How admirable are they themselves?

What is it that they teach and you have learned? Why are you speaking their words? How does that really benefit you - or does it? Why would you even want to have an afterlife? Would you then finally start to take matters into your own hands? Why not now?

(3) (...) When you come to know yourselves, then you will become known, and you will realize that it is you who are the sons of the living father. But if you will not know yourselves, you dwell in poverty and it is you who are that poverty.'

(11) (...) In the days when you consumed what is dead, you made it what is alive. When you come to dwell in the light, what will you do? On the day when you were one you became two. But when you become two, what will you do?'

Dead and alive, dark and light, rich and poor. Drunk and thirsty, blind and sight. Hidden and become manifest, covered and become uncovered. Two and one.

The metaphors are more than manifest in Thomas, bordering on riddles and sometimes surpassing them. The questions asked, constantly, are directed at questioning yourself and everything around you, continuously - yes. Parables rule the story from beginning to end, filled with allegories of nature; planting, sowing, harvesting, fishing, catching, and animals play a part as well: foxes, sheep, dogs, and so on

All this is what undeniably came to harass the religious institutes of that time, in the first centuries CE. All those mysteries and questions with hardly any answer provided.

Some must have interpreted it all as religious, probably viewed through a Judaic lens, undoubtedly enduring some hardships there. The story has two firm pillars within a setting resembling a Jewish rabbi and his disciples: cryptic and mystic sayings and parables on one side, targeted against Judaic religion on the other - with a lot of cryptic grey in between that leaves more than enough room for interpretation.

So chances are highly likely that the majority of readers and listeners would have gone with the much more familiar religious direction that Thomas can be taken into, rather than with the foreign and outlandish "the kingdom of heaven is here all around you, yet people don't see it" core message.

Had the text been left alone, multiple fractions probably would have come to life, each fighting with others over their interpretation of this Jesus, and perhaps in due time the entire movement would have collapsed under its own weight. But this Jesus made bold claims: phrases like 'It is I who am the light which is above them all' surely must have gotten some traction among Jews who saw a new Messiah in him, yet the ruling religious leaders can only have viewed him as offensive, blasphemous, and a great threat to religion in general, and Judaism in particular.

The Jesus of Thomas must have made a major impact, made people ask questions, embrace this very fresh view on religion, clothed in a Judaic setting with ample references to their habits and laws and the Tanakh itself: it stirred up Jews, and the anti-Pharisee attitude couldn't be overlooked - it attacked that system from within.

Yet it was an invisible enemy, impossible to fight, debate with, overrule, stone to death or whatever else Judaism was used to do with opponents - it was very much like a guerrilla tactic that took Judaism by surprise.

Hence the gospel of Mark was written, instructed and ordered by the Church - that latter I will never be able to prove, yet I will prove that the text of the four gospels was written with the sole goal to refute the Jesus of Thomas; who and what was behind that (somewhat regrettably) will remain a mere assumption of me.

There never was a disciple Mark, just as much as there never was a Jesus. For the sake of brevity I'll refer to the gospels by their authors' names or "gospel-writers", and to the Church - as a central and major body of organised religious institutes in any form and place in time - as Church. I'm well aware of the entire lack of Church existence up until the 2nd century CE, and Church organisation and control was not very impressive either before the 5th century CE. Likewise, I will happily use the terms Christians and Christianity as well as Jews and Judaism as those are words we are all familiar with, I reckon. On most occasions, their use will be either too strict or too general or historically incorrect or all of the above, but the average reader will perfectly understand which groups I want to single out by using those words

Who was it that it all began with? Not Caiaphas, although he is the high priest who gets the most credit in the gospels. Ananus ben Ananus is a likely choice but that is pure speculation based on the fact that he was a brother of Caiaphas and the last in line of the five sons of Annas. I have nothing about the level or form of organisation of the gospels although there clearly was some, spanning several decades - all I have and use are the texts of Thomas, the Tanakh and the New Testament.
I will neither spell out every single bit of Thomas, explaining and clarifying it; that is perhaps for another moment as it is too much to combine with this, even though occasionally some of the latter will seep through

Goal and scope

Having said that, this book is solely about the way in which the text of Thomas strikingly clearly led to Mark, and how the text of Mark undoubtedly led to the text of Luke, and both Mark as well as Luke undeniably inspired the text of Matthew, with then John writing his text, very firmly basing his mystical prose, almost poetry sometimes, on the solid foundations of the three who went before him.

Thomas as a source of inspiration on one side, the Tanakh and its prophecies on the other side (and nothing else in between, certainly no Jesus, disciples and miracles): that's how the gospels were written, invented, made up from scratch. With the gospel-writers trying frantically hard to use as much of Thomas as possible, while twisting and turning all of it into Church context. Trying equally hard to have Jesus fulfil as many prophecies as possible, while even bending and breaking some of those - and not seldom using "prophecies" that either weren't prophecies at all and / or already fulfilled.

Thus, purely as a reaction against the (spread of) words of the Jesus of Thomas, the very foundations for the Church and its supreme domination for more than 1,500 years were laid

Writing the gospel

A simple creation Mark could have been, where Jesus for instance is portrayed as an outsider preaching unintelligible ramblings and meeting his demise at the hands of an angry Jewish mob, or something like that, for uttering his riddling blasphemies. Or any other scenario leading to the same result: Jesus has to die, of course, his words have to cease to exist; and they have to be tainted, bent, broken, so no one wants to, can or will use them afterwards.

But that's not what happened.

We'll never know when the idea took form that (ab)using him as (mostly) Isaiah's Messiah would benefit the Church's agenda even more, but that is how it unfolded. The Jesus of Mark is labelled by God himself as the Son of God, and performs miracles and fulfils prophecies - that's easy to do on paper, without a doubt. As transient as every miracle is, no evidence was required. At the end of Mark, Jesus is dead, case closed. Job well done - for a first attempt

How does one go about to rewrite a story? What do you pick from it and what do you leave out? To what degree?

There's content and context to Thomas, as in every other story; and both are clearly distinctive and present in this case. As anything else, content can be divided in two: anti-Judaic and self-critical (which essentially is anti-dualistic). We can split both of those in two again and then once more, and we'll get 8 major focal points. The logia driving those are put behind each of them:

- Anti-Judaic
  - Directed against the Pharisees as an institute or group
    - Pharisees are hiding the real knowledge (39, 34, 50, 66, 74, 102)
    - Pharisees don't live according to their rules (43, 53, 65, 85, 102)
  - Directed against Judaic customs

- The concept of heaven in heaven is nonsense, it's right here on earth and everywhere, and anyone can attain it (3, 11, 12, 111)
- Typical Judaic customs such as fasting and praying are nonsense and even harmful (6, 14, 88, 93, 104)
- Self-critical
  - Relentlessly seek and question everything in sight
    - Look at everyone and everything around you with fully objective eyes (5, 8, 10, 16, 40, 55, 68, 78, 99)
    - Observe and recognise how your life unfolds (11, 17, 26, 36, 37, 47, 57, 87, 89, 97, 98, 101, 113)
  - Make the two one again
    - Provide yourself with the proper environment (2, 9, 15, 20, 21, 24, 27, 31, 45, 49, 50, 60, 69, 75, 94)
    - Become like a child (4, 13, 18, 19, 22, 29, 37, 46, 48, 79, 80, 86, 106)

With context the same method can be applied:

- Consisting mostly of parables filled with allegories
  - Human
    - Living and being dead
    - Dressing and disrobing
  - Natural
    - Throwing out nets and catching fish
    - Sowing and harvesting
- Rich use of contrasting metaphors
  - Physical
    - Dead and alive, rich and poor, old and young
    - Thirsty and drunk, hungry and fed, seeing and perceiving, hearing and understanding
  - Natural
    - Seed becomes plant, plant and bear fruit
    - Light and dark

What can be used here? And what must be used? There are quantities to these qualities that are immeasurable to us, we'll never know which of these formed a major issue back then that had to be dealt with on a larger scale than others. For example, it is well known that rich and poor made it into the gospels, as well as healing the sick - yet the latter couldn't possibly make it on this list, given the (lack of) attention it receives in Thomas

What about the other half of the gospels then? The prophecies that must and do drive the entire story behind Jesus, fulfilling the promises in the Tanakh? The good thing about prophecies is that there are more than enough of them, so prophecy fulfilment is not an issue - the bad thing is that there are so many of them, and they're not all completely in agreement with one another. And then there is fine print about some prophecies in some other prophecies, so merely selectively quoting a few is not going to help propel your Messiah into complete acceptance by all.

I think that, compared to selecting the exact right set and order of prophecies to fulfil, copying Thomas and pretending it was all Church property right from the very start is child's play: the complexity of prophecies is huge and their meaning is ruled by interpretation: most of them are allegoric and can't be used literally. I will somewhat regrettably yet surely to my relief not delve and dive into more than a few prophecies as it's more than enough to deal with as it is, although I'll lightly touch on the subject here and there - and there's a bit of irony in that last phrase

The basic gospel

The gospel of Mark narrates the following story of Jesus: it starts with John the Baptist baptising Jesus, who then gets tempted by the devil in the first half of chapter 1. Jesus calls his first disciples and performs some miracles in the second half, after which chapter 2 shows him performing even more miracles and doing a lot of preaching - a showcase of his ministry.

Halfway through chapter 3 he starts speaking in parables to his disciples and all other people, and chapter 4 ends with Jesus commanding the wind in a storm.

Chapter 5 takes him outside of Galilee, performing yet more miracles. Chapter 6 takes him back to Galilee where he teaches in the synagogue on Sabbath day. He fails to work many miracles there yet sends out his disciples to perform some, speaking in riddles while instructing them to do so. John the Baptist gets beheaded by Herod, and Jesus magically feeds 5,000.

Chapter 7 takes us among the Pharisees whom Jesus rebukes, and chapter 7 finishes with miracles mixed with parables. In chapter 8 Jesus feeds 4,000, and is proclaimed Christ by Peter. The first Passion Prediction follows.

Chapter 9 has Moses, Elijah and God appear in the Transfiguration and proclaim Jesus the son of God. Jesus performs more miracles, reiterates the prediction of rising after three days (sic) - the second Passion Prediction. Ending with parables again, chapter 10 follows: to Jerusalem!

More parables, and the third Passion Prediction. And it ends with the blind man proclaiming Jesus as son of David - and then getting his sight back.

Chapter 11 starts with Jesus making his praised entrance into Jerusalem. He clears out the temple, and defies the Pharisees once more. Chapter 12 has more parables yet, and Jesus is tempted once more by Pharisees.

Chapter 13 kicks off the Apocalyptic Discourse where Mark neatly matches prophecies from the Old Testament, mixed with some more parables.

Chapter 14 starts the Passion week with the conspiracy by the Pharisees. The Last Supper takes place, Jesus gets betrayed by Judas and arrested and, when interrogated, confirms he's 'Christ, the Son of the Blessed'.
Chapter 15 has Jesus sentenced to death, and he gets crucified. At the very end people find out that 'he has risen' and that's it

There.
Enough Messianic prophecies fulfilled. And a lot of logia quoted. And most importantly: a good part of the narrative is in parable-style, and Thomas context.
Good work really - honestly

The elaborate Mark, and his (ab)use of Thomas

In the chapters dealing with Mark, only those parts of logia will be quoted that directly apply. When all three gospel-writers together are discussed in the chapters on Luke and Matthew, every logion referenced will be quoted in full. Each logion is split in separate sentences and every sentence is numbered, for instance logion 113 consists of four sentences:

(113a) His disciples said to him, "When will the kingdom come?"
(113b) [Jesus said] "It will not come by waiting for it.
(113c) It will not be a matter of saying 'here it is' or 'there it is.'
(113d) Rather, the kingdom of the father is spread out upon the earth, and men do not see it."

A small word on the bible texts used. Purely for reasons of copyright I've picked the World English Bible (WEB), which has a few things I like less: it uses 'Good News' instead of 'Gospel', 'to stumble' instead of 'to sin', 'John the Baptizer' instead of 'John the Baptist' and 'Gehenna' for 'hell'. Which is alright really but not what we're used to - I'll just use the old-fashioned words and phrases in my comments.
The text of Thomas is the beautiful translation by Thomas O. Lambdin

Emphasis will be used where and when it helps, usually to stress the parts from the gospel-writers that match with those of Thomas, but sometimes just to highlight the parts that will be commented on

The very beginning of Mark sets the tone and direction:

*1:1 The beginning of the Good News of Jesus Christ, the Son of God.
2 As it is written in the prophets, "**Behold, I send my messenger before your face, who will prepare your way before you**: 3 the*

*voice of one crying in the wilderness, 'Make ready the way of the Lord! Make his paths straight!'" 4 John came baptizing in the wilderness and preaching the baptism of repentance for forgiveness of sins. 5 All the country of Judea and all those of Jerusalem went out to him. They were baptized by him in the Jordan river, confessing their sins. 6 **John was clothed with camel's hair and a leather belt around his waist**. He ate locusts and wild honey. 7 He preached, saying, "After me comes he who is mightier than I, the thong of whose sandals I am not worthy to stoop down and loosen. 8 I baptized you in water, but he will baptize you in the Holy Spirit." 9 In those days, **Jesus came from Nazareth of Galilee**, and was baptized by John in the Jordan. 10 Immediately coming up from the water, he saw the heavens parting and the **Spirit descending on him like a dove. 11 A voice came out of the sky, "You are my beloved Son, in whom I am well pleased**."*

Powerful, starting right off with Isaiah 40:3 in verse 3 and quoting Malachi 3:1 in verse 2:

*(Malachi 3:1 "**Behold, I send my messenger, and he will prepare the way before me**; and **the Lord**, whom you seek, **will suddenly come to his temple**; and the messenger of the covenant, whom you desire, behold, he comes!" says Yahweh of Armies.)*

*(Isaiah 40:3 **The voice of one who calls out, "Prepare the way of Yahweh in the wilderness! Make a level highway in the desert for our God**.)*

The vast majority of bibles state 'As it is written in Isaiah' yet unfortunately the WEB states what it says in verse 2 - I will not dwell on original translations, alleged scribal errors and whatnot, but I'll make this one exception at pointing out that history sometimes is deliberately rewritten to suit one's agenda. And that no bible is identical to another one.

John the Baptist is introduced right away, his clothes described in verse 6; identical to the prophet Elijah he's dressed in camel's hair and a leather belt (2 Kings 1:8) - it starts what I call Project Elijah which permeates all four gospels, playing a central and crucial role:

(2 Kings 1:8 They answered him, "He was a hairy man, and wearing a leather belt around his waist." He said, "It's Elijah the Tishbite.")

Again, and this will be the second to last bible translation comment in this entire book: other bibles say differently, such as the New International Version and the English Standardised Version:

(2 Kings 1:8 They answered him, "He wore a garment of hair, with a belt of leather about his waist." And he said, "It is Elijah the Tishbite.")

When John has baptised Jesus, a voice from heaven calls him his beloved Son - nothing left to the imagination there. Jesus' first words?

1:15 and saying, "The time is fulfilled, and God's Kingdom is at hand! Repent, and believe in the Good News."

That one verse right there, that's the central message Mark wants to send. The very first words Jesus speaks: I'm here, the prophecy is fulfilled. A new era starts. Bow to me, obey me, and acknowledge me as your Master. And believe what I say - because these are the true words of the true Jesus! "Believe in this gospel, not that other one" is what Mark reluctantly seems to not be willing to say...

Right after Mark's instruction to believe in his gospel, verses 16-17 deftly introduce the first garbled copy of a Thomas parable, somewhat a mixture of logion 3 and 8, reusing Thomas words to sketch a Thomasine context; hinting at the metaphors to come:

*1:16 Passing along by the sea of Galilee, he saw Simon and Andrew, the brother of Simon, casting a net into the sea, for they were fishermen. 17 Jesus said to them, "**Come after me, and I will make*** *you into fishers for men."*

Thus Mark's story sets out. He steers very hard in the direction of the fulfilment of (Isaiah's) prophecies, making Jesus Jewish property and heir, while dropping bits and pieces of Thomas context and content: and that really is what Mark is all about, as we'll see. Although his approach will change in due course, searching for different angles, trying to grow into his Thomas' skin.

Mark quickly moves on with Jesus performing miracles, adding more weight to his credibility as Messiah, leading up to chapter 2 that starts with the healing of the paralytic.

There Mark addresses the perhaps most burning issue of Thomas from the perspective of the Church: going against Jewish doctrine and customs. Jesus forgives the paralytic's sins and tells him to stand up. It's obvious that it borders on blasphemy to forgive one's sins, as only God can do so, but Mark doesn't elaborate on that - Luke and (especially) Matthew will be rubbing it all in, as you will come to notice. Mark takes a lot of things for granted, seemingly supposing fair to good knowledge of the Tanakh from his readers. The next scene takes us to Jesus sitting with tax collectors and sinners (I must admit I do cherish how those two types are clubbed together) who have been following him - another red flag there, Jesus is followed by sinners: Isaiah 53:12 fulfilled (a chapter that will be addressed in its entirety at the start of Luke). And we see how Thomas' reference to healing the sick (a very small part of logion 14b) is garbled:

2:17 When Jesus heard it, he said to them, "Those who are healthy have no need for a physician, but those who are sick. I came not to call the righteous, but sinners to repentance."

I'll comment on healing the sick at the end of Mark, and logion 14 we'll see plenty of times: it is not likely to have driven this verse all by itself.

A further spin follows right after, where Mark depicts Jesus' disciples abstaining from fasting - yet another address of Thomas, acting against Judaic customs - while neatly referencing logion 6 and 14 and quoting the only convenient part of logion 104, 104c. As an example it will be quoted in full here next to Mark's complete scene so it becomes visible how different the content and context of the complete Thomas logion are from the verses of Mark:

(104a) They said to Jesus, "Come, let us pray today and let us fast."
(104b) Jesus said, "What is the sin that I have committed, or wherein have I been defeated?
(104c) But when the bridegroom leaves the bridal chamber, then let them fast and pray."

*2:18 John's disciples and the Pharisees were fasting, and they came and asked him, "Why do John's disciples and the disciples of the Pharisees fast, but **your disciples don't fast**?" 19 Jesus said to them, "**Can the groomsmen fast** while the bridegroom is with them? As long as they have the bridegroom with them, they can't fast. 20 But the days will come when the bridegroom will be taken away from them, and then they will fast in that day.*

Considering the entire logion, Thomas' point is clear: fasting is undeserved punishment. His is a coherent story with the bridegroom and his bridal chamber a metaphor for his answer, while pointing at others who should fast and pray when the groom leaves that chamber. I could explain that the bridegroom is one with the bridal chamber and upon leaving becomes two, a man to a wife, thus dual, but that would make it all very lengthy and even more complicated: explaining all of Thomas would require a book of its own. As stated before, this book treats everything as pure text, which will suffice to allow the reader to witness how Thomas' text is incorporated into Church text and leading it all, driving it, causing it, creating it.

The logia of Thomas receive two major kinds of treatment: either they are copied mostly literally and fully and applied to a Church goal, or they are very selectively and partially copied in which way they "automatically" apply to a Church goal.

This being a fine example of the latter, Mark takes it all out of context and naturally leaves out the word 'pray'. He uses only a third of the logion and of that third not even all the same words, which then are applied to a different context - and a different direction and use. Extra points by the way for introducing the taking away of the bridegroom, which hints at Jesus being arrested or even crucified.

But a most important feat is accomplished: Jesus rebukes the Pharisees using Thomas' words - alea iacta est! It is the beginning of hostility towards Pharisees and attacking more of their customs, and it will become a central theme in Mark: Jesus is increasingly aggravating the Pharisees (by doing mostly good deeds) which eventually results in the Jews convicting and killing (an innocent) Jesus.

This is the solution of the gospel-writers for the first two important and difficult to handle themes of Thomas: his complete rejection of religious concepts, and his hostility towards the Pharisees and the scribes. Mark starts with Jesus making an exception for himself and his disciples regarding (only) fasting, but the three religious customs together will be combined with the hostility towards the Pharisees: killing two birds with one stone

What follows next are the only convenient parts logion 47e and logion 47d (in that order indeed):

(47d) And new wine is not put into old wineskins, lest they burst; nor is old wine put into a new wineskin, lest it spoil it.
(47e) An old patch is not sewn onto a new garment, because a tear would result."

*2:21 No one sews a piece of unshrunk cloth on an **old garment**, or else **the patch shrinks and the new tears away from the old**, and a worse hole is made. 22 No one puts new wine into old wineskins; or else the new wine will burst the skins, **and the wine pours out, and the skins will be destroyed; but they put new wine into fresh*** *wineskins.*"

A few things are noteworthy and exemplary of how Mark twists Thomas into his direction. First of all, the order of clothing and wine is reversed; perhaps to obfuscate the fact that Mark is swapping the old patch for a new patch, or simply because he deemed people to be more familiar with drinking wine than piecing together garments.

Emphasis is on the following parts that are commented on: Thomas uses an old patch on new clothes, but Mark wants to put this logion to use for his new religion and the old Judaism, so he turns that into a new ('unshrunk') patch on an old garment. Thomas doesn't specify at all how the new and old cloth would be incompatible and what would tear which or how, but Mark applies the small part of the new religion onto the large and old Judaism, and explains elaborately how that would not work out. On a side note: we'll get very familiar with what I call the pioneer's fate: the first of the gospel-writers to copy Thomas will either simply do a fairly literal copy and use the original clue (slightly twisted or not) to befit his goal, or do an elaborate copy involving the addition of many details as well as over-explanation. Why that is the case? I could fantasise about that but the point is that it is a clearly discernable pattern, and we will see Mark as well as Luke and Matthew struggle in identical ways.

The first part of the wine logion is left intact as that befits Mark's same analogy, putting new into old. The fermenting demands flexibility and the old skins don't have that anymore. How the old wine would spoil new skins beats me, and Mark circumvents that by happily leaving it out - only because old into new simply doesn't support his business case at all.

Mark is over-explaining things here, apparently uncomfortable with the allegories? Thomas is very concise and doesn't feel any need for explanation - let it be noted

As yet we're a mere two chapters in, and already we have it almost all: Jesus solidly introduced as Messiah (even God lending a hand there), and linked to Thomas in the two most important aspects: Jesus speaking in parables, and going firmly against Pharisee rules and regulations. A sincerely impressive start, it really is.

The image of Jesus in Thomas is vague, to be honest - what's his role? What's his origin? What's his destiny? Is he a teacher of disciples, or does he just fool around with them? Is he even with us, or against us?

For people trying to take him literally and following his example, he doesn't set many straight boundaries. Whereas the Jesus of Mark leaves absolutely nothing to the imagination - he is a Leader, a Ruler, a Performer of Miracles. Knows the Scriptures, and Lectures the Pharisees - I'm running out of capitals trying to do justice to his towering figure, and we're only two chapters down Marks' road. This Jesus is stiff competition for the Jesus of Thomas

The wrath of the Pharisees

Chapter 3 continues on the rebellion of Jesus - or rather, the "I can do as I please because I'm the Son of God" anti-Pharisee attitude. In a synagogue, of all places, on a Sabbath, he heals a withered hand. And Mark throws in the sword of Damocles right away:

3:6 The Pharisees went out, and immediately conspired with the Herodians against him, how they might destroy him.

The animosity is definite now; it's Jesus against the Pharisees and vice versa, and both parties have fully justifiable motives. Our hero is threatened with death, this early on in his story. One cannot help but identify and sympathise with him - he's only doing good and the bad men want him dead - although 'destroy' does leave something of an open ending, for now.

It is literary sociological marvel at its best, still working wonders in any good novel these days.

Chapter 3 ends with a boat load of Thomas parables after Jesus appoints his twelve disciples, then Jesus needs to argue his defence when the Pharisees accuse him of being possessed by Satan.

Starting from verse 24 through 26 with what very well may be inspired by logion 16, verse 27 is a literal copy of logion 35:

(16a) Jesus said, "Men think, perhaps, that it is peace which I have come to cast upon the world.
(16b) They do not know that it is dissension which I have come to cast upon the earth: fire, sword, and war.
(16c) For there will be five in a house: three will be against two, and two against three, the father against the son, and the son against the father.
(16d) And they will stand solitary."
(35) Jesus said, "It is not possible for anyone to enter the house of a strong man and take it by force unless he binds his hands; then

he will (be able to) ransack his house."

*3:24 If a kingdom is divided against itself, that kingdom cannot stand. 25 **If a house is divided against itself, that house cannot stand.** 26 If Satan has risen up against himself, and is divided, he can't stand, but has an end. 27 **But no one can enter into the house of the strong man to plunder unless he first binds the strong man; then he will plunder his house**.*

The binding of the hands seems significant in Thomas yet Mark leaves it out because binding Satan merely by his hands isn't a strong enough image to fit his context. Why is Mark using this logion? He wants to make the case that Jesus can't be possessed by Satan because Jesus is actually working against Satan, with the undoing of his possession of humans (by driving out demons): on three occasions already has Jesus driven out demons. At the same time Jesus argues for his own case of overthrowing Satan by suggesting that each soul un-possessed (by driving out a demon from someone) is limiting Satan in power, in a way binding him, restricting his might

Then follows a literal copy of logion 44. Mark deviously adds the eternal sin part in verse 29 - another tick in the Church box there. Indeed he's paraphrasing Thomas's 'either on earth or in heaven', and I have no idea what that heaven is doing there in Thomas, but it's an opportunity that simply can't be passed up:

(44) Jesus said, "Whoever blasphemes against the father will be forgiven, and whoever blasphemes against the son will be forgiven, but whoever blasphemes against the holy spirit will not be forgiven either on earth or in heaven."

*3:28 "Most certainly I tell you, all sins of the descendants of man will be forgiven, including their blasphemies with which they may blaspheme; 29 **but whoever may blaspheme against the Holy Spirit never has forgiveness, but is subject to eternal condemnation.**" 30*

-because they said, "He has an unclean spirit."

Again, Mark is cherry picking here, cautiously navigating around Thomas logia. Needless to say he can't state that blasphemy against the father or the son is alright. Just like before, when Mark leaves out of the word 'pray' in 2:20, ignores 'old wine spoils new skins' after 2:22 and drops 'hands' in 3:27, it is very clear that he copies Thomas selectively in such a manner to fit his purpose.
And I hope it's equally clear why Thomas would have nothing to gain by copying Mark and adding these words - unless you're really thinking of making the case that Thomas would copy Mark and add these 'noise words' to perhaps just show that he couldn't possibly have copied Mark, but that it could only be the other way around? It is perfectly logical to use 'pray' next to 'fast', both being religious practices - and we'll see how both are addressed later on in the gospels, just not here by Mark.
It is perfectly logical to look at a two-sided dilemma from both sides, and in that case pay attention to both old and new (wine).
And Luke and Matthew will show that all the five parts of this logion are used by them so they did have access to the whole of it, but just chose to selectively quote it when and where it befitted their occasions, and disperse its parts across their gospels.
It is perfectly logical to bind someone's hands, rendering him nearly powerless and leaving only his lower half mobility fully intact: that's enough to allow for plundering his house. In fact that is the entire point of the logion: the goal is to plunder the house but that's impossible because it's guarded by a strong man - who has a weak point, as everything does. Binding him is not taking advantage of a weak point; you might as well knock him out or even kill him when you are in the position to just bind a strong man. Even when doing so it would still be unclear which weak point was exploited, whereas merely binding his hands will exploit his weak point and thus allow the goal to be achieved, and it will be a relatively small effort compared to immobilising the entire powerful man.
And, of course, it is perfectly logical that Mark couldn't state that it is no problem to blaspheme against the Father or the Son

Could the opposite be argued? Shall I play the devil's advocate and try to argue that Thomas copied Mark in these verses?

Starting from the end of the three logia just discussed, why would Thomas copy the blasphemy verse from Mark and add that it is okay to blaspheme against the Father and the Son? How would that add extra meaning to his logion? Although it is obvious that he would profit from changing Mark's 'eternal condemnation' to 'on earth or in heaven'.

If Thomas copied the strong man verse from Mark, why would he add the hands? What goal would that have, what difference would it make? In Mark the binding of the man is the goal: defeating Satan is the entire objective, and that's achieved when he's bound - there is no house to plunder when that's done. So Thomas sees that unused extra goal in Mark, decides to copy the entire verse with everything in it and turn it into a real goal by turning Mark's goal into a means which he accomplishes by merely adding the words 'hands'? Truly, that is brilliant - honestly.

Mark only has the new wine into old skins. Would Thomas really have added the perspective from the other side of the coin - old wine into new skins - and then suddenly have realised that taking such an unbiased perspective would be aided by changing the new patch on old garment into and old patch on new garment, because... it helped his newly acquired neutral stance so greatly?

It is clear, every single time, why the gospel-writers take only bits and pieces of Thomas and twist those to their agenda - we know how and why they apply (only) those bits and to which goal.

It is unclear what Thomas were to gain by copying the gospel-writers - how exactly would he aid his case by leaving out the Church stuff? Would he really have gone through the trouble of working his way through the 85,000 words of the four gospels, deciding which bits he could reuse and piece together, so he could write his 5,000 words piece? What would be the goal of that, starting this "free yourself all by yourself" movement? By twisting the words of a supposedly real Messiah? What would be the motive behind that, how would that advance his case?

His would likely be a spiritual movement without guidance, teachers, temples - it wouldn't sustain a system, it couldn't be monetised like a religious system (or a spiritual institute, as rare as those are) - although the contemporary self-help culture shows otherwise. Yet the current self-help is a scattered and dispersed ecosystem impossible to organise and centralise, whereas true power and absolute control comes from Institutes with only one "door" and ultimate decision-making body - such as the Church.

It is rather inconvenient that the text of Thomas is relatively obscure, because that makes it difficult to argue what would benefit it and how; most of it can't be taken literally. Yet it is too facile to label Thomas as a unique text of (proto-)Gnosticism, thereby creating a very vaguely defined and relatively barely limited pool of concepts and ideas where most if not all undesired elements can be sunk into. It is a unique text - that is indisputable.

I will try to play the devil's advocate on occasion, when it is feasible. And the next logion is a perfect example of where and when it is completely unfeasible: logion 99 is next, with a devious twist: Mark labels all who follow Jesus as doing God's will - a not so slight difference. By not using a comma Thomas intends 'Those here who do the will of my father' to be a restrictive relative clause, singling out from the crowd a select subgroup, whereas Mark uses it as a non-restrictive relative clause: 'Those here, who do the will of my father' - which labels the entire crowd as doing the will of God. Pay attention to the lengthy introduction of Mark, sketching the entire situation before he can launch his version of the logion:

(99a) The disciples said to him, "Your brothers and your mother are standing outside."
(99b) He said to them, "Those here who do the will of my father are my brothers and my mother.
(99c) It is they who will enter the kingdom of my father."

*3:31 His mother and his brothers came, and standing outside, they sent to him, calling him. 32 **A multitude** was sitting around him, and* they **told him**, "Behold, **your mother, your brothers, and your sisters are outside looking for you**." 33 **He answered them**, "Who are my mother and my brothers?" 34 Looking around at those who sat around him, he said, "**Behold, my mother and my brothers! 35 For whoever does the will of God is my brother, my sister, and mother**."

The pioneer's fate again - I do like the scenery sketching by Mark, really, it does help me visualise, and I do see the multitude in front of me, the many men and women and children sitting around Jesus, some standing at the back. It does give Mark's Jesus character; it does animate him, it helps bringing him to life. Yet Mark copies only 99a and 99b and I've emphasised only the words that match those - the rest is extra.

A grand total of 5 (not counting the 'divided house' of logion 16) undisputed and literal copies of Thomas logia so far - as very safe as these are, they strengthen the story. Pure quantity, almost unaltered, placed into just (not always so) slightly different context. They stress that the new believers would hurt the old Judaic religion when forced onto it, underline that Satan does not possess Jesus, enforce that Jesus is strong, and label all followers of Jesus as doing the will of God. They are subtle but magnificently significant twists to advance Mark's case; this is what Mark should persevere if he wants to own Thomas' Jesus

The parables - explained

Chapter 4 continues the literal parables, again, all safe ones. Logion 9 is given a pioneer's twist in verse 6 with the rising and scorching sun (isn't that a beautiful image):

(9a) Jesus said, "Now the sewer went out, took a handful (of seeds), and scattered them.
(9b) Some fell on the road; the birds came and gathered them up.
(9c) Others fell on the rock, did not take root in the soil, and did not produce ears.
(9d) And others fell on thorns; they choked the seed(s) and worms ate them.
(9e) And others fell on the good soil and it produced good fruit: it bore sixty per measure and a hundred and twenty per measure."

*4:3 "Listen! Behold, **the farmer went out to sow, 4 and as he sowed, some seed fell by the road, and the birds came and devoured it. 5 Others fell on the rocky ground, where it had little soil**, and immediately it sprang up, because it had no depth of soil. 6 When the sun had risen, it was scorched; and because it had no root, it withered away. 7 **Others fell among the thorns, and the thorns** grew up, and **choked it**, and it yielded no fruit. 8 **Others fell into the good ground, and yielded fruit**, growing up and increasing. **Some produced thirty times, some sixty times, and some one hundred times as much**." 9 He said, "Whoever has ears to hear, let him hear."*

Emphasis is on the words that match with Thomas.
Thomas' seemingly odd 'worms' is left out, although the mere growing up of thorns which choke the seeds isn't a very plausible scenario: thorns do not grow leaves or other shade-providing extensions that would prevent seeds from growing. To make up for the missing worms Mark inserts the feeble 'and it yielded no fruit':

Mark is the poorest gospel-writer when it comes to syntax and frequently misses the occasion to use a proper conjunction, using a weak "and" instead.

The end of verse 8 ruins the 60 / 120 of Thomas, which is only a 100% percent difference between both outcomes - whatever it may mean. Mark ambitiously aims for 3,000%, 6,000% and 10,000% and thus makes the promise of how explosively successful seed in good soil will prosper (reward in heaven you'll get). The unanswered question that Mark however introduces with that is: those are percentages of what, exactly? The 'hundred times' highly likely comes from Genesis 26:12, which creates that same problem and it is not hard to see how Mark's lead himself there by Thomas's hundred and twenty:

(Genesis 26:12 Isaac sowed in that land, and reaped in the same year one hundred times what he planted. Yahweh blessed him.)

(62a) Jesus said, "It is to those who are worthy of my mysteries that I tell my mysteries.

*4:10 When he was alone, those who were around him with the twelve asked him about the parables. 11 He said to them, "**To you is given the mystery of God's Kingdom**, but to those who are outside, all things are done in parables, 12 that 'seeing they may see, and not perceive; and hearing they may hear, and not understand; lest perhaps they should turn again, and their sins should be forgiven them.'"*

In order to explain the parable, Mark uses logion 62a. The disciples now get implicitly labelled as 'worthy'. Mark promotes the disciples to inner crowd here; preparing for the future, and neatly following up in verse 12 with a reference to Isaiah 6:9 - two birds with one stone:

(Isaiah 6:9 He said, "Go, and tell this people, 'You hear indeed, but don't understand. You see indeed, but don't perceive.')

The word mystery is mentioned again, the disciples labelled as recipients of the mystery of God's Kingdom, and Thomas is combined with scripture by linking to Isaiah - Mark is fortifying very strongly here. And continues in verse 13 through 20 to explain the parable of verses 2 through 9:

4:13 He said to them, "Don't you understand this parable? How will you understand all of the parables?

This is the first time that Mark has Jesus explain a parable. The descriptions of those verses should be reversed into instructions, in order to understand the message Mark wants to send: those along the path are lost to Satan; the ones on rocky ground fail to endure tribulation and persecution; those among thorns fall prey to material desires; only 'the ones who hear the word and accept it' are worthy.
Simply believe what is said - that is what the Church wants. With that very explanation, yet another logion is impounded by the Church, regardless the extreme explicitness thereof

Logion 33b is next in verse 21, and Mark gets truly carried away. Verse 22 shows us logion 6c, followed by a pun on secret - the only time that that is mentioned in Thomas is in the opening subtitle. A secret coming to light? - using Thomas against Thomas here; now that is clever. After that, Mark can't resist adding the typical Thomas 'hear hear' that is part of logion 8, 21, 24, 63, 65 and 96, but not 33:

(33b) For no one lights a lamp and puts it under a bushel, nor does he put it in a hidden place, but rather he sets it on a lampstand so that everyone who enters and leaves will see its light."
(6c) For nothing hidden will not become manifest, and nothing covered will remain without being uncovered."

*4:21 He said to them, "**Is the lamp brought to be put under a*** *basket or under a bed? Isn't it put on a stand? 22 **For there is nothing hidden, except that it should be made known; neither was anything made secret, but that it should come to light.** 23 If any man has **ears to hear, let him hear.***"

The hidden place is turned into a bed as well - clarity instead of leaving room for interpretation. Mark skips the purpose of the lamp as that apparently doesn't fit the message he wants to carry across here and immediately follows up with logion 41:

(41) Jesus said, "Whoever has something in his hand will receive more, and whoever has nothing will be deprived of even the little he has."

4:25 For whoever has, to him more will be given, and he who doesn't have, even that which he has will be taken away from him."

Mark omits the hand, which seems significant in Thomas. Having something in your hand could be a tool, suggesting that you put effort into something and will likely produce something, or it could be indicating that you are offering something to trade or bargain with? Or is it a slighting remark at the Pharisees who offer just hollow words? It certainly does raise questions, which Mark likely also can't easily answer, and he's happy to leave it out.
Verses 26 through 29 are a thorough remake on Thomas logion 57a and 57b, and verse 29 is a literal copy of logion 21i. It is unconvincing that these verses also copy logion 57 but Luke and Matthew will provide the proof for that so I am counting it as a logion used by Mark:

(57a) Jesus said, "The kingdom of the father is like a man who had good seed.
(57b) His enemy came by night and sowed weeds among the good seed.
(21i) When the grain ripened, he came quickly with his sickle in his hand and reaped it.

*4:26 He said, "**God's Kingdom is as if a man should cast seed on the earth**, 27 and should **sleep** and rise **night** and day, and the **seed** should **spring up and grow, although he doesn't know how**. 28 For the earth bears fruit by itself: first the blade, then the ear, then the full grain in the ear. 29 **But when the fruit is ripe, immediately he puts in the sickle, because the harvest has come**."*

Odd and complicated copies as they seem, they're a prologue to verses 30 through 32, which are literal copies again of logion 20 - the parable of the mustard seed:

(20a) The disciples said to Jesus, "Tell us what the kingdom of heaven is like."
(20b) He said to them, "It is like a mustard seed.
(20c) It is the smallest of all seeds.
(20d) But when it falls on tilled soil, it produces a great plant and becomes a shelter for birds of the sky."

*4:30 **He said, "How will we liken God's Kingdom**? Or with what parable will we illustrate it? 31 **It's like a grain of mustard seed**, which, when it is sown in the earth, although **it is less than all the seeds** that are on the earth, 32 yet when it is sown, grows up, and **becomes greater than** all the herbs, and puts out great branches, **so that the birds of the sky can lodge** under its shadow."*

Emphasis is on the words matching with Thomas. The word parable is introduced in the second part of verse 30 as a prologue to the finish of chapter 4, where Mark explains the use of parables. Substituting 'kingdom of heaven' for 'God's Kingdom' in that same verse is yet another subtle twist that he will consistently repeat. Removing tilled soil, the very essence of this parable, is an omission far too easily made by Mark - I think it would befit the Church's agenda very well that you have to work (hard) to earn your share. Mark drops it as if it is just another word; which it most certainly is not, and that will be discussed in a separate chapter on parables.

Mark adds a bit too many details, as if he is deliberately trying to be different from Thomas. 'Sown in the earth' is a pleonasm as one wouldn't, for instance, sow on a table or a tree, nor does being the smallest of all seeds suddenly become a property gained from the sowing action. It is an unnecessary exaggeration to say 'less than all the seeds that are on the earth'; Thomas is perfectly concise there. Mark also adds 'greater than all the herbs' (not a significant feat, to be honest) and the over-explanatory 'great branches' yet without adding 'leaves' - how else would birds have shade? Thomas just leaves it all unspecified and only mentions shelter, and it is a perfectly sensible image how a great plant would provide shelter for birds.

Mark suffers the pioneer's fate again, adding insignificant and even distracting detail in an attempt to explain a perfectly concise parable

Before ending with Jesus commanding the wind and sea, chapter 4 kills two birds with one stone - again:

*4:33 With many such parables he spoke the word to them, as they were able to hear it. 34 **Without a parable he didn't speak to them; but privately to his own disciples he explained everything**.*

A repetition of verses 11 through 12, Mark once more stresses the fact that his disciples are above the crowd. Yet isn't it odd that the disciples need just as much explanation of the parables ('everything', really?) as the crowd, for the disciples allegedly have received the keys to wisdom, haven't they? They have been given the mystery of God's Kingdom?

Mark's plan here would have been much stronger if e.g. the disciples had taken turns explaining the parables, with of course a special role for some, like Peter, in order to prove worthiness. But let's not forget that Mark is conjuring a Church' Jesus out of thin air here, and doing a fine job as it is

Chapter 4 is strong, very strong. 8 logia added to 5 makes 13 logia now ticked off by mostly literally quoting them, with only subtle yet significant twists to some.

And where Mark can't find one entire logion to quote literally, he deftly combines more than one and shuffles parts of those into a more or less coherent group of verses. That works too, but is a means to which end? It takes a lot of knowledge of Thomas to be able to recognise parts of logion 57 in verses 4:26-28.

Mark also has no less than two repetitions of verses within the same chapter; the explanation of the parable of the sower adds extreme weight by instructing with utter clarity how believers must blindly accept the word of the Church, and the repeated stress on the parable explanation process in verses 4:33-34 emphasises that the disciples are true inner crowd and stand above all others - they are Jesus' managers and he is clearly prepping the transfer of it all to Peter.

Has Mark built a case? Oh yes. Is it clear? Yes, it is pretty clear. Jesus is owned now, and the amount and speed at which logia have been incorporated has been amazing. Mostly innocent and intelligible logia, admittedly, but enough clear and harmless food for thought for the average reader. Who will probably lose attention by now, after four whole chapters. So what's next?

But - wait. Incorporating the logia is a must, as those are unique to Thomas and must be (re)possessed. Using parables as much as possible is a double must, as that is Thomas' trademark. But explaining a parable? That is not how it works - at best a parable is hinted at by another parable every once in a while. Spelling it out completely, word by word? No, never - that is most certainly not how parables work, although they usually aren't nearly as complex as those of Thomas.

Especially the length at which Mark takes the 'explanation' is a dead give away of the fact that the use of parables is alien to Mark. Explaining the parables to the disciples, Jesus' trusted inner circle? That is even more peculiar, more so as Mark explicitly states in 4:34 that Jesus repeats the explanation process each time he uses a parable - how much wisdom did they really receive then?

Mark does make mistakes here and there, obviously. Some of his material will be rephrased and explicitly corrected, and some will just not be repeated.

Yet all of it, and that is very important to notice, is Mark's legacy for those who come after him: there are choices made at this point in time and as such Mark is writing Church history here. Jesus having to explain every parable to his disciples who supposedly have received the keys of knowledge is reluctantly repeated by every other gospel-writer who comes after him; such is the fate of writing history, even if you are making it all up

Chapter 5 takes a rest from Thomas, although Jairus' daughter touching his garments and the fuss about them that arises afterwards ("Who touched my clothes?") might be taken as an oblique reference to the multiple mentions of disrobing and garments in Thomas, but now featuring in a literal sense and thus further eliminating room for interpretation. It just might

Thomasine context and more experiments

In chapter 6, logion 31 is introduced in verses 1 through 3, where Jesus returns to his own country - it is obvious why Mark leaves out the physician part as none of those play any part in his gospel:

(31) Jesus said, "No prophet is accepted in his own village; no physician heals those who know him."

*6:3 Isn't this the carpenter, the son of Mary, and brother of James, Joses, Judah, and Simon? Aren't his sisters here with us?" So they were offended at him. 4 Jesus said to them, "**A prophet is not without honor, except in his own country**, and among his own relatives, and in his own house."*

Extra points there for deepening the character of Jesus and giving him a profession and relatives. Verse 5 is a bit of a disappointment, (not being able to do mighty works), as though Mark feels the need to prove verse 4 (which he does):

6:5 He could do no mighty work there, except that he laid his hands on a few sick people and healed them.

Five verses spent on one seemingly harmless and not so relevant logion, and not even the full one - what's the (hi)story behind that? Maybe Mark himself realised the inefficiency of incorporating logia this way, as verses 7 through 11 show an entirely new approach to assimilating the logia:

6:7 He called to himself the twelve, and began to send them out two by two; and he gave them authority over the unclean spirits. 8 He commanded them that they should take nothing for their journey, except a staff only: no bread, no wallet, no money in their purse, 9 but to wear sandals, and not put on two tunics. 10 He said to them, *"Wherever you enter into a house, stay there until you depart from there. 11 Whoever will not receive you nor hear you, as you depart from there, shake off the dust that is under your feet for a testimony against them. Assuredly, I tell you, it will be more tolerable for Sodom and Gomorrah in the day of judgment than for that city!"*

That is... mysterious! The clothing orders are strange, and so are the other instructions.
The two by two in verse 7 and the two tunics in verse 9 seem to imitate the numbers game Thomas is playing in general. Verse 8 might be a complete makeover of logion 36. Verse 9 yet especially verse 10 is a straight attempt at an authentic Thomasine riddle, as obvious as the statement itself seems. The first part of verse 11 resembles logion 14b, and the second part echoes logion 28e:

(14b) When you go into any land and walk about in the districts, if they receive you, eat what they will set before you, and heal the sick among them.
(28e) When they shake off their wine, then they will repent."

A slippery slope trying to point these verses to Thomas, I'll admit. But from either clear and straight instructions or parables Jesus now suddenly speaks in riddles. It is the first time he directs a parable towards humans, and I cannot suppress the feeling that Mark is trying something new here.
Chapter 6 continues with the elaborate tale about Herod having John the Baptist beheaded, an awful lot of text for a seemingly small feat that doesn't lead to anything further; but perhaps it serves to contribute to Project Elijah? When the disciples tell Jesus, Mark uses the first sentence of logion 60f in a very free style:

(60f) He said to them, "You too, look for a place for yourself within repose, lest you become a corpse and be eaten."

*6:31 He said to them, "**Come apart into a deserted place, and rest*** *awhile."* *For there were many coming and going, and they had no leisure so much as* **to eat.**

Is 'deserted' referring to logion 49a (Blessed are the solitary and elect), once again raising the disciples to their proper stature? Perhaps, but surely this must be logion 60? I am not counting it, it is only one out of a logion of six sentences and there is just not enough context. Again we see poetic freedom by Mark trying to assimilate Thomas' logia while his secondary goal for them remains the same: debunking them by placing them in a literal and pragmatic context, preferably mixed with his own agenda. Verse 32 is a repetition of verse 31, when the disciples do as they are told:

6:32 They went away in the boat to a deserted place by themselves.

Fourteen times in Mark Jesus embarks on a boat. Is that his remake of 'entering' so frequently used in Thomas? Or is the boat a vehicle that allows Mark to squeeze so many events across so many countries and regions in so little time? Or both?
Verse 34, again, hints at a logion, this time it's 107:

(107a) Jesus said, "The kingdom is like a shepherd who had a hundred sheep.

6:34 Jesus came out, saw a great multitude, and he had compassion on them, because they were like sheep without a shepherd, and he began to teach them many things.

An even subtler approach here, just throwing in the words sheep and shepherd, nothing more? Although of course sheep and shepherd are a familiar theme in the Tanakh with 179 and 89 verses of each (yet only 17 verses that have both sheep and shepherd), sheep without a shepherd are mentioned three times: Numbers 27:17, 1 Kings 22:17, and 2 Chronicles 18:16. Chronicles is an exact copy of Kings and Kings refers to Numbers, when Moses pleas with God to 'appoint a man over the congregation (...) that the congregation of Yahweh may not be as sheep which have no shepherd.'. Still, one major reference is enough for not being able to attribute this one to Thomas, and major it is: in Numbers, God responds to Moses' plea by appointing Joshua, who will become leader of the Israelite tribes after Moses' death - that certainly is a remarkable event, highly likely to be part of common religious knowledge.

Verses 38 through 44 confront us with the same new Markan poetic freedom:

6:38 He said to them, "How many loaves do you have? Go see."
*When they knew, they said, "**Five, and two fish**." 39 He commanded*
them that everyone should sit down in groups on the green grass.
*40 **They sat down in ranks, by hundreds and by fifties**. 41 He took*
*the **five loaves and the two fish**, and looking up to heaven, he*
blessed and broke the loaves, and he gave to his disciples to set
before them, and he divided the two fish among them all. 42 They
*all ate, and were filled. 43 They took up **twelve baskets full of***
***broken pieces and also of the fish**. 44 Those who ate the loaves*
*were **five thousand men**.*

When reading the words five and two of verse 38 and 41, logion 16c comes to mind. The hundreds and fifties of verse 39 resemble the sixty per measure and a hundred and twenty per measure of logion 9e. And the five thousand of verse 43 may point to the riddles of logion 23.

Again, I don't feel comfortable interpreting these verses this way, and I'm not counting them as logia used by Mark. Yet again, they repeat the efforts presented earlier in chapter 6. From (almost) literally copying logia Mark has traversed to combining parts of logia, and has now gone completely out of his comfort zone to clubbing together bits and pieces of logia and garbling them into seemingly sense-making content.

To be perfectly honest, his numbers make more sense than Thomas' numbers - they are simple and pragmatic numbers and juxtaposing the five bread and two fish to the five thousand people, the idea behind and impact of these verses here becomes strikingly clear

Jesus then walks on water, and the last part of logion 37b is paraphrased:

(37b) Jesus said, "When you disrobe without being ashamed and take up your garments and place them under your feet like little children and tread on them, then will you see the son of the living one, and you will not be afraid"

*6:50 for **they all saw him, and were troubled**. But he immediately spoke with them, and said to them, "Cheer up! It is I! **Don't be afraid**."*

Stretching it? I'd be inclined to disagree although I'm not counting this one either towards Mark's score. And with a final new Markan poetic freedom, chapter 6 ends:

6:56 Wherever he entered, into villages, or into cities, or into the country, they laid the sick in the marketplaces, and begged him that they might just touch the fringe of his garment; and as many as touched him were made well.

Villages, cities, the sick, garment - a beautiful resume and conclusion of this chapter. Repetition is once more used, and with utter pragmatism the allegories of Thomas are debunked. The sick are just physically sick, the garments just garments, houses and villages and cities just that: houses and villages and cities.
It is a new Mark, and he has found a new angle, now confident of the work done and taking it one step up. On the other hand, tackling the riddling figures and numbers of Thomas and turning them into sobering outcomes is a monumental task; and a job seemingly accomplished.
By reassembling the slightly more nasty bits and pieces of Thomas into Church-fitting contexts, Mark has definitely entered phase two

here. Yet I can count only one logion (logion 31) that can stand on its own, and the total now sits at 14

Chapter 7 starts out with a lengthy introduction of the Pharisees and their religious customs, but not after stressing that they caught (some of his) disciples eating with unwashed hands:

7:2 Now when they saw some of his disciples eating bread with defiled, that is unwashed, hands, they found fault.

Mark uses the word 'defiled' here and explains it as meaning unwashed - a reference to the so very pointed and damaging logion 14c. Mark sketches the context very thoroughly before planting his own versions of logia among the carefully targeted strike at the Pharisees here; explicitly labelling Isaiah 29:13 as directed against the Pharisees in verses 6 and 7:

*7:6 And he said to them, "Well did Isaiah prophesy of you hypocrites, as it is written, "'This people honors me with their lips, but their heart is far from me; 7 in vain do they worship me, teaching as doctrines the commandments of men.' 8 "For you set aside the commandment of God, and **hold tightly to the tradition of men-the washing of pitchers and cups**, and you do many other such things."*

Equally out of context is the strange 'washing of pitchers and cups' as a supposedly very important tradition of the Jews; a reference to logion 89 ('Why do you wash the outside of the cup [...]') which will follow later on.
It is a lengthy introduction but more than worth it! Combining the Pharisee rebuking of Thomas with Isaiah works very well, although 'and you do many other such things' is neither particularly aggressive nor strong. However, this is the official declaration of war by Jesus: accusing the Pharisees of not following the commandments of God is not a mere slap on the wrist.
Mark continues, combating the various confusing father and

mother references of Thomas by combining them with the ten commandments:

7:10 For Moses said, 'Honor your father and your mother;' and, 'He who speaks evil of father or mother, let him be put to death.' 11 But you say, 'If a man tells his father or his mother, "Whatever profit you might have received from me is Corban,"'" that is to say, given to God, 12 "then you no longer allow him to do anything for his father or his mother, 13 making void the word of God by your tradition which you have handed down. You do many things like this."

Once more combining Thomas and scripture leads to puzzling statements here, and once more Mark ends it with the feeble 'you do many things like this'. And still, it's a build up to much more. I will quote 14a and 14b as well so that the context of Thomas becomes completely clear:

(14a) Jesus said to them, "If you fast, you will give rise to sin for yourselves; and if you pray, you will be condemned; and if you give alms, you will do harm to your spirits.
(14b) When you go into any land and walk about in the districts, if they receive you, eat what they will set before you, and heal the sick among them.
(14c) For what goes into your mouth will not defile you, but that which issues from your mouth - it is that which will defile you."

*7:14 He called all the multitude to himself, and said to them, "Hear me, all of you, and understand. 15 There is nothing from outside of the man, that going into him can defile him; but **the things which proceed out of the man are those that defile the man**. 16 If anyone has ears to hear, let him hear!"*

Disregarding 14a and 14b and just considering 14c, except for leaving out the mouth there is not much of a difference between Mark and Thomas here, is there? Of course, it is crystal-clear why

Thomas has 14c and that it is an explanation of the reason behind the instruction in 14b to 'eat what they will set before you'. Mark however happily takes the opportunity to copy only one sentence out of a logion - thereby dragging it out of context - and even of that one sentence he copies only half, thereby dragging it all completely out of context.

Mark continues and once more uses the house context - 34 of those throughout his gospel - and for the second time has Jesus explain a parable in full. We know what happened last time he did that, so brace yourselves for the similarly ugly transformation of logion 45 - I'm including 45b here even though it's evidently ignored:

(45b) A good man brings forth good from his storehouse; an evil man brings forth evil things from his evil storehouse, which is in his heart, and says evil things.
(45c) For out of the abundance of the heart he brings forth evil things."

7:17 When he had entered into a house away from the multitude, his disciples asked him about the parable. 18 He said to them, "Are you also without understanding? Don't you perceive that whatever goes into the man from outside can't defile him, 19 because it doesn't go into his heart, but into his stomach, then into the latrine, making all foods clean?" 20 He said, "That which proceeds out of the man, that defiles the man. 21 **For from within, out of the hearts of men, proceed evil thoughts**, *adulteries, sexual sins, murders, thefts, 22 covetings, wickedness, deceit, lustful desires, an evil eye, blasphemy, pride, and foolishness. 23 All these evil things come from within, and defile the man."*

Looking at that sheer endless list; I do wonder how much time and fierce debate it took them to come up with exactly those, and decide that it wasn't long enough yet to feel obliged to explicitly state that it wasn't an exhaustive list but merely an inclusive one. The sad truth is that this one time Mark actually starts off with using logion 14c in the right context. Yes indeed, you can't be defiled by what goes into your mouth, because that enters the stomach and not the heart - that is, among others, exactly what Thomas means. But then he leaves out the difference in Thomas between the good man and the evil man: the good heart and the evil heart, and generalises it all in order to bring about the central and focal Church message that all men (and women, of course - sometimes suddenly they're equal to men) are evil.

Mark explaining parables...

The context of Thomas is perfectly clear, yet Mark highly selectively quotes this finely balanced Thomas logion in order to phrase the very core of Christian religion: original sin. But Mark deserves full credit here for framing Thomas' words into this pivotal point of the Church agenda

Chapter 7 concludes with more mixed Thomas context; Mark now even has a seemingly ordinary woman produce one, and a bit more context is needed to understand the story:

(93a) [Jesus said] "Do not give what is holy to dogs, lest they throw them on the dung-heap.

7:24 From there he arose, and went away into the borders of Tyre and Sidon. He entered into a house, and didn't want anyone to know it, but he couldn't escape notice. 25 For a woman, whose little daughter had an unclean spirit, having heard of him, came and fell down at his feet. 26 Now the woman was a Greek, a Syrophoenician by race. She begged him that he would cast the demon out of her daughter. 27 But Jesus said to her, "Let the children be filled first, for **it is not appropriate to take the children's bread and throw it to the dogs.***" 28 But she answered him, "Yes, Lord. Yet even the dogs under the table eat the children's crumbs." 29 He said to her, "For this saying, go your way. The demon has gone out of your daughter." 30 She went away to her house, and found the child having been laid on the bed, with the demon gone out.*

Verse 27 is a remake of logion 93a, and Jesus rewards the woman with the expulsion of the demon, simply for stating this puzzling remark. All this makes sense in the Church context as she is labelled a Gentile - but that will be discussed during Luke and Matthew. If you don't believe that these verses are a remake on logion 93 I can hardly blame you, yet you'll be convinced when those of Luke and Matthew are discussed - I'm counting this one

What about the style and score of chapters 6 and 7? Uncomfortable is a good word to describe it. One literal logion copied, that is to say, half of it. Four logia inferred if you are trying to be open-minded (or full of fantasy, depending on your viewpoint), another two literal logia combined for one purpose, and this last one, half of a logion, barely recognisable.
Mark surely hasn't travelled back on his newly found path. I count 3 logia in chapter 7 to add to the grand total of 14: 17 now.
In case you wonder why a score is kept at the end of chapters: I do like to be completely transparent, and the process of evaluating and "ticking off" logia to be entirely and easily traceable. It is little work to go through only one chapter and check the logia and compare those to the score, and I prefer totalling it per chapter rather than at every logion

Jesus is Christ

Chapter 8 verses 1 through 10 repeat verses 6:34-44, with a very vague - if obstinate - hint of logion 8c:

(8c) He threw all the small fish back into the sea and chose the large fish without difficulty.

8:6 He commanded the multitude to sit down on the ground, and he took the seven loaves. Having given thanks, he broke them, and gave them to his disciples to serve, and they served the multitude. 7 They had a few small fish. Having blessed them, he said to serve these also. 8 They ate, and were filled. They took up seven baskets of broken pieces that were left over.

The size of the fish really is irrelevant to the story as it's equally incredible to feed four thousand people with a (guesstimated) dozen or so large fish. My attempt to relate this to Thomas is slightly tongue-in-cheek, I am not counting this one yet it is a telling "miracle" without a doubt.

The next verses serve to temper expectations with an oblique reference to either logion 113a or logion 51a or both, replacing his disciples with the Pharisees: the kingdom won't come any time soon:

(113a) His disciples said to him, "When will the kingdom come?"
(51a) His disciples said to him, "When will the repose of the dead come about, and when will the new world come?"
(51b) He said to them, "What you look forward to has already come, but you do not recognize it."

8:11 The Pharisees came out and began to question him, seeking from him a sign from heaven, and testing him. 12 He sighed deeply in his spirit, and said, "Why does this generation seek a sign? Most certainly I tell you, no sign will be given to this generation." 13 He left them, and again entering into the boat, departed to the other side.

Are these verses derived from Thomas or not? It could be anything really, it is to be expected that people are curious for signs with a Messiah in front of them. Thomas saying that the kingdom is already here is of little use to Mark so he would clearly leave that out; only if 51a were largely copied would I have enough distinctive words to attribute it.

Mark seems to have recuperated when he performs a true miracle: making sure of Jesus' mystery by truly mystifying it:

*8:14 They forgot to take bread; and they didn't have more than one loaf in the boat with them. 15 He warned them, saying, "Take heed: beware of the yeast of the Pharisees and the yeast of Herod." 16 They reasoned with one another, saying, "It's because we have no bread." 17 Jesus, perceiving it, said to them, "Why do you reason that it's because you have no bread? **Don't you perceive yet, neither understand? Is your heart still hardened? 18 Having eyes, don't you see? Having ears, don't you hear**? Don't you remember? 19 When I broke the five loaves among the five thousand, how many baskets full of broken pieces did you take up?" They told him, "Twelve." 20 "When the seven loaves fed the four thousand, how many baskets full of broken pieces did you take up?" They told him, "Seven." 21 **He asked them, "Don't you understand yet**?"*

No of course they don't understand, I don't understand either; it's as clear as mud. This is the first time Mark makes Jesus unintelligible. What is Mark's goal here, throwing more Thomasine at it?

Logion 96b names the yeast in the loaves but yeast (or rather, leaven) is a popular Tanakh theme with 67 occurrences. The riddling 'Having eyes do you not see, and having ears do you not hear?' might refer to logion 28c or the first two sentences of logion 17, a and b, but it's a lot more likely that it refers to Isaiah 6:9-10:

(Isaiah 6:9 He said, "Go, and tell this people, 'You hear indeed, but don't understand. You see indeed, but don't perceive.' 10 Make the heart of this people fat. Make their ears heavy, and shut their eyes; lest they see with their eyes, hear with their ears, understand with their heart, and turn again, and be healed.")

Just as a hardened heart pertains to the ample references to the Pharaoh in the book of Exodus, but most importantly Isaiah 63:17:

(Isaiah 63:17 O Yahweh, why do you make us wander from your ways, and harden our heart from your fear? Return for your servants' sake, the tribes of your inheritance.)

The repetition of the question about understanding, as well as the phrase itself, are lovely Thomasine one-liners invented by Mark; he has his weaknesses in copying Thomas but sure does some good stuff - these riddles might inspire readers with awe, and keep up the mystery - stressing the need for teachers and guides to interpret Jesus' words.

Verses 8:22 through 26 have Jesus perform yet another miracle, healing yet another blind. Neatly ending with another instruction to not tell anyone (we all know how that works out, don't we) and using a Thomasine 'don't enter into the village' for that.

It is obvious by now that the multitude of references to senses in Thomas has been integrated into Mark, and undergone a miraculous process: from pure metaphors, each and every one of them, they have been assembled into pragmatic literals in Mark. Where Thomas means perceiving by seeing, Mark considers it a mere optical process. Where Thomas' hearing means understanding, Mark uses it as purely auditory. Unless, of course, Mark is quoting Isaiah...

Finally and fortunately, verses 8:27 through 30 almost literally copy the convenient parts of logion 13: 13a, 13b, 13c and 13i. With the inevitable twists:

(13a) Jesus said to his disciples, "Compare me to someone and tell me whom I am like."
(13b) Simon Peter said to him, "You are like a righteous angel."
(13c) Matthew said to him, "You are like a wise philosopher."
(13d) Thomas said to him, "Master, my mouth is wholly incapable of saying whom you are like."
(...)
(13i) Thomas said to them, "If I tell you one of the things which he told me, you will pick up stones and throw them at me; a fire will come out of the stones and burn you up."

*8:27 Jesus went out, with his disciples, into the villages of Caesarea Philippi. On the way he asked his disciples, "**Who do men say that I am?**" 28 They told him, "**John the Baptizer, and others say Elijah, but others, one of the prophets.**" 29 He said to them, "But who do you say that I am?" Peter answered, "**You are the Christ.**" 30 **He commanded them that they should tell no one about him.***

John the Baptist and Elijah get thrown in of course, work our way through to the prophecy we must... It is no coincidence that these two get clubbed together: that's part of Project Elijah, another important point in Mark. In Luke and Matthew we will see how more nitty-gritty details of the Isaiah prophecy are handled, and at some point they have to do with John and Elijah and the rather obnoxious prophecy of Malachi 4:5:

(Malachi 4:5 Behold, I will send you Elijah the prophet before the great and terrible day of Yahweh comes.)

It was rather difficult to fulfil that prophecy as Elijah was taken up to heaven around the 9th century BCE. This is a splendid example of a prophecy that is equally as required to fulfil as it is impossible: whoever might show up claiming to be Elijah, there would be no one else to credibly confirm that he in fact is Elijah. He could raise someone from the dead, that would certainly lend him credibility, because Elijah raised a widow's son (1 Kings 17:17-24). Jesus does exactly the same in Luke 7:12-15, which adds to the confusion about who's the new Elijah.

It has become clear that from the very beginning John the Baptist has been chosen to be portrayed as Elijah, and the name-dropping of the two right here serves to further that cause.

Mark shows good understanding of story telling here: where Peter is first in Thomas, labelling him merely an angel (or messenger), in Mark it is Peter who must come last because he has the final say in it, stating the most important message: Jesus is the Messiah, the Christ, the anointed one.

Jesus next predicts his own end for the first time in Mark. Matthew will correct him for saying 'after three days' instead of 'on the third day'; one of Mark's minor mistakes.

Chapter 8 ends with logion 55:

(55b) And whoever does not hate his brothers and sisters and take up his cross in my way will not be worthy of me."

*8:34 He called the multitude to himself with his disciples, and said to them, "Whoever wants to come after me, **let him deny himself**, and **take up his cross**, and **follow me**. 35 For whoever wants to save his life will lose it; and whoever will lose his life for my sake and the sake of the Good News will save it. 36 For what does it profit a man, to gain the whole world, and forfeit his life? 37 For what will a man give in exchange for his life? 38 For whoever will be ashamed of me and of my words in this adulterous and sinful generation, the Son of Man also will be ashamed of him, when he comes in his Father's glory, with the holy angels."*

Hating of brothers and sisters is too cryptic and undesired and turned into 'deny himself', and it's steered into the proper direction in verse 38: Judgment Day. Good effort from Mark to change the negative 'not worthy of me' into the very tempting 'follow me'.

I can count only 2 logia in chapter 8, which brings the total to 19

Lost in addressing tough issues

Chapter 9 starts with a remake of logion 1; experiencing or tasting death is nowhere to be found in the Tanakh so Thomas is a highly likely source:

(1) And he said, "Whoever finds the interpretation of these sayings will not experience death."

*9:1 He said to them, "Most certainly I tell you, there are some standing here who will **in no way taste death** until they **see God's Kingdom come with power**."*

The epileptic boy reuses some of the key Thomas words, wrapping this miracle in Thomas context: childhood, fire and water, destroy:

9:21 He asked his father, "How long has it been since this has come to him?" He said, "From childhood. 22 Often it has cast him both into the fire and into the water to destroy him. But if you can do anything, have compassion on us, and help us."

Verses 25 through 26 feature dumb, deaf, enter, corpse, dead:

9:25 When Jesus saw that a multitude came running together, he rebuked the unclean spirit, saying to him, "You mute and deaf spirit, I command you, come out of him, and never enter him again!" 26 After crying out and convulsing him greatly, it came out of him. The boy became like one dead, so much that most of them said, "He is dead."

Both Luke and Matthew drop all this context of the epileptic boy. Whether they just grew bored with the details or disliked them is impossible to tell, but it is a fine example of an occasion where Mark is being reduced to a mere mention: Mark spends 11 verses on the epileptic boy, very precious space: 0.16% of all his 680 sentences. Luke spends 5 out of his 1,150 verses (0.043%) where Matthew uses 5 out of his 1,070 (0.047%) - about a quarter of Mark's portion. It is a pioneer's fate as well and we will see it occurring quite often: (parts of) Mark being appended, corrected, fixed or just completely ignored and left out

Verses 35 through 37 teach the disciples humility, garbling logion 4b, logion 28a (or is that Isaiah 63:11?), and logion 22. Namedropping 'servant' adds to the Church's case

(4b) For many who are first will become last, and they will become one and the same."
(28a) Jesus said, "I took my place in the midst of the world, and I appeared to them in flesh.
(22c) They said to him, "Shall we then, as children, enter the kingdom?"

*9:35 He sat down, and called the twelve; and he said to them, "**If any man wants to be first, he shall be last of all**, and servant of all." 36 He took a little child, and **set him in the middle of them**. Taking him in his arms, he said to them, 37 "**Whoever receives one such little child in my name, receives me**, and **whoever receives me, doesn't receive me, but him who sent me**."*

Mark has Jesus equate himself to the kingdom here, by equating himself to God. The first logion is fairly clear to see and the only one that's being counted.
The children entering the kingdom is another grand theme of Thomas, and difficult to address - what did he mean by it? Mark is exploring that here, and chapter 9 ends with Mark again using the image of children, and the last part of logion 22d, completely rewritten. The occurrence of hands, feet and eyes is still there, but once again they're meant literally and directed towards Judgment Day:

(22d) Jesus said to them, "When you make the two one, and when you make the inside like the outside and the outside like the inside, and the above like the below, and when you make the male and the female one and the same, so that the male not be male nor the female female; and when you fashion eyes in the place of an eye, and a hand in place of a hand, and a foot in place of a foot, and a likeness in place of a likeness; then will you enter the kingdom."

*9:42 Whoever will cause one of these little ones who believe in me to stumble, it would be better for him if he were thrown into the sea with a millstone hung around his neck. 43 If **your hand** causes you to stumble, cut it off. It is better for you to enter into life maimed, rather than **having your two hands** to go into Gehenna, into the unquenchable fire, 44 'where their worm doesn't die, and the fire is not quenched.' 45 If **your foot** causes you to stumble, cut it off. It is better for you to enter into life lame, rather than **having your two feet** to be cast into Gehenna, into the fire that will never be quenched- 46 'where their worm doesn't die, and the fire is not quenched.' 47 If **your eye** causes you to stumble, cast it out. It is better for you to enter into God's Kingdom with one eye, rather than **having two eyes** to be cast into the Gehenna of fire, 48 'where their worm doesn't die, and the fire is not quenched.'*

I will admit it is not that easy to make a case for logion 22d here. If you can recognise 22c in 9:37 it sure helps.
Mark certainly is running wild now. Twisting and bending logia is to be expected, but garbling Thomas to this extent is questionable. Verses 44, 46 and 48 are literal copies of the very last phrase of Isaiah:

(Isaiah 66:24 "They will go out, and look at the dead bodies of the men who have transgressed against me; for their worm will not die, nor will their fire be quenched, and they will be loathsome to all mankind.")

The word 'Gehenna' is not used by Isaiah but it's a well-known reference in the Tanakh to refer to hell. Who will recognise Thomas in this? Few. And who will recognise Thomas and believe that it's Thomas? Even fewer - Mark misses the mark here, confusing means with goals, it seems.

It is interesting to see Mark's mission revealed in these verses right here: copy Thomas, copy prophecies (preferably Isaiah) and thence create a true Messiah - but that's a delicate business and just doing both at the exact same time and place doesn't really work. Granted, Mark can't do much else but make a mess of the original Thomas right here in 22d, and adding Isaiah does strengthen the doom and gloom of these verses. They add weight to his Jesus and provide a nice angle for Jews, but won't sway anyone who's heard or read Thomas

Chapter 10 continues logion 22d, this time the first part, tackling another difficult theme of Thomas: making the two one. Where Thomas uses this as an instruction to liberate oneself from duality, of course, once more, Mark redirects it in a literal sense. I am going to copy a lot more than just the four verses:

*10:1 He arose from there and came into the borders of Judea and beyond the Jordan. Multitudes came together to him again. As he usually did, he was again teaching them. 2 Pharisees came to him testing him, and asked him, "Is it lawful for a man to divorce his wife?" 3 He answered, "What did Moses command you?" 4 They said, "Moses allowed a certificate of divorce to be written, and to divorce her." 5 But Jesus said to them, "For your hardness of heart, he wrote you this commandment. 6 But from the beginning of the creation, **God made them male and female**. 7 For this cause **a man** will leave his father and mother, and **will join to his wife**, 8 and the two will become one flesh, so that they are no longer two, but one flesh. 9 What therefore God has joined together, let no man separate." 10 In the house, his disciples asked him again about the same matter. 11 He said to them, "Whoever divorces his wife and marries another commits adultery against her. 12 If a woman* *herself divorces her husband and marries another, she commits adultery."*

That is a really brilliant find, highly creative - and addressing a Thomas theme just as a theme in stead of (ab)using a logion works really well.

Using Genesis 1:27 in verse 10:6 and Genesis 2:24 in verse 10:8 and then concluding 'so that they are no longer two, but one flesh' is strong, very strong - although that extra explanation is giving Mark away. Mark is repeating what he said just letters before, as if he wants to make extra sure that the reader "gets it".

As a side effect, in an attempt to use Thomas' theme of making two one, the divorce is singled out, and another Jewish custom bites the dust - two birds with one stone, but this time not without consequences. Mark doesn't hold back here and is very strict, and we'll see Matthew build in an escape or two. Luke, strangely, spends one meagre verse on it - seemingly reluctantly even, and without reference to 'two' nor 'one', or anything from the Tanakh.

A pioneer's life, Mark - it is hard sometimes isn't it? Out of the blue this statement on divorce appears: there has been no talk about man, woman, relationships, or anything remotely close to marriage or divorce - surely it's a nice pretext that the Pharisees are testing him and that it is supposed to be them who drop the divorce topic on Jesus, but that's not the point. And thus Matthew hurries to squeeze in a verse or two into his sermon on the mount before repeating Mark's verses - with escape clauses added to them on both occasions.

Concerning Matthew copying these verses of Mark: when we get there you will see how Mark has lead him into temptation, and at that point you'll wonder how you could have overlooked that right here

Verses 13 through 16 repeat 9:37, with verse 16 being another touchy gesture from Mark: Jesus takes the children in his arms, and blesses them. Unsure whether Mark invented a scenery here that has been used thousands of times since, but leaders embracing children - it is a most powerful image:

*10:13 They were bringing to him little children, that he should touch them, but the disciples rebuked those who were bringing them. 14 But when Jesus saw it, he was moved with indignation, and said to them, "Allow the little children to come to me! Don't forbid them, for **God's Kingdom belongs to such as these**. 15 Most certainly I tell you, **whoever will not receive God's Kingdom like a little child, he will in no way enter into it**." 16 He took them in his arms, and blessed them, laying his hands on them.*

(22b) He said to his disciples, "These infants being suckled are like those who enter the kingdom."
(22c) They said to him, "Shall we then, as children, enter the kingdom?"

Logion 22b and 22c are used here, which are similar to logion 46b (which will be discussed later). Logion 22 must have made quite an impact, given the attention and hair-splitting it receives in two chapters and three collections of verses. Yet Mark is neatly handling Thomas' theme of children here, another puzzling riddle for the gospel-writers to deal with: become like children in order to enter the kingdom - what on earth would that mean? Mark adds extremely little to Thomas here, advancing from Thomas' "enter the kingdom as a child" to "receive the kingdom like a (little) child". Mark continues on the riches, introducing his famous camel-needle comparison, and another Thomasine allegory is destroyed: rich means financially wealthy, poor is the opposite of rich; behold the inverse of logion 54:

(54) Jesus said, "Blessed are the poor, for yours is the kingdom of heaven."

*10:23 Jesus looked around, and said to his disciples, "**How difficult it is for those who have riches to enter into God's Kingdom!**" 24 The disciples were amazed at his words. But Jesus answered again,*

64

*"**Children, how hard it is for those who trust in riches to enter into God's Kingdom**! 25 It is easier for a camel to go through a needle's eye than for a rich man to enter into God's Kingdom."*

Mark repeats his copy of logion 54, prefixing it with calling his audience children; Mark is working hard to get the children theme going: 6 verses with that word in it, in 50 consecutive verses. Mark wraps it up greatly with another garbled reshuffling of logia:

*10:29 Jesus said, "Most certainly I tell you, there is no one who has left house, or brothers, or sisters, or father, or mother, or wife, or children, or land, for my sake, and for the sake of the Good News, 30 but he will receive one hundred times more now in this time: houses, brothers, sisters, mothers, children, and land, with persecutions; and in the age to come eternal life. 31 **But many who are first will be last; and the last first**."*

House, brothers, sisters, mother, father, children, land - Mark fluidly interjects Thomas context here in order to have Jesus promise an afterlife to his followers. Mark finishes with a repetition of logion 4b to keep the mystery cloaked - and salvation up to interpretation by the clergy of course.

The next verses give us the third Passion Prediction, followed by the Position in the Kingdom. The left and right hand of logion 62 might be referenced here although that certainly is stretching it, but the drinking of the cup is a splendid combination of logion 13f and logion 108a (and I am counting it):

(13f) Because you have drunk, you have become intoxicated from the bubbling spring which I have measured out."
(108a) Jesus said, "He who will drink from my mouth will become like me.

10:39 They said to him, "We are able." Jesus said to them, "You shall indeed drink the cup that I drink, and you shall be baptized with the baptism that I am baptized with; 40 but to sit at my right hand and at my left hand is not mine to give, but for whom it has been prepared."

Wrapping up chapter 10, counting 5 logia in chapters 9 and 10 (totalling 24), servant has become a central theme as well now, and Mark makes it very explicit:

10:43 But it shall not be so among you, but whoever wants to become great among you shall be your servant. 44 Whoever of you wants to become first among you, shall be bondservant of all. 45 **For the Son of Man also came not to be served, but to serve, and to give his life as a ransom for many."**

Repose

With chapter 10 alluding no more to Thomas, it's time for a repose (pun intended).

Mark has advanced to a literary stage where there is a whole lot more grey than in the beginning. Whereas there undoubtedly is a connection between e.g. verses 2:20-22 and logion 47 as they are almost literally the same, the use of Thomas logia by Mark now is a lot harder to demonstrate.

Am I trying to read Thomas into Mark? To be quite frank, maybe I am - but that entirely depends on the exact definition of "reading into".

I am inclined to believe that the rise and spread of Thomas instigated the Judaic religious institutes of that time to invent some response, which finally ended up in Catholicism. But I am absolutely convinced that the text of Thomas led to the gospels, for many reasons which will slowly unfold.

Although my case seems to be solid so far, I am only halfway Mark and must admit that I am lost in a sea of shrapnel since chapters 6 and 8: trying to tie Mark to Thomas since that point has come to look an awful lot like mindreading

My sincere goal still is to be as objective as I can, yet I can only guarantee as much of that as I can - which almost sounds Thomasine, doesn't it? Naturally, I am reading Mark through Thomas' lens here, trying to identify logia, phrases, themes from Thomas, and I will do the same when I am going through Matthew and Luke. I will verify my findings when in doubt, as I for instance have done with tasting or experiencing death, and just as I have done with the word 'servant' which turned out to occur less frequent in the four gospels than in the Tanakh. When counting average occurrences per verse: 203 verses out of 8,235 (0,025%) containing the word 'servant' versus 1,117 out of 31,317 (0,036%) - the Tanakh contains about 50% more occurrences of that word than the New Testament.

As another example, let's take verse 10:38 through 40: there is no use trying to tie the right and left hand back to Thomas; these notions are so widespread that they could have come from anywhere. But the drinking of the cup? There are parallels to Isaiah 51:17 and 51:22 there, when it comes to drinking the cup. However, Isaiah mentions wrath, fury, and it's God's cup.

Jeremiah chapter 25 verses 15, 17 and 28? That's the cup of wrath as well. The Book of Lamentations mentions drinking from the cup - of desolation.

Yet a "positive cup" filled with relatively good (in the long run, and compared to the other cups mentioned above), and people drinking from the same cup Jesus drinks of? That is undeniably linked to Thomas and Thomas alone in the so very powerful logion 108

The remainder of Mark

A turning point perhaps, Mark drastically returns to his initial approach: incorporating fairly literal logia in order to twist them into just the right direction. No more complicated scenery sketching and turning context into content, he is at two-thirds of his story and has been working towards this very end all the time. Chapter 11 and further will give us a dozen logia!
Chapter 11 starts with logia 48 and / or 106 (I will count them as one), mixed with Psalms 46:2 ('the mountains are shaken into the heart of the seas'); a bit of extra context is provided:

(48) Jesus said, "If two make peace with each other in this one house, they will say to the mountain, 'Move Away,' and it will move away."
(106) Jesus said, "When you make the two one, you will become the sons of man, and when you say, 'Mountain, move away,' it will move away."

11:20 As they passed by in the morning, they saw the fig tree withered away from the roots. 21 Peter, remembering, said to him, "Rabbi, look! The fig tree which you cursed has withered away." 22 Jesus answered them, "Have faith in God. 23 For most certainly I tell you, whoever may **tell this mountain,** *'****Be taken up and cast into the sea****,' and doesn't doubt in his heart,* **but believes** *that what he says is happening; he shall have whatever he says.*

One could make the case that the mountain and sea are wholly inspired by Psalms 46:2, but speaking to a mountain? That is undeniably linked to Thomas alone; most surprisingly so there appears to be no one speaking to mountains in the Tanakh.
Mark adds the believing part, which he stresses again in the next verse; simply believe that which you prayed for, you have received - this chapter certainly is about faith.

Chapter 12 and the parable of the tenants gives us logion 65. Mark introduces verse 5 which breaks Thomas' three act structure of servants sent as well as the treatment they receive; in Thomas only the third servant is killed:

(65a) He said, "There was a good man who owned a vineyard.
(65b) He leased it to tenant farmers so that they might work it and he might collect the produce from them.
(65c) He sent his servant so that the tenants might give him the produce of the vineyard.
(65d) They seized his servant and beat him, all but killing him.
(65e) The servant went back and told his master.
(65f) The master said, 'Perhaps he did not recognize them.'
(65g) He sent another servant.
(65h) The tenants beat this one as well.
(65i) Then the owner sent his son and said, 'Perhaps they will show respect to my son.'
(65j) Because the tenants knew that it was he who was the heir to the vineyard, they seized him and killed him.
(65k) Let him who has ears hear."

*12:1 He began to speak to them in parables. "**A man planted a vineyard**, put a hedge around it, dug a pit for the wine press, built a tower, **rented it out to a farmer**, and went into another country. 2 When it was time, he **sent a servant** to the farmer **to get from the farmer his share of the fruit of the vineyard**. 3 They **took him, beat him, and sent him away empty**. 4 Again, he **sent another servant** to them; and they threw stones at him, wounded him in the head, and **sent him away shamefully treated**. 5 Again he sent another; and they killed him; and many others, beating some, and killing some. 6 Therefore still having one, **his beloved son, he sent** him last to them, **saying, 'They will respect my son.'** 7 But those farmers said among themselves, 'This is the heir. Come, let's kill him, and the inheritance will be ours.' 8 **They took him, killed him**, and cast him out of the vineyard.*

Mark adds lots, basically anything not emphasised, and also leaves out a lot. Mark needs verse 5 in order to build up for his main twist: the son and heir, who is meant to be Jesus so Mark adds 'beloved'. The expansion in verse 1 serves as a reference to Isaiah 5:2; Isaiah's chapter starts as follows:

(Isaiah 5:1 Let me sing for my well beloved a song of my beloved about his vineyard. My beloved had a vineyard on a very fruitful hill. 2 He dug it up, gathered out its stones, planted it with the choicest vine, built a tower in the middle of it, and also cut out a wine press in it. He looked for it to yield grapes, but it yielded wild grapes.)

Note the renting out to a (single) farmer; another of Mark's mistakes.
Mark adds yet another twist to the story by finishing it off in verse 9 with the wrath of God after the son is killed. In Isaiah chapter 5 the vineyard gets destroyed and maybe that inspired Mark to this twist, as it would make no sense for the owner to destroy his own vineyard as a punishment for the tenants who abused his servants and even killed his son - now would it:

*12:9 What therefore will the lord of the vineyard do? He will come and destroy the farmers, and will give the vineyard to others. 10 Haven't you even read this Scripture: '**The stone which the builders rejected was made the head of the corner**. 11 This was from the Lord. It is marvelous in our eyes'?"*

**(66a) Jesus said, "Show me the stone which the builders have rejected.
(66b) That one is the cornerstone."**

Logion 66 seems out of place here in verse 10. It might be an oblique reference to Isaiah 28:16 but it is a literal copy of Psalms 118:22-23. What is the reason for its placement right here? The most plausible explanation is that in Thomas logion 66 immediately follows logion 65, but that argument could be turned around for the same reason.

Why is it obvious that Mark copied Thomas instead of vice versa? Next to the obvious addition of details from Isaiah 5, Mark adds that the son is cast out of the vineyard, literally (r)ejected - a superfluous detail added to the story unless it serves a certain purpose: Luke and Matthew will give away that this is an invention of Mark and extraneous to its source, Thomas.

There is one riddle in Thomas right here, that remains to puzzle me:

(65f) The master said, 'Perhaps he did not recognize them.'

Who is meant by 'he'? At that point, five actors in total have come to the stage: the 'good man', the 'tenant farmers', the 'tenants', the 'servant' and the 'master'. The tenant farmers and tenants must be the same, but it is not so relevant whether that actually is the case. The scene unfolds between the servant who went back and told the master (or does it, really?), and that very servant can only be the servant who got sent, seized, beat and almost killed.

So there is only one 'he' to refer to, from the point of view of the master: the 'good man'. That is, if the master is still in the direct company of the servant and not making this comment to someone else; and even if the latter were the case, the master could still be referring to the good man with 'he'.

Then who is this master? If he is the same person as the good man, he can only be meaning to say "Perhaps the servant didn't recognise the tenants" which would be odd, because there's no hint at all in the entire logion that anyone sent would know any of the tenants. The only other possibility is that the master is someone else than the good man, and means to say "Perhaps the good man didn't recognise the tenants (for what they are)". A true puzzle

Mark seems to be in a hurry to throw in as many logia as he can, while reserving almost all space for his final acts: justifying the end of Jesus in fulfilling the prophecies - or vice versa. Verses 12:13 through 17 indicate the likes of that, giving us logion 100:

(100a) They showed Jesus a gold coin and said to him, "Caesar's men demand taxes from us."
(100b) He said to them, "Give Caesar what belongs to Caesar, give God what belongs to God, and give me what is mine."

*12:13 They sent some of the Pharisees and the Herodians to him, that they might trap him with words. 14 When they had come, they asked him, "Teacher, we know that you are honest, and don't defer to anyone; for you aren't partial to anyone, but truly teach the way of God. Is it lawful to pay taxes to Caesar, or not? 15 Shall we give, or shall we not give?" But he, knowing their hypocrisy, said to them, "Why do you test me? **Bring me a denarius**, that I may see it." 16 They brought it. He said to them, "**Whose is this image and inscription**?" They said to him, "**Caesar's**." 17 Jesus answered them, "**Render to Caesar the things that are Caesar's, and to God the things that are God's**." They marveled greatly at him.*

It is an awful lot of text to deal with one straightforward logion, even though it starts the last three trick questions of the Pharisees. It also seems rather pointless to acknowledge that Jesus truly teaches the way of God, and then ask him about laws of men - but maybe that's the whole point, and I am missing it.
Once more it is so very evident how beautifully concise Thomas is, and to what lengths Mark goes in order to explain it all and try to put everything into the right context - which is there already anyway. It is trivial whether the coin really has Caesar on it or not, but it is significant that it is gold, not silver: money is not the issue here. Thomas means to say that Caesar, like God, is just another powerhouse that needs to be pleased; if it takes gold to do so, so be it.
Needless to say, 'give me what is mine' - the entire clue of the logion - is completely left out

Equally hasty is verse 27, it seems, concluding the scolding of the Sadducees about raising the dead. Instead of terribly lengthy, this one is terribly short:

*12:26 But about the dead, that they are raised; haven't you read in the book of Moses, about the Bush, how God spoke to him, saying, 'I am the God of Abraham, the God of Isaac, and the God of Jacob'? 27 **He is not the God of the dead, but of the living**. You are therefore badly mistaken."*

The quote from verse 12:26 is a literal copy from Exodus 3:6 and verse 27 could very well point to Isaiah 8:19, but another tick off the box for mentioning living versus dead and associating God with the living - there is no God of the dead or of the living in the entire Tanakh.

Next Mark tackles the love thy neighbour issue of logion 25, putting it second to loving God. It is odd that only this very phrase makes it in here in combination with 'love God' - out of the so many other commandments that could have been included: common sense and good storytelling dictate that it should either be one commandment, three, ten or any other number. But with only two, the weight between the both of them is divided equally and given the weight of that very first commandment, the other must be very important:

(25) Jesus said, "Love your brother like your soul, guard him like the pupil of your eye."

*12:28 One of the scribes came, and heard them questioning together, and knowing that he had answered them well, asked him, "Which commandment is the greatest of all?" 29 Jesus answered, "The greatest is, 'Hear, Israel, the Lord our God, the Lord is one: 30 you shall **love the Lord your God with all your heart**, and with all your soul, and with all your mind, and with all your strength.' **This is the first commandment**. 31 **The second is** like this, '**You shall love your neighbor as yourself**.' There is no other commandment greater than these."*

Verse 32 through 34 have the scribe repeat it, and stress that this surpasses the Jewish custom of burnt offerings and sacrifices (a copy of 1 Samuel 15:22). Another tick off the box; yet another rejection of yet another Jewish custom; and it's fair to assume that Thomas mentioning the neighbour in his logion is the sole driver for this odd juxtaposition, where the utmost important commandment is almost equated to another one that ranks somewhere at the bottom.

Logion 102 gets only its header turned into verses 38 through 40 - or does it:

(102) Jesus said, "Woe to the pharisees, for they are like a dog sleeping in the manger of oxen, for neither does he eat nor does he let the oxen eat."

*12:38 In his teaching he said to them, "**Beware of the scribes**, who like to walk in long robes, and to get greetings in the marketplaces, 39 and the best seats in the synagogues, and the best places at feasts: 40 those who devour widows' houses, and for a pretense make long prayers. These will receive greater condemnation."*

A hazy attempt by Mark? Or a failed attempt by me to find Thomas in Mark? I'm going with the latter for now, as it is clear that the Pharisees and scribes have to be sneered at. It is not until Luke that the 'Woe to the Pharisees' from Thomas is literally copied.

Rich versus poor are portrayed in the widow's gift; another Thomas theme is safely stowed away by associating rich with an abundance of money, and defining poor as the opposite of that. Logion 71 then appears in the prediction of the destruction of the temple:

(71) Jesus said, "I shall destroy this house, and no one will be able to build it [...]."

*13:1 As he went out of the temple, one of his disciples said to him, "Teacher, see what kind of stones and what kind of buildings!" 2 Jesus said to him, "Do you see these great buildings? **There will not be left here one stone on another, which will not be thrown** *down."*

Verse 1 is an obvious and poor pretext for throwing in verse 2 and copying logion 71.
We then see a literal copy of logion 113a, which starts a lengthy monologue about the signs of the end of the ages. Alas, as the rest of the logion is left out, leaving us with a fragment that is too generic to attribute, it is not enough to go on and count it:

(113a) His disciples said to him, "When will the kingdom come?"

*13:3 As he sat on the Mount of Olives opposite the temple, **Peter, James, John, and Andrew asked him privately, 4 "Tell us, when will these things be**? What is the sign that these things are all about to be fulfilled?"*

Is there a hint of logion 68 in verse 13, perhaps? Luke and Matthew will prove that such is the case and I am counting it for now. Thomas' 'Blessed' is substituted by the promise that those who endure to the end will be saved

(68a) Jesus said, "Blessed are you when you are hated and persecuted.

*13:13 **You will be hated by all men** for my name's sake, but he who endures to the end **will be saved**.*

Logion 79c gets a mention in the verses about the desolating sacrilege, the logion is inversed (for good pragmatic reasons, I think):

(79c) For there will be days when you will say, 'Blessed are the womb which has not conceived and the breasts which have not given milk.'

*13:17 But **woe to those who are with child** and to **those who nurse***

babies in those days!

What follows is a remake of the only other sentence of logion 113 that can be reused by Mark, 113c:

(113c) It will not be a matter of saying 'here it is' or 'there it is.'

13:21 Then if anyone tells you, 'Look, here is the Christ!' or, 'Look, there!' don't believe it.

That logion sentence is really nicely rephrased by Mark, who turns Thomas' 'not [...] a matter of' into an instruction that is perfectly in line with his theme of faith: 'don't believe it'.
Verses 30 through 31 incorporate logion 11a into an extremely odd twist to Mark's own words in verse 8:12, where he told the Pharisees that this generation would not see a sign:

(11a) Jesus said, "This heaven will pass away, and the one above it will pass away.

*13:28 "Now from the fig tree, learn this parable. When the branch has now become tender, and produces its leaves, you know that the summer is near; 29 even so you also, when you see these things coming to pass, know that it is near, at the doors. 30 **Most certainly I say to you, this generation will not pass away until all these things happen**. 31 Heaven and earth will pass away, but my words will not pass away. 32 **But of that day or that hour no one knows, not even the angels in heaven, nor the Son, but only the Father**.*

Perhaps it is about time now to install true fear into the hearts of believers? Then again verse 32 seems to contradict these last verses again.
It's a Catch 22 really, the whole business of threatening people into obedience with a looming Doomsday: if you prophesise the end of the world only a few years or decades ahead, you'll be proven wrong soon and your scheme will fall through. Yet if you put it at

e.g. a few centuries from now most people might just disregard it as not enough of their concern.

The best bet is to avoid any and all transparency and send out mixed messages, and use those to 'dualise' people back and forth between the various messages. That way they'll busy themselves adding weight to one message by subtracting it from another and vice versa, instead of standing still, reflecting on the entire concept of the messaging itself, and wondering about the very essence of that.

Yet Mark is also trying to do something else here: 'learn this parable'. Only copying the parables of Thomas might have been giving away something, perhaps? After three quarters of his gospel Mark feels confident enough to come up with a parable of his own, and it is a fine one really. It has allegory, with the comparison of pending summer to the day of judgment, and similar to Thomas it has animate objects. The subject itself, the branch of the fig tree, performs action and undergoes transformation. Just as it is inevitable that summer will come when trees produce leaves is the fact that the long awaited day of judgment will come, is what Mark is implying.

This is his only parable but it is a promising one - we will see that Matthew but especially Luke will produce parables of their own as well, and they will be quite different

Logion 21e and 21f appear in verses 33 through 37, where Mark has God personify the owner of the house. Bear with me please; Luke and Matthew will prove that this logion is the source by adding other parts of it:

(21e) Therefore I say, if the owner of a house knows that the thief is coming, he will begin his vigil before he comes and will not let him dig through into his house of his domain to carry away his goods.
(21f) You, then, be on your guard against the world.

*13:33 **Watch, keep alert**, and pray; for you don't know when the*

*time is. 34 "It is like a man, traveling to another country, having left his house, and given authority to his servants, and to each one his work, and also commanded the doorkeeper to keep watch. 35 Watch therefore, for **you don't know when the lord of the house is coming**, whether at evening, or at midnight, or when the rooster crows, or in the morning; 36 lest coming suddenly he might find you sleeping. 37 What I tell you, I tell all: **Watch**."*

After this enormous end sprint, chapter 14 is dedicated to Mark entirely. With only very few Thomas words: (the strange man with) the jar, guest room, the cup at the memorial meal (not the Gethsemane one, that is Isaiah's), shepherd and sheep, spirit and flesh. A different hand seems to hold the pen here, or is it way beyond copying Thomas with all eyes fixed on the prophecies? Chapter 15 is well underway when logion 42 might be found in verse 15:

(42) Jesus said, "Become passers-by."

*15:21 They compelled **one passing by**, coming from the country, Simon of Cyrene, the father of Alexander and Rufus, to go with them, that he might bear his cross.*

Become passers-by, Thomas said. Is Mark turning that into 'Carry my cross' in this way? It is the last reference to Thomas that could possibly be found in the original ending at verse 8 of chapter 16. Luke 23:26 and Matthew 27:32 repeat the event but both omit the term 'passer-by' as well as the intimate detail about his lineage. Counting 12 logia for chapters 11 through to the very last, the grand total for Mark stands at 36.
The last three chapters of Mark, exclusively dealing with writing Jesus as Messiah into and out of history, show virtually nothing of Thomas

Mark evaluated

So, how has Mark fared? For a first counter strike he has done amazingly well in my opinion - Jesus has successfully been personified and brought to life, is solidly owned by the Church through ample references to the Tanakh, and conveniently muted for eternity (with the new end of 16:9-20 added later on - we'll get there soon). The tricky parts of Thomas, being the allegoric references to life and death, spirit and flesh, eating and drinking, have all been quite perfectly straight-jacketed into solely literal interpretations, all of which are now an intrinsic part of the Church Jesus, his teachings and his life.

The entire atmosphere of Thomas, with continued references and allegories to entering houses, children, garments, light and dark, rich and poor, it is all there. Mark's own invention might be Jesus getting in and out of a boat, and it fits nicely into Thomasine context.

The allegoric seeing and hearing have been quite naturally wielded into the miracles Mark has Jesus perform: healing and curing blind, deaf and mute people, the sick in general - it has all found a consistent place in Mark. It is very unlikely that Thomas inspired it but servants and serving have been pushed to the top: serving is what Jesus does, so serving is what his followers must do in order to honour him: follow the leader.

Mark has addressed the theme of children, albeit not very convincingly: where Thomas basically states 'become like a child to enter the kingdom', Mark has very uneventfully rephrased that as 'receive God's Kingdom like a little child in order to enter it'.

On the theme of making the two one, Mark has struck gold: from Exodus he quotes God creating male and female, whose uniting in matrimony makes them one again.

The anti-Judaic attitude has been put to great use, with Jesus ignoring Sabbath rules and regulations, attacking the Pharisees for their alleged hypocrisy, forbidding divorce while at it, and putting that all into the greater scheme of God disregarding the Jews - even using prophecies to justify that.

Everything in the gospels is aimed at acting out Isaiah chapter 53:

*53:1 **Who has believed our message***? *To whom has Yahweh's arm been revealed? 2 For he grew up before him as a tender plant, and as a root out of dry ground. He has no good looks or majesty. When we see him, there is no beauty that we should desire him. 3 **He was despised and rejected by men, a man of suffering and acquainted with disease**. He was despised as one from whom men hide their face; and **we didn't respect him**. 4 Surely **he has borne our sickness and carried our suffering**; yet we considered him plagued, struck by God, and afflicted. 5 But he was **pierced for our transgressions**. **He was crushed for our iniquities**. **The punishment that brought our peace was on him; and by his wounds we are healed**. 6 All we like sheep have gone astray. Everyone has turned to his own way; and **Yahweh has laid on him the iniquity of us all**. 7 He was oppressed, yet **when he was afflicted he didn't open his mouth**. As a lamb that is led to the slaughter, and as a sheep that before its shearers is silent, so he didn't open his mouth. 8 **He was taken away by oppression and judgment**. As for his generation, who considered that **he was cut off out of the land of the living** and **stricken for the disobedience of my people**? 9 They **made his grave with the wicked**, and with a rich man in his death, although **he had done no violence, nor was any deceit in his mouth**. 10 Yet it **pleased Yahweh to bruise him. He has caused him to suffer**. When you make **his soul an offering for sin**, he will see his offspring. He will prolong his days and Yahweh's pleasure will prosper in his hand. 11 **After the suffering of his soul, he will see the light** and be satisfied. My righteous servant will justify many by the knowledge of himself; and he **will bear their iniquities**. 12 Therefore **I will give him a portion with the great**. He will divide the plunder with the strong; because **he poured out his soul to death** and was **counted with the transgressors**; yet he **bore the sins of many** and made **intercession for the transgressors**.*

It is easy to fulfil prophecies when you're making up a story, and Mark effortlessly fulfils many of these. Luke as well as Matthew felt the need to amplify his prophecy fulfilments: simply counting verses that contain the words 'prophe', 'written', 'fulfil' and 'it is said', and then checking every single verse - a method that has been consistently applied to all four - Mark has 13 verses, Luke fulfils 21, Matthew 28 and John 17.

A very blunt and crude method for sure, it is worth some but not much - diving into prophecies would make this all even more complex and tedious. I merely want to state that Luke and Matthew (and John) will match or outdo Mark on the subject of prophecies as well.

Mark seems to be written by someone well versed in scripture. The error in Mark 1:2 to name Isaiah as a prophet while quoting Malachi as well as Isaiah (obscured in later bible translations by simply swapping 'Isaiah the prophet' for 'prophets', like in this translation) seems like one made comfortably, without actually feeling the obligation to check and verify, nor fearing that anyone else would

Truly, considering the fact that Mark did it all from scratch, he has written a masterpiece here. And he does show growth, gradual maturity, in handling his various tasks and topics. Starting out with literally copying the more harmless logia, he doesn't wait long to twist them to his own agenda - ever so slightly. Then he becomes bolder, and starts rewriting logia almost entirely. Halfway through he has mastered the art of interjecting Thomas themes around his own message, painting his own context in Thomas' style. And he also starts mashing up his own Thomasine parables - with mixed results, to be honest.

However, after chapter 5 Mark takes a rest from Thomas and spends it all on miracles; in chapters 6 through 8 Mark gets lost, experimenting with only painting Thomas context into his content. Only 7 logia in three chapters, with an additional handful if you have a vivid imagination. Chapters 9 and 10 persist, when suddenly chapter 11 gives us back the Mark as we know him and we are handed out 12 logia in the final chapters

So, what's the score? Dozens of logia more or less copied, turned, twisted, referenced, used and most importantly all abused in order to fit the Church goal. A grand total of 36 logia that can be accounted for without much if any dispute and over a dozen others that are subject to interpretation.

If I go for quantity and ruthlessly split the text of Thomas in its 308 separate sentences, then I find 24% of Thomas material in Mark, and that is not a lot at all - although it is clear that no gospel-writer could have possibly copied every single logion sentence. Counting separate logia the score is 36 out of the 114 logia, 32%: a pretty good score for a first attempt but by no means a glorious victory. Mark is the tiniest of the four gospels; while we are bean counting let's put them side-to-side (rounded):

Mark: 15,500 words, 700 lines, 80,000 characters including spaces.

Luke: 26,500 words, 1,175 lines, 135,000 characters including spaces.

Matthew: 24,500 words, 1,100 lines, 125,000 characters including spaces

John: 20,000 words, 900 lines, 100,000 characters including spaces

On the other hand it would be nitpicking to belittle the relatively small quantity of Thomas logia copied - the quality of Thomas now owned (or should I say, impounded) by Mark is more than sufficient to bring Jesus to life. It is safe to state that Mark breathes the atmosphere of Thomas wholeheartedly, that Thomas' themes are now his, and that most of Thomas' metaphors have been successfully and unequivocally turned to undoubtedly and undeniably literal pragmatic use by Mark

Am I missing something in Mark? Yes and no. Could Mark really have copied all 114 logia? Not at all, not even close.

Logia such as *(87) 'Jesus said, "Wretched is the body that is dependant upon a body, and wretched is the soul that is dependent on these two."'* will never make it into any scripture, and neither will the similarly vague logia 7 and 29, and many others like it: first of all because they're unintelligible to the casual observer, and second of all because there's nothing to gain in incorporating them.

Then there is another kind of logion, the dangerous one like logion 50:

(50) Jesus said, "If they say to you, 'Where did you come from?', say to them, 'We came from the light, the place where the light came into being on its own accord and established itself and became manifest through their image.' If they say to you, 'Is it you?', say, 'We are its children, we are the elect of the living father.' If they ask you, 'What is the sign of your father in you?', say to them, 'It is movement and repose.'"

Each and every part of it is untouchable; it can't be put into Church context at all. Where Mark happily uses only (parts of) sentences of a logion, ones such as this forbid each and every use.
Then there are others like that:

(77) Jesus said, 'It is I who am the light which is above them all. It is I who am the all. From me did the all come forth, and unto me did the all extend. Split a piece of wood, and I am there. Lift up the stone, and you will find me there.'

And we will see that, while these are too dangerous for Mark, and even Luke and Matthew, John will dare lay his hands on it, as befits his part in the Church play. John is the mystic, fairly identical to Thomas in style - at least a whole lot closer to Thomas than to his fellow gospel-writers, John continuously repeats his Jesus monologue and message

But - there is one major but. When we take a close look at what Mark copied, and zoom in on how and what he copied, we see an awful lot of compromises: logia loosely copied in words, usually completely mixing them up, and then even followed by putting them into (quite) a different context.
Logia barely recognisable as such, logia completely unrecognisable: I have not counted those, but only the really traceable and (fairly) literal logia.

Mark seems to have forgone his primary goal: to copy Thomas as much as he can, to cloak and soak his text in Thomas. Yes he has the style, the metaphors, the sceneries full of Thomas allegoric words, but he has failed hard to build a solid Thomas base and case by throwing in logia that are literal copies without completely turning and twisting them to serve his purpose. He doesn't mimic Thomas, doesn't mirror him, and doesn't do all the psychological things that need to be done. When you spin a story you have to take one's words, literally, and put them in your context - that's the main goal and the very simple and essentially only tool.

Have a look at a typical USA presidential debate, for instance, and you'll catch my drift: repeat your opponent's words, and rip and drag them out of context. "Did you not say...!" is what the vile attack on such an occasion is started with, and you see the look on the victim's face when it happens; a mixture of surprise, impotence and despair. And off they go, the aggressors, yipping like a hyena, proud of the bloody victory - putting someone's literal words in an entirely different context is perhaps the most powerful way to silence someone

And indeed, next to a very thick Church Jesus it is a very thin Thomas that Mark recreated. Surely he did a great job bringing Jesus to life but at the same time he's killed Thomas: it simply is not credible enough for enough people who know Thomas that this really is the Jesus of Thomas

Is there anything else? Yes, for sure. From a Church point of view Mark has won this battle gloriously - but is it enough? Enough for what, really? Enough to claim Jesus? Yes, he's Isaiah's prophecy come to life - and death. Enough for a religion? Not quite. There is one ritual but there are no customs, no signs to recognise and share such as songs, hymns, and what not. But that's really too much to ask for at this stage, and brevity of text: this battle was all about owning the Jesus of Thomas, turning him into a credible person that actually was alive and seen, witnessed - and that battle has been won victoriously.

The way to do so was to turn him into a credible Messiah and then kill him - whether that was meant to offend the Jews and guarantee their lack of support or not is another question, which I will certainly not even try to answer.

Given the apparent sloppiness of the prophecies used, was Jesus even meant to start a viable religion at this point in time? Jesus doesn't "carry over" to Peter like he does in Matthew, but that may be one of Mark's omissions. The behaviour of the disciples in the last hours during his arrest isn't particularly memorable, and the end of Mark's gospel is rather disheartening, with an angel telling that he has risen and will see them in Galilee (the original end is with verse 8 of chapter 16)

So, let's see how Matthew and Luke fill in the gaps Mark left. Only describing the last few years of Jesus' life does not provide the proper context to the character. Even though Mark did a great job erecting his own Jesus, Thomas isn't absolutely owned yet. Especially Mark's last three chapters were far from Thomas-like nor wholly satisfying, and we all know that the end of a story is what remains most fresh in a human mind...

Mark's omissions

What did leave Mark out and thus really needs to be addressed?
Not being judgmental, but what does Jesus' story lack, necessitate?

Jesus is just dropped on us as an adult. No idea about his age,
clothing, physique - nothing. He came from Nazareth, that we
know, but even John the Baptist (and only John, of all the people in
all of the four gospels) has his clothing described - not Jesus. No
background, no parentage, no lineage, no youth.
Jesus also leaves us just like that:

*16:5 Entering into the tomb, they saw a young man sitting on the
right side, dressed in a white robe, and they were amazed. 6 He said
to them, "Don't be amazed. You seek Jesus, the Nazarene, who has
been crucified. He has risen. He is not here. Behold, the place where
they laid him! 7 But go, tell his disciples and Peter, 'He goes before
you into Galilee. There you will see him, as he said to you.'" 8 They
went out, and fled from the tomb, for trembling and astonishment
had come on them. They said nothing to anyone; for they were
afraid.*

The oldest copies of Mark that don't include anything else but these
verses, date from the 4th century CE, and the longer ending is first
cited in other books around the end of the 2nd century CE. There
are actually two alternative endings: a short one and a long one,
which together appear in six Greek manuscripts and dozens of
Ethiopic copies. The short ending:

*But they reported briefly to Peter and those with him all that they
had been told. And after this, Jesus himself (appeared to them and)
sent out by means of them, from east to west, the sacred and
imperishable proclamation of eternal salvation.*

A quicky, apparently. 'Briefly' they reported 'all that' they had been told - how is that? They haven't been told much of course, but still: in this ending Jesus is seen after his death, instructing them to spread the gospel - in essence it is the exact same story as the longer ending. The only difference is that the longer one effectively writes Jesus into history and out of sight by having him 'received into heaven sitting at the right hand of God'.

So, not a very satisfying end after Jesus' death at the moment of Mark's publication and many centuries afterwards

John the Baptist - the most important prophet of all, the only one ever witnessing the coming of a Messiah - likewise is dropped on us just like that, and doesn't develop much character. He deserves a whole lot more attention than he has gotten from Mark, that is for sure. We know by now that John is supposed to be Elijah in disguise, but that story also has quite an unsatisfying ending. Jesus' last words on Elijah?

9:13 But I tell you that Elijah has come, and they have also done to him whatever they wanted to, even as it is written about him."

Then the name turns up twice more, when bystanders comment on Jesus' words after his 'My God, my God, why have you forsaken me?':

15:35 Some of those who stood by, when they heard it, said, "Behold, he is calling Elijah." 36 One ran, and filling a sponge full of vinegar, put it on a reed, and gave it to him to drink, saying, "Let him be. Let's see whether Elijah comes to take him down."

I think this is an attempt by Mark to show that the bystanders watching Jesus die were "the typical" Jews who didn't believe he was the Messiah, among others because they didn't believe that Elijah had preceded him. It seems as if Mark once again wants to stress that it were the Jews who killed the Messiah - but it hurts his case, doesn't really help to successfully close Project Elijah

Mark also doesn't introduce himself or try to give weight to his "testimony". He could be anyone writing anything about Jesus

Luke and Matthew take Mark's forced heirship head-on

Luke and Matthew serve to complete Mark's Jesus. I will treat them as one as I view them as one (rather large) editorial to Mark. Luke followed Mark and Matthew followed Luke, yet both had different audiences

We will see that they try to accomplish three things: introduce new Thomas logia that didn't make it into Mark, add more prophecies to Mark's Church Jesus, and fix Mark's Thomas (and Mark's Church Jesus). The former two are the main goal, of course, next to supplementing the life of Jesus with some proper human context: where did he come from? What was his youth like?

Matthew starts out at the very beginning, with Abraham, trying to link Jesus back to his origins in the first two chapters, naming him king of the Jews. Luke spends his first three chapters on John and Jesus and ends chapter 3 with the beginning of chapter 1 of Matthew yet continuing it a bit further, counting down back to Adam and God. Luke takes the opportunity to fixate Jesus in time down to a precise year, and both use a word starting with 'prophe' 6 times in their first three chapters.
Luke is a few chapters ahead of Matthew most of the time and we will just follow Luke and handle the verses and logia in his order. Logia will be quoted in full

A longer word on the first three chapters of both is in order. Luke starts with justifying his writings and pretends to write his entire gospel for and to an unknown 'Theophilus', literally translated "friend of god". Then he follows up with an angel - none other than Gabriel himself - elaborately foretelling Zacharias, John's future father, the birth of John the Baptist. His wife Elizabeth is old and barren so this comes as a surprise to Zacharias, who at the same time is instructed to call his son John. Gabriel later pays a visit to

Mary who appears not only to be equally as childless as Elizabeth, but also related to her.

Luke spends the huge number of 80 verses in his chapter 1 on mostly John and then spends the entire chapter 2 on the actual birth, and a bit of youth, of Jesus.

Needless to say these scenes are meant to fix Mark's omissions, or rather, to respond to the questions which apparently remained unanswered afterwards. Mark's legacy is filled with issues and problems and two of them are addressed here. First there is Elijah who would precede the Messiah, according to Malachi 4:5 (and apparently something that was greatly stressed by the Jews) - so in Luke Gabriel elaborates on his own prediction of John's birth by also saying that John will go before him 'in the spirit and power of Elijah', neatly quoting Malachi 4:6 right after that:

*1:13 But the angel said to him, "Don't be afraid, Zacharias, because your request has been heard. Your wife, Elizabeth, will bear you a son, and **you shall call his name John**. 14 You will have joy and gladness, and many will rejoice at his birth. 15 For he will be great in the sight of the Lord, and he will drink no wine nor strong drink. **He will be filled with the Holy Spirit**, even from his mother's womb. 16 **He will turn many of the children of Israel to the Lord their God**. 17 **He will go before him in the spirit and power of Elijah**, 'to turn the hearts of the fathers to the children,' and the disobedient to the wisdom of the just; to prepare a people prepared for the Lord."*

Even Gabriel is a team member of Project Elijah now, it seems. Will it help? That is not the last of his actions, as apparently John's name, like that of Jesus, needs even more explanation:

*1:59 On the eighth day, they came to circumcise the child; and **they would have called him Zacharias, after the name of his father**. 60 **His mother answered, "Not so; but he will be called John."** 61 They said to her, "There is no one among your relatives who is called by this name." 62 They made signs to his father, what he would have him called. 63 He asked for a writing tablet, and wrote, "**His name is***

John." They all marveled. 64 His mouth was opened immediately and his tongue freed, and he spoke, blessing God.

For doubting Gabriel's foretelling Zacharias was turned mute 'and not able to speak until the day that these things will happen', so it is clear that Zacharias doesn't "speak" wholly of his own accord here - there is quite an act performed around the naming of John. The Elijah problem increased after Mark, apparently? This is quite a scene, and an obvious attempt to answer questions regarding John's name, and to address them by insinuating that it was a divine instruction to name him so.

Was John not an ordinary name then? Not at all, there is no John in the entire Tanakh.

Luke ends chapter 1 with Zacharias possessed by the Holy Spirit and filling twelve verses with praising God, and ends with an almost casual verse that seems a mere afterthought - we'll come to that later:

1:80 The child was growing and becoming strong in spirit, and was in the desert until the day of his public appearance to Israel.

A second issue is Jesus' name: again Luke has Gabriel appear and sent to Nazareth, instructing Mary to name her child Jesus - two birds with one stone:

*1:30 The angel said to her, "Don't be afraid, Mary, for you have found favor with God. 31 Behold, you will conceive in your womb and give birth to a son, **and shall name him 'Jesus.'** 32 **He will be great and will be called the Son of the Most High**. The Lord God will give him the **throne of his father David**, 33 and he will **reign over the house of Jacob forever. There will be no end to his Kingdom."** 34 Mary said to the angel, "How can this be, seeing I am a virgin?"*

That all does, however, bear strong resemblance to Isaiah 9:6-8:

(Isaiah 9:6 For a child is born to us. A son is given to us; and the

*government will be on his shoulders. **His name will be called Wonderful Counselor, Mighty God, Everlasting Father, Prince of Peace**. 7 **Of the increase of his government and of peace there shall be no end, on David's throne**, and on **his kingdom**, to establish it, and to uphold it with justice and with righteousness from that time on, **even forever**. The zeal of Yahweh of Armies will perform this. 8 **The Lord sent a word into Jacob, and it falls on Israel**.)*

How does Matthew handle these two issues? He stunningly ends his chapter 1 with (just) an angel instructing Joseph, not Mary, to call his child Immanuel, and two verses later Joseph names it Jesus:

*(Matthew 1:22 Now all this has happened that it might be fulfilled which was spoken by the Lord through the prophet, saying, 23 "Behold, the virgin shall be with child, and shall give birth to a son. They shall call his name Immanuel," **which is, being interpreted, "God with us**." 24 Joseph arose from his sleep, and did as the angel of the Lord commanded him, and took his wife to himself; 25 and didn't know her sexually until she had given birth to her firstborn son. **He named him Jesus**.)*

Verse 1:23 is a literal copy of Isaiah 7:14 except for the emphasis; that is an addition by Matthew and an extra excuse for not naming Jesus Immanuel. The father does the naming in stead of the mother, Matthew is moved to primary canon position, and naming Jesus as Jesus by Joseph thus becomes a divine instruction fulfilling the prophecy that he would be called Immanuel: case closed, as easy as that

Did Mark just forget to mention that Jesus was born from a virgin?

In chapter 2 Matthew ambitiously fulfils three prophecies about the origin of Jesus: he's from Bethlehem of Judea, Egypt, and Nazareth. Matthew's elaborate story is as follows: wise men come to Jerusalem to worship the newly born King of the Jews - a great excuse for Herod being able to know about Jesus being born. Then

Herod, 'troubled, and all Jerusalem with him' asks his own priests and scribes where Jesus would be born, and they merely cite the prophet Micah: Bethlehem - they clearly have no second knowledge at that time, which is very plausible of course.

Herod asks the wise men to tell him where he can find the King so he can worship him, but they are warned in a dream to not do so and go back to their country "another way".

Matthew then has Herod (Herod the Great or Herod I, Roman king of Judea, and father of the later Herod Antipas of Galilee who in Luke sends Jesus back to Pilate) 'become exceedingly angry' and kill all the newborns in Bethlehem. Joseph however has been warned by an angel and takes Jesus to Egypt of all places; and according to Matthew the killing fulfils a prophecy:

(Matthew 2:17 Then that which was spoken by Jeremiah the prophet was fulfilled, saying, 18 "A voice was heard in Ramah, lamentation, weeping and great mourning, Rachel weeping for her children; she wouldn't be comforted, because they are no more.")

That's not a prophecy although indeed written in Jeremiah, and concerns Rachel figuratively weeping over her "children" after the Babylonians destroyed Jerusalem and the captives from Jerusalem were assembled in Ramah before being moved to Babylon - in 586 BCE:

(Jeremiah 31:15 Yahweh says: "A voice is heard in Ramah, lamentation and bitter weeping, Rachel weeping for her children. She refuses to be comforted for her children, because they are no more.")

What Matthew is leaving out here are the verses immediately following this one - and the reason for that doesn't need to be explained:

(Jeremiah 31:16 Yahweh says: "Refrain your voice from weeping, and your eyes from tears, for your work will be rewarded," says

*Yahweh. "**They will come again from the land of the enemy. 17
There is hope for your latter end," says Yahweh. "Your children
will come again to their own territory**.)*

Needless to say that no matter how one looks at this "prophecy", it
couldn't possibly apply to the very dead children of the alleged
Bethlehem massacre - who most certainly wouldn't be doing any
coming back, not from the land of the enemy nor to their own
territory.
The fleeing to Egypt fulfils another prophecy, according to
Matthew:

*(Matthew 2:14 He arose and took the young child and his mother by
night and departed into Egypt, 15 and was there until the death of
Herod, that it might be fulfilled which was spoken by the Lord
through the prophet, saying, "Out of Egypt I called my son.")*

That last sentence is from Hosea 11:1 and relates to the exodus of
the people of Israel:

*(Hosea 11:1 "**When Israel was a child, then I loved him**, and called
my son out of Egypt.)*

Whereas the Ramah "prophecy" could - with a mindset of being
exceptionally generous and most forgiving - be attributed to
Matthew regrettably having access to only that one verse, such
doesn't apply here - unless that generosity and forgiveness were to
be extended even further, supposing Matthew to have access to
only the third and last phrase of Hosea 11:1.
It is beyond a doubt that Matthew is knowingly and willingly making
up prophecies here, and these are not the last, and most certainly
not the least that we will see

Finally, Matthew has another angel appear to Joseph to tell of
Herod's death, upon which Joseph returns to Galilee:

*(Matthew 2:**22 But when he heard that Archelaus was reigning over Judea in the place of his father, Herod, he was afraid to go there.** Being warned in a dream, he withdrew into the region of Galilee, 23 and came and lived in a city called Nazareth; **that it might be fulfilled which was spoken through the prophets that he will be called a Nazarene.**)*

In order to escape the reign of Archelaus it apparently suffices to go to Galilee, where Herod Antipas reigns, who just like Archelaus is yet another son of Herod the Great - and even goes by the same name as his father? To yet again fulfil a prophecy, one of which not even a single word can be found in the entire Tanakh? Being called a Nazarene?

Matthew thus starts his gospel with angels and dreams pushing prophecies into place: Jesus is named Jesus, in stead of Immanuel as Micah's prophecy foretold; the wise men don't return to Herod, thus triggering the Bethlehem massacre (allegedly fulfilling Jeremiah's Ramah prophecy which wasn't a prophecy and already had taken place); Joseph flees to Egypt with Jesus (allegedly fulfilling Hosea 11:1 which wasn't a prophecy and already had taken place); Joseph and Jesus return to Israel, specifically Nazareth, in stead of Judea (allegedly fulfilling a prophecy about a Nazarene that's nowhere to be found).

Jesus being a Nazarene highly likely is a convoluted translation error from Hebrew (which I'll elaborate on much later). Yet Mark started the whole Nazarene story so there's no turning back now, and even John will suffer from that - hence why I'll address the Nazarene issue after John.

Let's not omit that Luke also starts his gospel with angels and dreams pushing prophecies into place: an angel - the angel himself, Gabriel - foretells the birth of John the Baptist who is to be Elijah in disguise (thus fulfilling a proper prophecy by Malachi about Elijah paving the way for the Messiah). Then Gabriel continues to Mary to tell her the good news, and the way Gabriel tells that it's an almost literal copy of Isaiah 9:6

The odd thing is that in the first two chapters of Matthew there is only one proper prophecy, namely the Messiah being called Immanuel, and that only proper prophecy is broken by Matthew who has Joseph name the child Jesus in stead - all other prophecies are just completely made up. It was apparently impossible to use double names and name Jesus "Jesus Immanuel" or "Immanuel also known as Jesus" or anything the like. Similarly, it was apparently impossible to name John "John Zacharias (the Baptist)" or "Zacharias John (the Baptist)", just as for instance Simon Peter was called Simon Peter - Mark even has 'Simon (to whom he gave the name Peter)' - or Judas was called Judas Iscariot.
Now why would that be?

It has become an excessively long introduction, and not a single logion in sight. It does, however, strongly pertain to the Jesus of Thomas, just as it does show what we can expect from Matthew when it comes to quoting from scripture in order to give ample body to the Jesus of the Church

Luke starters

The first copy (logion 79a) can be found in chapter 1, and Luke perhaps uses a reference to Deuteronomy 7:13 and 28:4:

(79a) A woman from the crowd said to him, "Blessed are the womb which bore you and the breasts which nourished you."
(79b) He said to her, "Blessed are those who have heard the word of the father and have truly kept it.
(79c) For there will be days when you will say, 'Blessed are the womb which has not conceived and the breasts which have not given milk.'"

1:42 She called out with a loud voice and said, "Blessed are you among women, and blessed is the fruit of your womb!

Luke has another go at it in chapter 11, which is a literal copy of 79a and 79b:

11:27 It came to pass, as he said these things, a certain woman out of the multitude lifted up her voice, and said to him, "Blessed is the womb that bore you, and the breasts which nursed you!" 28 But he said, "On the contrary, blessed are those who hear the word of God, and keep it."

It could be considered doubtful whether 1:42 comes directly from Thomas, indeed it could even be argued that Thomas himself got his logion from Genesis 49:25 as the blessing of wombs and breasts only occurs there, once, in the entire Tanakh. With Luke splitting this logion and Mark and Matthew repeating only 79b and 79c (as will be discussed later), we will never know beyond a doubt

Verse 1:44 shows similarities with logion 84a, which is new, and equally uncertain:

(84a) Jesus said, "When you see your likeness, you rejoice.

1:44 For behold, when the voice of your greeting came into my ears, the baby leaped in my womb for joy!

Luke does however reference logion 111b in 2:26:

(111b) And the one who lives from the living one will not see death."

*2:26 It had been revealed to him by the Holy Spirit that **he should not see death before he had seen the Lord's Christ**.*

Again, it is hard to prove that Luke's 2:26 uses logion 111b, as a large part of the gospel-writers' task is to debunk Thomas by taking his logia out of context, paraphrasing and rephrasing them as much as possible or needed, and fitting them into their own context and to their purpose - and this cryptic logion is a likely candidate there. At some point it is just bean counting Thomas words used and redirected, and it comes close to second-guessing.
Taking this verse as an example, how likely is it that 'seeing death' is just a coincidental way to refer to dying? See(ing) death appears 4 times in the entire bible: Book of Psalms chapter 89 verse 48, Luke 2:26, John 8:51 and Book of Hebrews 11:5 - only one book from the Tanakh, and its verse is not tempting:

89:48 What man is he who shall live and not see death, who shall deliver his soul from the power of Sheol? Selah.

Did both Thomas as well as Luke draw from Psalms? Possible, but of all the references to the Tanakh Luke could have picked, this is a meagre one: no prophecy, no foretelling, it is a mere question in between others.
Back to Luke, and a (first) solid case. Luke 4:23-24 turns around logion 31:

(31) Jesus said, "No prophet is accepted in his own village; no physician heals those who know him."

*(Mark 6:4 Jesus said to them, "A prophet is not without honor, except in his own country, and **among his own relatives, and in his own house**.")*

*4:23 He said to them, "Doubtless you will tell me this parable, '**Physician, heal yourself! Whatever we have heard done at Capernaum**, do also here in your hometown.'" 24 He said, "Most certainly I tell you, no prophet is **acceptable** in his hometown.*

*(Matthew 13:57 They were offended by him. But Jesus said to them, "A prophet is not without honor, except in his own country **and in his own house**.")*

All three gospel-writers together! Wherever verses are cited that don't belong to the current gospel subject, they're enclosed in round brackets and preceded by the appropriate book. With two or three gospel-writers citing their verses and versions of a logion, the use of emphasis (by making text bold) is intended to increase legibility and understanding of the differences and similarities

Let's first settle the Capernaum matter: it's an obvious error by Luke, as Jesus still has to go there, and in fact will do so only seven verses later (!), where he will perform the exact same miracles that Mark has him perform in Capernaum: driving out the unclean spirit, healing Simon's mother-in-law and healing all other sick. Matthew unfortunately is preoccupied with seeing yet another prophecy fulfilled by Jesus' stay in Capernaum and only vaguely mentions the sick being healed so doesn't offer any reflection on his version of Jesus in Capernaum. But let's not dwell on that.

Back to the logion and verses: while naturally leaving out the physician part it befits Mark to simply stick to Thomas, adding 'own house' and the relatives: a reference to Jesus' relatives mentioned in the verse before. Matthew refers to the exact same persons yet leaves out the relatives. The physician proverb Luke mentions is highly likely an attempt to get closer to Thomas, next to the use of the word 'acceptable' - Luke introduces both and also embraces the concise version without the word house - and it seems that none of it made the cut in Matthew.

This is one of the patterns we will see in Luke and Matthew: Luke usually sticks very close to Thomas, Matthew backs out from that and undoes most if not all, at least with regards to literal and thus traceable Thomas words. It would almost seem as if Matthew came after Mark and then Luke came after that, ignoring the both of them and mainly following Thomas to the letter, all on his own - but Luke usually uses some of Mark's words and Matthew uses some of Luke's

I will count one logion for both Luke and Matthew for all these four chapters, certainly not a flying start. The count will start again by the way, and just keep in memory that Mark has 36 logia.

Next is chapter 5, and the first we encounter is about healing the sick.

The healing of the sick has become one of the central themes for the gospel-writers. Why? For the only one mention of healing the sick in Thomas, there are dozens in each of the four gospels. The mention in Thomas is undoubtedly no instruction to heal physically sick; his disciples weren't doctors. There are a few mentions of sick in the Tanakh, but none justify this grand theme - unless you have a look at Isaiah chapter 53 (and that we already did) that prophesies the fate of the Messiah; verses 3 and 4 are the ones:

*(Isaiah 53:3 He was despised and rejected by men, a **man of suffering** and **acquainted with disease**. He was despised as one from whom men hide their face; and we didn't respect him. 4 Surely **he has borne our sickness and carried our suffering**; yet we considered him plagued, struck by God, and afflicted.)*

I will stick to naming these verses as most likely inspiration for the gospel-writers to deal so abundantly with the theme of healing the sick, and will leave it at that: it certainly doesn't originate from Thomas

Luke chapter 5 follows Mark chapter 2 (and Matthew's chapter 9 follows both):

(14a) Jesus said to them, "If you fast, you will give rise to sin for yourselves; and if you pray, you will be condemned; and if you give alms, you will do harm to your spirits.
(14b) When you go into any land and walk about in the districts, if they receive you, eat what they will set before you, and heal the sick among them.
(14c) For what goes into your mouth will not defile you, but that which issues from your mouth - it is that which will defile you."

(Mark 2:17 When Jesus heard it, he said to them, "Those who are healthy have no need for a physician, but those who are sick. I came not to call the righteous, but sinners to repentance.")

5:31 Jesus answered them, "Those who are healthy have no need for a physician, but those who are sick do. 32 I have not come to call the righteous, but sinners to repentance."

*(Matthew 9:12 When Jesus heard it, he said to them, "Those who are healthy have no need for a physician, but those who are sick do. 13 **But you go and learn what this means: 'I desire mercy, and not sacrifice,'** for I came not to call the righteous, but sinners to repentance.")*

Emphasis is on the differences. All gospel-writers stay perfectly in sync here, although Matthew adds a reference to Hosea 6:6, likely meant to also infer Hosea 6:7, thus comparing the Pharisees and scribes to covenant breakers; even better - we'll see that Matthew is very fond of scripture, implicitly referencing it where he can and not even shying away from explicitly rubbing it in:

*(Hosea 6:6 For **I desire mercy, and not sacrifice**; and the knowledge of God more than burnt offerings. 7 But they, like Adam, have broken the covenant. They were unfaithful to me, there.)*

Please do note very carefully that Matthew is perfectly able to read, comprehend, and literally quote scripture, as testified right here. Let me repeat that: is it perfectly crystal-clear on this occasion that Matthew can literally quote scripture? That Matthew can likely read beyond one single verse and appreciate the context of that one single verse? It is, isn't it?
The order could be anything here, given the very close resemblance in all, although it is unlikely that Matthew's addition would be accidentally left out by someone else, as it's interjected in the verse

Luke follows up with the bridegroom parable (logion 104c). In Thomas the bridegroom is a sign of non-duality, the bridegroom belongs into the bridal chamber. When he leaves it he becomes a man to a wife and all the duality hell breaks loose. Of course, the gospel-writers take it literally and personify Jesus as the bridegroom, leaving out the entire bridal chamber reference - not to mention the 'pray':

(104a) They said to Jesus, "Come, let us pray today and let us fast."
(104b) Jesus said, "What is the sin that I have committed, or wherein have I been defeated?
(104c) But when the bridegroom leaves the bridal chamber, then let them fast and pray."

*(Mark 2:18 John's disciples and the Pharisees were fasting, and they came and asked him, "Why do John's disciples and the disciples of the Pharisees **fast, but** your disciples don't fast?" 19 Jesus said to them, "Can **the groomsmen** fast while the bridegroom is with them? **As long as they have the bridegroom with them, they can't fast.** 20 But the days will come when the bridegroom will be taken away*

*from them, and then they will fast **in that day**.)*

*5:33 They said to him, "Why do John's disciples often **fast and pray, likewise** also the disciples of the Pharisees, but yours eat and drink?"34 He said to them, "Can you make **the friends of the bridegroom** fast while the bridegroom is with them? 35 But the days will come when the bridegroom will be taken away from them. Then they will fast **in those days**."*

*(Matthew 9:14 Then John's disciples came to him, saying, "Why do we and the Pharisees fast often, but your disciples don't fast?" 15 Jesus said to them, "Can **the friends of the bridegroom mourn** as long as the bridegroom is with them? But **the days** will come when the bridegroom will be taken away from them, and then they will fast.)*

Emphasis is on the differences. Thomas' is a coherent story that starts with a question; Jesus follows up with an answer in the form of a question that clearly indicates he has no intention whatsoever of praying and fasting. Then he names one single (and perhaps only) occasion on which others would fast and pray - but not he himself. The gospel-writers selectively pick only one and a half sentence out of the logion and bend that to their cause, fixating only on the fasting and naturally not including the praying. The one preceding verse tells it all; Mark and Matthew pretend that the whole subject is fasting, but Luke, moving closest to Thomas, includes the word 'pray' - and then just like the others addresses only the fasting part in his answer and ignores the praying. Luke is giving away that they read a part of Thomas that they chose to omit.

Mark tries to explain the reason for fasting in the second half of his first verse, which is a bit overdoing it (and a pioneer's fate), and juxtaposes 'the days' to 'that day', erroneously implying that the fasting (and likely also the taking away) will last only one day. Luke fixes that by changing 'that day' to 'those days' and Matthew neatly finishes it by changing the first 'fast' to 'mourn' and 'while' to 'as long'.

That is another pattern that will become explicitly clear and evident: the gradual transformation of the Church story between Mark, Luke and Matthew. Whenever the three share a logion Mark's version will usually be relatively crude and clumsy and contain one or more errors, sometimes quite painful ones. Luke usually goes his own way - following Thomas to the letter where possible - but fixes Mark's errors, and Matthew comes last and combines the best of both worlds into a usually perfectly fluid set of verses, wrapped in wonderful words.

Right here, Matthew decisively leaves no room for interpretation that fasting will begin only after Jesus is taken away from us by simply removing the indication of time at the end of the sentence - a most elegant solution.

Luke could have come behind Matthew although it is clear that Luke read Thomas, and that both came after Mark, given the corrections to Mark that both share. 'Groomsmen' becomes 'friends of the groom', both leave out the extra explanatory sentence and share the plural form of Mark's 'that day'. Yet Matthew copies Mark's question, not that of Luke (ignoring Luke's 'likewise'). Retains 'Jesus said to them' over 'He said to them', and has the exact same last sentence as Mark (ignoring the action imposed on the groomsmen in Luke who uses 'Can you make [...]'). Would Luke willingly leave out Matthew's great find of omitting the indication of time at the end of the final sentence?

A clear but not definite order of gospels: Thomas, Mark, and then likely Luke followed by Matthew - or vice versa

Logion 47 is next: Thomas is lovely concise and complete here: he first posits his theorem that no one can handle two objects simultaneously (47a) and elaborates on that in serving two masters at the same time (47b). Then he zooms in on the aspect of time by exemplifying one side of the coin (47c), building a case for the fact that it takes time to transition from old to new. Switching to inanimate objects he then handles the compatibility of the old and the new, while shedding light on both sides: they are mutually incompatible because new destroys old and old spoils new (47d).

And then in (47e) he falls back on the example in (47c) with this time looking at the other side of the coin: (47c) shows that old doesn't immediately desire new, (47e) shows that new doesn't desire or endure (a piece of) the old.

Thomas is perfectly balanced, unbiased, looking at old and new from both sides, starting with the general observation that there can be only one at a time: either old or new, never both.

As stated before when discussing Mark, not surprisingly the gospel-writers completely omit the old wine hurting the new skins, and likewise turn the old patch on a new garment into a new patch on an old garment. Doing so they make their version fit with the image of Christians being applied to Judaism (which would hurt) while leaving ample room for Jews flocking to Christianity (old wine drinkers can very well have an appetite for new):

(47a) Jesus said, "It is impossible for a man to mount two horses or to stretch two bows.
(47b) And it is impossible for a servant to serve two masters; otherwise, he will honor the one and treat the other contemptuously.
(47c) No man drinks old wine and immediately desires to drink new wine.
(47d) And new wine is not put into old wineskins, lest they burst; nor is old wine put into a new wineskin, lest it spoil it.
(47e) An old patch is not sewn onto a new garment, because a tear would result."

*(Mark 2:21 No one sews **a piece of unshrunk cloth** on an old garment, or else the patch shrinks and the new tears away from the old, and a **worse hole is made.** 22 No one puts new wine into old wineskins; or else the new wine will burst the skins, **and the wine pours out, and the skins will be destroyed**; but they put new wine into fresh wineskins.")*

*5:36 He also told a parable to them. "No one puts a piece from a new garment on an old garment, or else he will **tear the new,** and* *also the piece from **the new will not match the old**. 37 No one puts new wine into old wine skins, or else the new wine will burst the skins, **and it will be spilled, and the skins will be destroyed**. 38 But new wine must be put into fresh wine skins, and both are preserved. 39 **No man having drunk old wine immediately desires new, for he says, 'The old is better.'"***

Emphasis is on the differences. This being the third time in a row that such is stated, it usually is when there are more than two pieces of text compared. When not, the emphasis is on what the two pieces of text share, unless there is no emphasis at all because the two pieces of text are so identical that emphasis wouldn't add any value. In that case, emphasis might be used to show the difference(s) between the two texts. The volume determines where emphasis is applied: if differences between any number of text are small, emphasis will stress the differences.

Where Mark focuses on the old (hole) getting damaged if the patch fails, Luke pays attention to the new (patch)! Even more surprising is that by adding verse 39, Luke adds 47c to his version of Mark - with a slight comment at the end. Should that be read 'After Jewish religion no one desires Jesus'? That can't be the general idea, I think - fortunately Luke retains the so very crucial word 'immediately' - in this bible translation. Yet it is no small wonder that Matthew leaves out 47c entirely as it is so openly pointing to Jews being converted to Christianity. Again, Matthew makes it all concise, also by leaving out the odd explanation Luke introduces by stating that the new patch will not match the old. And again, Luke shows that they read a part of Thomas that they chose to omit.

What is Luke doing here?

*(Matthew 9:16 No one puts **a piece of unshrunk cloth** on an old garment; for the patch would tear away from the garment, and a **worse hole is made**. 17 Neither do people put new wine into old wine skins, or else the skins would burst, **and the wine be spilled, and the skins ruined**. No, they put new wine into fresh wine skins, and **both are preserved**.")*

Luke and Matthew share the 'both are preserved' and Mark and Matthew share the 'worse hole is made'.

This is a crucial allegory for the gospel-writers, positioning their new religion next to Judaism. It is a perfect example of how, why and where the gospel-writers twist and turn Thomas, and why Thomas is first and not the other way around.

Whereas Thomas also puts emphasis on negative effects of the old being applied to the new (with regards to the wine; the tear will likely be in the patch but that's inconclusive), the gospel-writers only stress the new wine being spilled and the new garment being torn. The underlying message is that the new religion and the old Judaism are incompatible, with the new - their primal focus point - being wasted and damaging the old if it were to be applied onto it. In that light, the unbiased metaphor of the two masters doesn't add to their specific business case at this point either, and is simply left out - to be used by Luke and Matthew in an entirely different context at a later point in time.

Thomas is balanced, impartial, unbiased, purely showing the incompatibility between two, not picking any side - and that's the very opposite of what the so strongly polarising gospel-writers are aiming for.

Let it also be noted that Thomas doesn't explain at all why or how the patch would tear the garment or vice versa, which indeed is an absolutely trivial detail if you're not interested in or biased towards either piece of cloth. That little void results in the gospel-writers taking turns in order to fill it with an explanation, each varying rather greatly from the other. Whenever the gospel-writers show vast differences among themselves, they are handling content that is entirely of their own yet very closely related to Thomas content. I call that the gospel sandbox: material that doesn't directly originate from either of their two pillars (copying Thomas and fulfilling scripture), and as such isn't subject to more or less strict rules. Especially Matthew will play around in the gospel sandbox, sometimes even grossly ignoring or elaborating on material from his predecessors.

Regarding this logion and these verses, the order is strikingly clear: Thomas, Mark, Luke, Matthew: it couldn't possibly be any other way.

Or could it? Is it feasible that Thomas takes these so extremely one-sided and biased verses and turns them into his beautifully unbiased logion? No. Both Luke (16:13) and Matthew (6:24) will prove that they had access to the complete logion when they use the two masters metaphor at a later point. They also prove right here that they very well knew about the old wine put into new skins because of using the word 'destroyed' (or 'ruined') in their own extra reason for not putting new wine into old skins, with all three adding the detail of the wine being poured out or spilled. The skins being destroyed or ruined are highly likely inspired by Thomas' 'spoil', the word that only occurs in the last phrase of 47d which is deliberately not used by all three.

How useful is it to add that the skins are destroyed or ruined, after having stated that they (have been) burst?

This concludes Luke chapter 5; 3 logia counted in it, amounting to a total of 4

Luke's beatitudes and Matthew's sermon

Luke starts off chapter 6 with his disciples and him breaking Sabbath rules. Luke's beatitudes cover six logia; five of these are new, and some will make it into Matthew's sermon on the mount (although all will be copied by Matthew in his entire gospel). Both beatitudes as sermon are ideal monologues for reiterating traditional Jewish law or scripture as well as adding logia that Mark omitted: two birds with one stone

Logion 54 is new:

(54) Jesus said, "Blessed are the poor, for yours is the kingdom of heaven."

*6:20 He lifted up his eyes to his disciples, and said, "Blessed are you who are poor, for **God's Kingdom** is yours.*

*(Matthew 5:3 "Blessed are the poor **in spirit**, for theirs is the **Kingdom of Heaven**.)*

Luke uses the literal copy, yet swaps 'heaven' for 'God'. Matthew undoes that last change and adds 'in spirit' in order to leave nothing up to interpretation: the meek who think humble and lowly of themselves, those will fit the mould of the Church.
The order could be anything. Could Luke (or Thomas) have ignored Matthew's 'in spirit'? Yes, possibly.
Mark and Luke will take and swap Thomas' 'kingdom of heaven' for 'God's Kingdom'. Matthew will, every single time, side with 'Kingdom of Heaven' and appear to be reverting to Thomas by doing so. I think the general idea was to leave nothing up to interpretation and thus turn Thomas' neutral 'heaven' into God with a capital G. When Christianity slowly unfolded and the Trinity made its introduction (only Matthew names it once in his penultimate

verse), Matthew didn't want to label it kingdom of God, Father, Son, Holy Spirit and whatnot, and reverted to heaven again. Or not - reasons are unclear to me but it's a fact that wherever Mark and Luke use 'kingdom of God' in their Thomas copies (and that's wherever Thomas uses 'kingdom of heaven'), Matthew uses 'kingdom of heaven'.

I will not emphasise this difference every time, as these changes are applied consistently

Logion 69 gets quoted in full in the order of c, a and b by Luke and Matthew, and is also new:

(69a) Jesus said, "Blessed are they who have been persecuted within themselves.
(69b) It is they who have truly come to know the father.
(69c) Blessed are the hungry, for the belly of him who desires will be filled."

*6:21 Blessed are you who hunger now, for you will be filled. Blessed are you who weep now, for you will laugh. 22 **Blessed are you when men hate you, and when they exclude and mock you**, and throw out your name as evil, **for the Son of Man's sake**. 23 **Rejoice in that day**, and leap for joy, for behold, **your reward is great in heaven**, for their fathers did the same thing to the prophets.*

Verse 22 is inspired by Isaiah 66:5 '[...] "Your brothers who hate you, who cast you out for my name's sake, have said [...]' - and the phrase 'within themselves' is conveniently left out, of course:

*(Matthew 5:6 Blessed are those who hunger **and thirst for righteousness**, for they shall be filled.*
(...)
*10 Blessed are those who have been persecuted **for righteousness'** sake, for theirs is the Kingdom of Heaven. 11 "**Blessed are you when people reproach you, persecute you**, and say all kinds of evil against you **falsely**, for my sake. 12 **Rejoice**, and be exceedingly*

*glad, for **great is your reward in heaven**. For that is how they persecuted the prophets who were before you.)*

Luke addresses the crowd and starts out with 'you' in his first few verses which makes it complicated to turn them into general guidelines for all; once again Matthew profits from that and fixes it, likely inspired by Luke's convenient '(But) I tell you' from his beatitudes.

Of course, both gospel-writers must twist it towards their cause and stress the reward in heaven; they also take the opportunity to tick off the scripture box another time by mentioning that the prophets were equally hated and persecuted - well done. Needless to say that 'within themselves' would give a whole different meaning to their verses. Surprisingly, Luke doesn't come up with reusing Thomas' 'persecute' yet Matthew does - didn't Matthew notice that Luke was quoting Isaiah?

Again, Matthew leaves no room for interpretation, adding 'for righteousness', in both verse 6 and 10 - and throws in 'thirst' as well. Luke also leaves unclear whether the reason for hate ('for the Son of Man's sake') is justified or not, so Matthew fixes that with the word 'falsely'. Nitpicking? Not in Matthew's book - he strives for perfection every single time. Likewise, Matthew drops Luke's 'in that day' as it could be suggesting that the hate, exclusion and persecution will last only one single day.

Thomas, Luke, Matthew - without a doubt. Logion 69, which starts Luke's beatitudes, will also start Matthew's sermon on the mount. Logion 95 is used by Luke, in two versions, of which the first one is the direct copy:

(95) Jesus said, "If you have money, do not lend it at interest, but give it to one from whom you will not get it back."

*6:34 If you **lend to those from whom you hope to receive**, what credit is that to you? Even sinners lend to sinners, **to receive back as much**.*

Luke turns Thomas' instruction into a question and hints at 'interest' with his last phrase, and precedes this verse with a similar idea yet one that expresses a particular liberal idea of property and ownership:

*6:30 Give to everyone who asks you, and **don't ask him** who takes away your goods **to give them back again**.*

Matthew happily drops verse 30, combining both versions into one clear instruction:

*(Matthew 5:42 Give to him **who asks you**, and don't turn away him **who desires to borrow from you**.)*

The 'interest' is avoided by both, which is an interesting fact (I just couldn't resist). Both use the word only once in their entire gospel, in their parable of the coins, as a suggestion from the main character. And that is an odd one, as the Tanakh stimulates lending to the poor yet explicitly forbids charging interest for it, which among others is based on Exodus 22:25, Leviticus 25:36-37 and Deuteronomy 23:19 (with the first books explicitly mentioning 'poor') although Deuteronomy 23:20 allows charging interest to 'foreigners'.

Merely repeating Thomas (who actually could very well be considered paraphrasing the Tanakh with his logion) would add nothing new for the gospel-writers so they take it one step further: Luke is the first copier and thus experiments, suffering the pioneer's fate with just letting goods be taken away. Matthew profits and ends up with one nice verse that surpasses both Thomas and the Tanakh: he implies to not only lend to the poor (certainly without charging interest) and explicitly states to lend to anyone who merely asks.

Luke reuses his general idea in chapter 14 but Matthew doesn't reuse it; doing good intended as an overt afterlife investment probably was frowned upon:

*14:12 He also said to the one who had invited him, "When you make a dinner or a supper, don't call your friends, nor your brothers, nor your kinsmen, nor rich neighbors, or perhaps they might also return the favor, and pay you back. 13 But when you make a feast, ask the poor, the maimed, the lame, or the blind; 14 and you will be blessed, because they don't have the resources to repay you. **For you will be repaid in the resurrection of the righteous**."*

Thomas, Luke, Matthew - no doubt there. Could Luke possibly have come after Matthew? Only if he were intent on explicitly making his highly peculiar point of 6:30 regardless of what Matthew said - but then why would he follow that up with 6:34 and 14:14 which clearly are rather superfluous statements when seen in the light of 6:30? What is the possibility of Thomas copying Luke or Matthew then, inserting 'interest' in his logion (with the alleged intent of creating his version of the Church Jesus)? Only if he were both too creative as well as completely ignorant of Jewish law and the Tanakh - and that is an impossible case to argue

Another new logion is literally copied in verse 39; logion 34:

(34) Jesus said, "If a blind man leads a blind man, they will both fall into a pit."

6:39 He spoke a parable to them. "Can the blind guide the blind? Won't they both fall into a pit?

(Matthew 15:14 Leave them alone. They are blind guides of the blind. If the blind guide the blind, both will fall into a pit.")

Luke or Matthew? The order could be anything, even Thomas could have come last. The term 'parable' is extremely loosely wielded by Luke here (it is a mere allegory and certainly not a story), and we will see more of that later on, as Luke and Matthew also feel the need to come up with parables of their own in their attempt to 'be Thomasine'

Right after that we find a literal copy of logion 26:

(26a) Jesus said, "You see the mote in your brother's eye, but you do not see the beam in your own eye.
(26b) When you cast the beam out of your own eye, then you will see clearly to cast the mote from your brother's eye."

*6:41 Why do you see the speck **of chaff** that is in your brother's eye, but don't consider the beam that is in your own eye? 42 Or how can you tell your brother, '**Brother**, let me remove the speck **of chaff** that is in your eye,' when **you yourself don't see** the beam that is in your own eye? You hypocrite! First remove the beam from your own eye, and then you can see clearly to remove the speck **of chaff** that is in your brother's eye.*

Emphasis is on the words that Luke has as extra, compared to Matthew.
Luke stretches it a bit in making it personal, addressing an invisible audience (although likely still talking to the Pharisees and scribes). And Matthew follows him almost literally - to my surprise:

(Matthew 7:3 Why do you see the speck that is in your brother's eye, but don't consider the beam that is in your own eye? 4 Or how will you tell your brother, 'Let me remove the speck from your eye,' and behold, the beam is in your own eye? 5 You hypocrite! First remove the beam out of your own eye, and then you can see clearly to remove the speck out of your brother's eye.)

Once again, Matthew perfects what Luke says in very subtle ways. The double occurrence of 'brother' disappears, as does the somewhat awkward and overdone mention of 'when you yourself do not see'. Matthew is by far the most eloquent of all the three. Could it be possible that Matthew came before Luke and that Luke decided to undo his condensed beauty? Luke may have insisted on adding his 'chaff' to Matthew, and might have disliked 'and behold'.

Both do a fairly literal copy of Thomas and advance their case by directing that towards the Pharisees, yet since Thomas doesn't have any such case it could also be argued that he came last and thus had to leave out that little detail. The two arguments I have for Thomas being first is that he is by far the most concise and has two sentences: one with a repetition of 'see', and one repeating 'cast' (and containing the same 'see' in a whole different meaning). Luke and Matthew miss that beauty and turn the first sentence into 'see' and 'consider' (breaking the repetition) while Luke suffers the pioneer's fate by superfluously adding an intermediate sentence with 'remove' and 'see' that Matthew omits.

It is evident that Thomas usually is the most articulate and concise, beautifully mastering the Wizardry of Words, and that Matthew is close competition in that field. But none of that can ever be a sole argument for either of them being last; although I do frequently argue for Matthew being last while he makes everything concise and beautiful and is so very eloquent - but only because he then uses words from Mark as well as Luke.

Why is Thomas so beautiful? The mote is the imperfection or misconceptions you perceive someone else to have, their opinions - called truths - that don't correlate to yours. The beam is the collection of your own truths that you equally take for granted, considering them to be logical and correct. You see some of the other and focus on them but disregard all of your own - hence the difference in size. The first 'see' literally means seeing, focussing, whereas the second 'see' means observing, perceiving.

The second sentence uses the word 'cast' for a very specific reason: it means to distance yourself from something rather than removing something, taking something out: the action of 'cast' is targeted towards changing yourself whereas the action of 'remove' is targeted towards changing something else.

You have to consider your own truths, concepts, perceptions, and cast those from you that don't survive close scrutiny - and then you will really 'see' - that the mote that you focussed on in someone else's eye was only bothering you because you felt your own semi-truths threatened by them: their truths made you doubt your truths, and that felt rather inconvenient. But now you've really 'seen' how your collection of truths is merely a heritage that has accumulated during your life by reacting to actions of others and yourself, you value them quite differently - and distance yourself from them. They're a large part of the 'world' of Thomas.

And when you have done so, it has become impossible to feel threatened by other people's truths. The mote from your brother's eye wasn't in his eye, it existed only in your mind

Everything Thomas talks about is about you: me. What the gospel-writers are doing here with this very logion is exactly the opposite of what Thomas does. There's only one hypocrite, and that is you: me

Brace yourselves for another lengthy commentary; what I hinted at during Mark regarding original sin is about to be revealed.

The best word to describe my state is bewilderment, when I first read Luke's verses 6:43-45, a complete literal copy of logion 45. The emphasis is on the shocking part alone:

(45a) Jesus said, "Grapes are not harvested from thorns, nor are figs gathered from thistles, for they do not produce fruit.
(45b) A good man brings forth good from his storehouse; an evil man brings forth evil things from his evil storehouse, which is in his heart, and says evil things.
(45c) For out of the abundance of the heart he brings forth evil things."

6:43 For there is no good tree that produces rotten fruit; nor again a rotten tree that produces good fruit. 44 For each tree is known by its own fruit. For people don't gather figs from thorns, nor do they gather grapes from a bramble bush. 45 ***The good man out of the good treasure of his heart brings out that which is good, and the evil man out of the evil treasure of his heart brings out that which is evil, for out of the abundance of the heart, his mouth speaks.***

What is this now? Luke once more turns to the literal copy of Thomas, but didn't Mark do his best to twist and turn logion 45 into original sin by leaving out the so exceptionally essential and equitable 45b?

*(Mark 7:17 When he had entered into a house away from the multitude, his disciples asked him about the parable. 18 He said to them, "Are you also without understanding? Don't you perceive that **whatever goes into the man from outside can't defile him**, 19 because it doesn't go into his heart, but into his stomach, then into the latrine, making all foods clean?"20 He said, "That **which proceeds out of the man, that defiles the man. 21 For from within, out of the hearts of men, proceed evil thoughts**, adulteries, sexual sins, murders, thefts, 22 covetings, wickedness, deceit, lustful desires, an evil eye, blasphemy, pride, and foolishness.)*

That is what Mark did: intentionally leaving out 45b so he could build a case for original sin on top of Thomas. Is Luke spoiling everything by making himself known as a Thomas reader yet not a Mark reader, or is he missing Mark's deliberate twist, or is this just plain sabotage - or if none of those then what is it? Clearly Luke's verse 45 follows logion 45b and 45c to the letter, just as his verse 44 is a direct copy of logion 45a, although swapping fruits and changing the plants. This is not original sin, this is a Thomas-like subtle nuanced version that doesn't fit the Church's agenda at all. What does Matthew have to say on this?

*(Matthew 7:15 "Beware of false prophets, who come to you in sheep's clothing, but inwardly are ravening wolves. 16 By their fruits you will know them. Do you gather grapes from thorns or figs from thistles? 17 Even so, every **good tree produces good fruit**, but the **corrupt tree produces evil fruit. 18 A good tree can't produce evil fruit, neither can a corrupt tree produce good fruit**. 19 Every tree that doesn't grow good fruit is cut down and thrown into the fire. 20 Therefore by their fruits you will know them.)*

Nothing, or everything? Luke's message is there but in completely different metaphors: Matthew uses the fruits and plants of Thomas yet leaves out 45b entirely - in chapter 7, where he talks about false prophets. In his chapter 12 he has another go at it:

*(Matthew 12:33 "Either make the tree good and its fruit good, or make the tree corrupt and its fruit corrupt; for the tree is known by its fruit. 34 You offspring of vipers, how can you, being evil, speak good things? For out of the abundance of the heart, the mouth speaks. 35 The **good man out of his good treasure brings out good things**, and the **evil man out of his evil treasure brings out evil things**. 36 I tell you that every idle word that men speak, they will give account of it in the day of judgment. 37 For by your words you will be justified, and by your words you will be condemned.")*

Nuance - again? From Matthew? The context in Matthew here, however, is prepping people for Judgment Day while at the same time addressing and rebuking the Pharisees, who are labelled as evil - part of the plan of course. So Pharisees are bad trees and evil persons, others are or can be good trees and good persons - fair enough then.
The context of chapter 7 is false prophets who can be recognised by their (bad) fruits and will be cut down and thrown into the fire at, presumably, a given point in time. There presumably are also good prophets so Matthew is in need of a comparison between good and bad - fair enough.
Matthew's rebound however comes in chapter 15 when he elaborates on his own 15:11, a literal copy of 14c which in Thomas also has no context in itself, just like 45c:

*(Matthew 15:10 He summoned the multitude, and said to them, "Hear, and understand. 11 That which enters into the mouth doesn't defile the man; but **that which proceeds out of the mouth, this defiles the man**."*
(...)
17 Don't you understand that whatever goes into the mouth passes

*into the belly and then out of the body? 18 But the things **which proceed out of the mouth come out of the heart, and they defile the man. 19 For out of the heart come evil thoughts**, murders, adulteries, sexual sins, thefts, false testimony, and blasphemies. 20 These are the things which defile the man; but to eat with unwashed hands doesn't defile the man.")*

Matthew sets the record straight, according to the Church agenda - all words that leave the mouth are evil because they come from the heart that is all evil. And he does make a highly significant other point which I'll address at the end of this paragraph.
It has been a rocky ride, however, with a messy result.
Luke doesn't help much with his beatitudes, which sometimes are hard to correlate and connect to one another: the context in which he makes the literal and balanced copy is difficult to sketch although Luke's verses seem to belong to a wider set of instructions about the teacher-disciple paradigm.
Nonetheless, the gospel-writers once more show their true nature here, selectively quoting and misquoting when and where it befits them. Matthew deliberately leaves out the balanced sentence when he wants to make the case for original sin (all men are evil because all hearts produce evil); yet when he wants to single out the Pharisees from the crowd, or distinguish between false prophets and true ones, suddenly there appear to be also good people with good hearts?
And in order to make both cases the exact same logion suffices, simply by also quoting that one sentence that purposely got left out before?
How extremely unlikely is it that Thomas was last here?
Once again we see a completely coherent narrative in Thomas that starts beautifully unbiased: the grapes and figs sentence in 45a shows that some objects inherently belong somewhere, and 45b elaborates on that while switching from the allegory of plants to humans: good men have a good storehouse, evil men an evil one, and the storehouse is in the heart. So far so good - but the rest of the logion is extremely one-sided, ending with the context-free last

sentence in 45c that is very much unlike Thomas. Can I offer an explanation for 45c? No. Will I try to wiggle my way out of this by making up editorial changes or additions by evil scribes and translators, or come up with other conspiracies? No. Even with the last phrase of 45b naming 'evil', had logion 45c not contained that same single word, it all would have been perfectly Thomasine. Still, if Thomas would have stolen from the gospel-writers it is completely inconceivable that he would have missed the opportunity to reuse the magnificent phrase of Luke: 'for out of the abundance of the heart, his mouth speaks'.

In any case, this is an example of very bad gospel management and orchestration. In the current official canonical order, people will first read Matthew and read a nuanced version in chapter 7 (the false prophets), then another nuanced version in chapter 12 (the Pharisees), and then suddenly all nuances disappear and original sin gets thrown in their faces in chapter 15 (people in general). Then Mark will reassure their sense of original sin by repeating the last verses of Matthew's chapter 15, yet Luke will end it all with his clean and honest, and beautifully nuanced, almost literal copy of Thomas - that even surpasses that of Thomas...

Which is the highly significant point I mentioned? It is Matthew fixing a grave error of Mark:

*(Mark 7: 18 He said to them, "Are you also without understanding? Don't you perceive that whatever goes into the man from outside can't defile him, 19 because it doesn't go into his heart, but into his stomach, then into the latrine, **making all foods clean**?")*

With one stroke of the pen the overenthusiastic Mark tosses aside all the Jewish laws on food, making them null and void - that must have made a gigantic impact. Matthew hurries to control the damage, and turns it into:

(Matthew 15: 19 For out of the heart come evil thoughts, murders, adulteries, sexual sins, thefts, false testimony, and blasphemies. 20

*These are the things which defile the man; **but to eat with unwashed hands doesn't defile the man**.")*

No need to wash your hands before eating - that is an infinitely insignificant sacrifice compared to ruthlessly abolishing all the numerous and intricate food laws of the Jews, all of them delicately detailed directions directly from God himself. Matthew doesn't just save the day here, I think this comes close to saving the planet from a Christian-Jewish point of view: declaring all foods clean could have lead to people interpreting it as forbidding every observation of the Jewish food law, and that would certainly have created an impossible barrier for every Jewish convert

I count 6 logia in chapter 6; a grand total of 10

The dance around Elijah

Mark didn't have Jesus meet John the Baptist, but as fortunate as storytelling goes, Luke grants Jesus the opportunity to indirectly meet and greet with John who sends his messengers to Jesus in order to verify that Jesus truly is the Messiah. Apparently, after witnessing the Holy Spirit descending from heaven on Jesus and hearing a voice from heaven say "You are my beloved Son" in Luke 3:22, John still isn't wholly convinced? Even I'd be convinced. Granted, Luke doesn't explicitly state that John witnesses the event, nor do Mark or Matthew. In Luke, Jesus is praying when the Holy Spirit visits him and the voice from heaven speaks, events that are narrated by an invisible witness:

3:21 Now when all the people were baptized, Jesus also had been baptized, and was praying. The sky was opened,

Both Mark and Matthew have Jesus himself see the Holy Spirit descend directly after he surfaces from the water, and then the voice speaks. Is it unlikely that John the Baptist is nearby when Jesus supposedly finishes the supposed last part of baptism? What is clear, is what is completely unclear: the whereabouts of John the Baptist when he does his baptising; is he right next to the one being baptised? Standing, sitting, lying on the ground even? Or is he at a distance and if so, how great is that distance - I could go on for many pages...

However, this new occasion lends itself for fulfilling more (Isaiah) prophecy as well as contributing to Project Elijah, next to introducing more Thomas, so it's a win-win really. Here is the perfectly literal copy of logion 78:

(78a) Jesus said, "Why have you come out into the desert?
(78b) To see a reed shaken by the wind?
(78c) And to see a man clothed in fine garments like your kings

and your great men?
(78d) Upon them are the fine garments, and they are unable to discern the truth."

*7:24 When John's messengers had departed, he began to tell the multitudes about John, "What did you go out into the wilderness to see? A reed shaken by the wind? 25 But what did you go out to see? A man clothed in soft clothing? Behold, those **who are gorgeously dressed, and live delicately, are in kings' courts**.*

*(Matthew 11:7 As these went their way, Jesus began to say to the multitudes concerning John, "What did you go out into the wilderness to see? A reed shaken by the wind? 8 But what did you go out to see? A man in soft clothing? Behold, those **who wear soft clothing are in kings' houses**.)*

The entire logion 78 is almost literally copied - and Matthew follows Luke almost to the letter, which is highly unusual. Substituting the word 'desert' for 'wilderness' is a favourite of course, 249 occurrences in the Tanakh of the latter versus 51 for 'desert'.
The purpose here (the scene unfolds further on) is to convince the audience that John is Elijah, thus conveniently dismissing the need for his presence any further, and just to refresh your memory: Malachi 4:5 predicted that Elijah would precede the Messiah. Elijah made an appearance during the Transfiguration in Mark but at this point, in Luke as well as in Matthew, the transfiguration is yet to come, and this is their chance to build a much stronger case beforehand.
In verse 5 Luke conflates 78c and 78d but leaves out the phrase about being able to discern the truth. Matthew doesn't like Luke's positive label of the clothing nor the 'live delicately' and merely repeats the 'soft clothing'. A pioneer's fate, I will often repeat this, yet it is a great compliment coming from Matthew that he sticks so close to a first try. And while we're at it, I'll bring up the gospel sandbox once more: Luke's poetic variation on Thomas in verse 25 is subject to that same liberal treatment by Matthew - and only that

part.

Thomas, Luke, Matthew, without the slightest doubt.

But there is more. A quite literal copy of logion 46 follows immediately, naturally leaving out the Thomas prerequisite of becoming like a child, as well as the first phrase of 46a:

(46a) Jesus said, "Among those born of women, from Adam until John the Baptist, there is no one so superior to John the Baptist that his eyes should not be lowered (before him).
(46b) Yet I have said, whichever one of you comes to be a child will be acquainted with the kingdom and will become superior to John."

7:26 But what did you go out to see? A prophet? Yes, I tell you, and much more than a prophet. 27 This is he of whom it is written, 'Behold, I send my messenger before your face, who will prepare your way before you.' 28 "For I tell you, among those who are born of women there is not a greater prophet than John the Baptizer, yet he who is least in God's Kingdom is greater than he."

(Matthew 11:9 But why did you go out? To see a prophet? Yes, I tell you, and much more than a prophet. 10 For this is he, of whom it is written, 'Behold, I send my messenger before your face, who will prepare your way before you.' 11 Most certainly I tell you, among those who are born of women **there has not arisen** *anyone greater than John the Baptizer; yet he who is least in the Kingdom of Heaven is greater than he.)*

Emphasis on the differences again; Luke and Matthew reuse the same Malachi 3:1 that Mark used in his 1:2.

Matthew perfects Luke by using 'arisen', which is far more powerful of course, and working towards their claim: John is the "reincarnation" of Elijah, which Luke has made explicit in 1:17 and both Luke and Matthew worked out further in their chapter 3.

Matthew (alone) then resorts to literally adding names and numbers:

*(Matthew 11:12 From the days of John the Baptizer until now, the Kingdom of Heaven suffers violence, and the violent take it by force. 13 **For all the prophets and the law prophesied until John. 14 If you are willing to receive it, this is Elijah, who is to come**. 15 He who has ears to hear, let him hear.)*

Quite daunting - especially the begging for acceptance of this shrewd proposition, but sometimes it just has to be rubbed in hard, it seems.
Who could possibly believe that these are the words of Jesus, the Messiah? The Saviour?
If I were The Son Of God, I wouldn't nor couldn't be particularly bothered with the trivialities of the hundreds of prophecies foretold regarding My Coming. This isn't Jesus speaking, this is the Church at work in an ultimate attempt to push their agenda, desperate to wrap up Project Elijah after all their apparently failed or at least unaccepted attempts to have Elijah return and precede the Messiah as Malachi foretold.
John the Baptist wasn't foretold, Elijah was. And in the same way that the name of Jesus wasn't quite the same as 'Immanuel', John the Baptist is very different from 'Elijah'. The solution to giving the name of Jesus to someone who was supposed to be named Immanuel was simply conceived by having an angel ordering Joseph and Mary to do so, and an identical treatment was received by John the Baptist, whose highly uncommon name plainly required to be also addressed by Luke in his very first chapter.
This right here is the Church on its knees, and it's difficult to resist feeling compassion

Luke by the way crams verses 12 and 13 into his 16:16, his chapter on possessions, as an apparent afterthought. Then again Luke appears to have very little business with the Jews and seems to be solely serving those who believe in the Jesus of Thomas.
Matthew tries to Thomasine it all by wrapping it up with verse 15 ('hear hear!'), which, quite frankly, works for me - a fine find. Still,

Matthew can neither leave it up to chance nor resist spelling it all out in his version of the transfiguration:

*(Matthew 17:10 His disciples asked him, saying, "Then why do the scribes say that Elijah must come first?" 11 Jesus answered them, "Elijah indeed comes first, and will restore all things; 12 **but I tell you that Elijah has come already, and they didn't recognize him, but did to him whatever they wanted to.** Even so the Son of Man will also suffer by them." 13 **Then the disciples understood that he spoke to them of John the Baptizer.**)*

There. Leave it to Matthew to leave absolutely nothing to the imagination

John the Baptist

Quite a deviation, but necessary; a bit overdue perhaps but now is a good time: the last sentence of Luke 7:28 and Matthew 11:11 ('yet he who is least in the Kingdom of Heaven is greater than he') is left rather unattended and remains to puzzle Christian commentators up to this day - did that get caught in the crossfire? What did Thomas mean by it? But most importantly: what did the gospel-writers mean by it - they don't give any reason at all whatsoever for this quite puzzling statement.
It triggers me to make an important statement on John the Baptist. If I stick to my own rules of taking each text as it is and not delving into original texts, alleged scribal errors whether accidental or intentional, and so on, I must conclude that John the Baptist is a figment of Thomas' imagination.
There is no mention of John the Baptist in the Tanakh, nor baptism or anything the like: baptising came either from Thomas or from the gospel-writers.
What is baptism, even? (Am I really going to do this? Yes I sure am, and you'll wonder (sic) along with me on the path, because baptism is nothing like that what you think it is)

*(Mark 1:4 John came baptizing in the wilderness and preaching the baptism of repentance for forgiveness of sins. 5 All the country of Judea and all those of Jerusalem went out to him. **They were baptized by him in the Jordan river, confessing their sins**. 6 John was clothed with camel's hair and a leather belt around his waist. He ate locusts and wild honey. 7 He preached, saying, "After me comes he who is mightier than I, the thong of whose sandals I am not worthy to stoop down and loosen. 8 **I baptized you in water, but he will baptize you in the Holy Spirit**.")*

That's it. Immersion (the literal translation of the Greek word) in water, while you confess your sins. The (ultimate) goal? Unknown. The frequency? Unknown. The origin? Unknown - although attempts have been made to compare it to the Judaic tvilah, which was an immersion in water for ritual purification. Undoubtedly, that is one of the least original ideas since the invention of spirituality and religion by mankind, as cleansing one's naked body from head to toe with a fluid like water is a perfectly sensible, harmless, cheap and pragmatic way of doing exactly that: cleansing oneself by making sure that every single piece of the body is touched, refreshed, wiped clean.

It can be witnessed, verified, attested, checked, repeated if necessary - touching every part of your body with water is an almost evolutionary fact of life and rite. The sweat lodge of the indigenous people of the Americas, the bathing of Hinduism; Cleopatra bathing in donkey milk, Achilles being immersed in the Styx - I think it's a safe bet that every culture and religion has some story on complete immersion into something.

Back to baptism: being baptised for forgiveness of sins... how would that operate on Jesus?

Why does Jesus get baptised? He's free from sin, according to the prophecies - why did he get baptised? There isn't a reason at all to baptise Jesus. Isn't there?

*(Malachi 3: 1 "Behold, I send my messenger, and he will prepare the way before me; **and the Lord, whom you seek, will suddenly come***

to his temple; *and the messenger of the covenant, whom you desire, **behold, he comes**!" says Yahweh of Armies.)*

The Lord will come to the temple of the messenger? Now that's interesting: Jesus comes to John the Baptist because prophecy foretells so - but why don't the gospel-writers mention that, why do they miss out on a chance to fulfil scripture? Maybe Matthew will shed some light on that, prone as he is to fulfil scripture any which way he can. Note the last emphasised part: it will tempt John the gospel-writer into having John the Baptist exclaim '1:36 and he looked at Jesus as he walked, and said, "Behold, the Lamb of God!"'. What else does Mark have to say about baptism? He limits his treatment of the act of baptism to what is strictly necessary, with Jesus merely:

*(Mark 1:10 Immediately **coming up from the water**, he saw the heavens parting and the Spirit descending on him like a dove.)*

That's it. No ritual, no acts, no words from either John or Jesus; just come up from the waters and you're baptised. Is that the complete ritual? What comes before that? And does nothing come after that? Mark has Jesus use the word two times, which doesn't particularly clarify its use and application:

*(Mark 10:38 But Jesus said to them, "You don't know what you are asking. Are you able to drink the cup that I drink, and to be **baptized with the baptism that I am baptized with**?" 39 They said to him, "We are able." Jesus said to them, "You shall indeed drink the cup that I drink, and you shall be **baptized with the baptism that I am baptized with**;)*

Riddling that is, baptising others with the baptism that Jesus has been baptised with. That almost suggests that the baptism of Jesus could be reused and applied to others; is there perhaps a particular unique way in which someone is baptised? Is a device created for it, especially and only for that occasion? And is Jesus here implying that that unique way of baptism or device could be reused for his disciples, reapplied to them?

Mark then spends only one more set of verses on baptism:

*(Mark 11:29 Jesus said to them, "I will ask you one question. Answer me, and I will tell you by what authority I do these things. 30 The baptism of John-was it from heaven, or from men? Answer me." 31 They reasoned with themselves, saying, "If we should say, 'From heaven;' he will say, 'Why then did you not believe him?' 32 If we should say, 'From men'"-they feared the people, **for all held John to really be a prophet**. 33 They answered Jesus, "We don't know." Jesus said to them, "Neither do I tell you by what authority I do these things.")*

A bit of partners in crime here? Jesus rubs John's back so Jesus benefits even more from everything John does for him? Mark stresses that John is a prophet so that John's claim of Jesus being the Messiah acquires even more weight, credibility, praise and following? Perhaps that could be the case, but again we find no details whatsoever on what baptism is.

Baptism could be anything if it were up to Mark. And in fact it entirely is up to Mark, as his gospel witnesses the very birth of baptism - it is fair to claim that right there it is the first time in the history of mankind that the term baptism is used and written down; the verb isn't in Thomas. There is no mention of it in the Tanakh either.

And baptism could be anything at this point, the end of Mark: digging a hole then filling it with water and immersing oneself or someone else in it; letting someone face the water and then gently nudging him into the water or shoving him with a foot or arm, with whatever force; having two persons grab someone by hands and feet and them tossing him into the water: anything is feasible. Drowning someone until almost passing out, thereby mimicking the concept of death and rebirth? As dangerous as that would be, at this point in time it is still perfectly feasible - completely and utterly perfectly feasible.

Nothing is inconceivable about baptism at this point in time as nothing that Mark writes about it could contradict it; because that's exactly what Mark says about baptism: nothing, nothing at all, only that sometimes it involves - not necessarily ends with - emerging from the water.

I am not being difficult here; I am just reading what I read with an open and blank mind, as if I were living in the first centuries CE while consulting all the documentation in the world available to me on the very subject of baptism.

What does Luke do? Luke adds at least something of a goal by telling that John:

1:3 He came into all the region around the Jordan, preaching the baptism of repentance for remission of sins.

A baptism of repentance for remission of sins! That's quite a difference from forgiveness: remission implies that once baptised your sins are all gone, you're even, starting anew with a blank slate. Your sins aren't just forgiven by someone, they have completely disappeared as if they never existed.

Luke gives examples of John's preaching, turning his next verses into somewhat of a mini-stry:

*3:7 He said therefore to the multitudes who went out to be baptized by him, "**You offspring of vipers, who warned you to flee from the wrath to come**? 8 Therefore produce fruits worthy of repentance, and don't begin to say among yourselves, 'We have Abraham for our father;' for I tell you that God is able to raise up children to Abraham from these stones! 9 Even now the ax also lies at the root of the trees. Every tree therefore that doesn't produce good fruit is cut down, and thrown into the fire." 10 The multitudes asked him, "What then must we do?" 11 He answered them, "**He who has two coats, let him give to him who has none. He who has food, let him do likewise**." 12 Tax collectors also came to be baptized, and they said to him, "Teacher, what must we do?" 13 He said to them, "**Collect no more than that which is appointed to you**." 14 Soldiers* *also asked him, saying, "What about us? What must we do?" He said to them, "**Extort from no one by violence, neither accuse anyone wrongfully. Be content with your wages**." 15 As the people were in expectation, and all men reasoned in their hearts concerning John, whether perhaps he was the Christ, 16 John answered them all, "**I indeed baptize you with water, but he comes who is mightier than I, the strap of whose sandals I am not worthy to loosen. He will baptize you in the Holy Spirit and fire**, 17 whose fan is in his hand, and he will thoroughly cleanse his threshing floor, and will gather the wheat into his barn; but he will burn up the chaff with unquenchable fire." 18 **Then with many other exhortations he preached good news to the people**,*

John isn't being particularly nice to all who come to him for baptism but baptises all of them anyway, according to his actions in 3:21. As we can see here, he hands out a few instructions on how people can avert the wrath of God, which apparently is still needed after this baptism that completely wipes clean your slate of sins. Was it a one time only remission of sins then, that which you got from baptism, just forgiving your sins up until then? It would appear that Luke applies it as something similar to confession of sins

3:21 Now when all the people were baptized, Jesus also had been baptized, and was praying. The sky was opened, 22 and the Holy Spirit descended in a bodily form like a dove on him; and a voice came out of the sky, saying "You are my beloved Son. In you I am well pleased."

Jesus is baptised by John like all other people and is praying. There's no coming out of the water, just this: after baptism you pray. Is it a gross exaggeration to claim that everyone prays after baptism? No, it could be very well possible, based on every single bit of text about baptism so far. Nowhere does it say that people pray after being baptised yet nowhere does it say that they don't - it could just have been an unmentioned detail up to this point, and Jesus might very well be praying as part of baptism - although it also might exclusively have to do with only his baptism. Or it is just a completely unrelated event.

What else does Luke say about the use and application of this baptism?

*7:29 When all the people and the tax collectors heard this, they declared God to be just, **having been baptized with John's baptism**. 30 But the Pharisees and the lawyers rejected the counsel of God, **not being baptized by him themselves**.*

According to Luke, John has a baptism with which he baptises you, just as according to Mark Jesus will or at least can baptise you with the baptism Jesus has been baptised with. On that same topic, later on Luke states something even more startling and surprising:

*12:49 "I came to throw fire on the earth. I wish it were already kindled. 50 But I **have a baptism to be baptized with**, and how distressed I am until it is accomplished!*

Jesus has at that point already been baptised, by John. And now he announces that he has another baptism to be baptised with - by John or by someone else? This is yet another new and unknown application of baptism, that it noticeably can be applied twice to the same person - or only to Jesus? Who was going to baptise Jesus for a second time then, given the fact that John was dead when Jesus spoke those words?

This is an incredibly significant statement by Luke; as incredible as it is that Jesus has been baptised, being free from sins as he is, it is impossible, absolutely inconceivable that Jesus would actually announce any baptism that involves himself. Such could only mean that not only Jesus will sin at some point in the future, but he even knows about it - and is perfectly content with it, even looking forward to it!

The details that are supplied on baptism by Mark and Luke are minute, but they are confusing and sometimes even greatly distressing. In stead of baptism becoming more clear, it becomes less clear, obscure even.

That is everything Luke has on baptism; now how about Matthew? Like Mark, Matthew starts with dressing up John in 3:4, and just like Mark Matthew also is conveniently cladding John identical to Elijah in camel's hair and a leather belt (2 Kings 1:8).

Matthew also has John baptise people, people who are 'confessing their sins'. And he has a slightly different baptism of Jesus:

*(Matthew 3:13 Then Jesus came from Galilee to the Jordan to John, to be baptized by him. 14 But John would have hindered him, saying, "**I need to be baptized by you, and you come to me**?" 15 But Jesus, answering, said to him, "**Allow it now, for this is the fitting way for us to fulfill all righteousness**." Then he allowed him. 16 Jesus, when he was baptized, went up directly from the water: and behold, the heavens were opened to him. He saw the Spirit of God descending as a dove, and coming on him. 17 Behold, a voice out of the heavens said, "This is my beloved Son, with whom I am well pleased.")*

No praying after baptism here, so the two aren't necessarily always related. The phrase 'the fitting way for us to fulfil all righteousness' is puzzling, but it seems a conversation piece between two brothers in arms, who unquestionably know each other or at least each other's role in the grander scheme of things, as well as what and why they are doing what they're doing right here. It is even slightly intimate in some way - and alas, utterly unrelated to and devoid from any specifics of baptism.

My guess is that 'righteousness' here is implying scripture, and that Matthew is pointing to Malachi 3:1 that was mentioned during Mark's baptism of Jesus, which said that the Lord would come to the temple of the messenger. Why no one, not even Matthew, grabs this opportunity to fulfil scripture is beyond me. A simple and obvious explanation could be that there is none to point at, but then the riddle of the righteousness fulfilment remains. Or will it?

Why did Mark have Jesus baptised? The Messiah comes to the

temple of the forerunner, is what Malachi said:

*(Malachi 3: 1 "Behold, I send my messenger, and he will prepare the way before me; **and the Lord, whom you seek, will suddenly come to his temple**; and the messenger of the covenant, whom you desire, behold, he comes!" says Yahweh of Armies.)*

John the Baptist doesn't have a temple, and the gospel-writers couldn't have supplied him with one because that would obviously have had to remain in its place and it would have become well known with all the people having to visit him there - what other purpose would the temple of John the Baptist serve? It would have had to be a large temple, perhaps the size of a church or even cathedral, or people would have stood in line for it for many kilometres - at least that is what one would suspect, based on the text of the gospels.

All the events in the life of Jesus, all the miracles, everything: they all are perfectly transient. Temporary, short-lived, ephemeral, impermanent - and so on. Driving out demons, healing people, raising one or two (three, actually) from the dead who will die eventually anyway; magically conjuring food out of thin air that hours later has been digested and disappeared: nothing that Jesus does persists for longer than a few hours. The veil of the Temple that is allegedly torn is the only exception, yet an event that can't be witnessed or confirmed because it covers the most sacred of the entire Temple and only the High Priest is allowed to visit it - once a year. Naturally, there is no record of the event outside the gospels. Nothing that Jesus does can be proven - and that is great, because that means it can't be disproven either: it can't be disproven that the Temple veil did not tear, nor can it be disproven that Jesus raised people from the dead, nor can it be disproven that he cured hundreds of sick people. So John the Baptist isn't assigned a temple by the gospel-writers, because it should have been located at a place easily accessible to multitudes of people, in plain sight of many: it could be disproven that there ever was a temple at that location.

Hence, Jesus has to visit John wherever he is, and the gospel-writers carefully omit the location: "in the river Jordan" says Mark, a river that is 250 kilometres long. Luke states "all the region around the Jordan", even less precise (even though "the river Jordan" is more than imprecise enough), and Matthew states that Jesus came to the Jordan to John. What is he to do there? Whatever the Lord is to do in the temple of the messenger - it doesn't say, only that it is 'suddenly', and that it is.

Jesus and John could have had a conversation, but about what? It would deepen John's character, but most importantly it would settle the matter between which of the two really was Elijah - of all the things incredible it would have been more than most incredible that neither of the two would bring up the topic. That is why there is no conversation at all between the two, and why John sends his messengers to Jesus so the gospel-writers can use that as a pretext to come up with the logion about John the Baptist.

So Mark, desperately searching for an angle, a way to shape and fulfil just another terribly inconvenient prophecy, probably has a mental breakdown - and in a momentary lapse of reason, Mark has Jesus baptised.

At that point, Church history is written, the event is fixed, Mark's legacy extended, and Jesus is to be baptised by the others as well - period. As easily as Mark could have forgotten to mention that Mary was a virgin, it really is impossibly implausible to omit an incredibly significant event - even when that is a significantly incredible event. The baptism of Jesus couldn't be undone, yet the clever and cunning Matthew turns their weak point to a strong point and takes on all challenges at the same time: he does let Jesus and John have a conversation with each other, and he does infer scripture. Matthew certainly doesn't quote Malachi 3:1 nor uses any other words to infer scripture, but only has Jesus say the very vague 'Allow it now, for this is the fitting way for us to fulfill all righteousness.'

It is clear by now: yet another one of Mark's errors, a part of his legacy, is to baptise Jesus - which is a move that undermines the credibility of baptism, as the entire goal of baptism is repentance, the remission of sins. Although it is not spelled out by the first three gospel-writers, Jesus was supposed to be free of sin. John is the only one to spell it out, although not literally:

*(John 1:9 **The true light that enlightens everyone was coming into the world**. 10 He was in the world, and the world was made through him, and the world didn't recognize him. 11 He came to his own, and those who were his own didn't receive him. 12 But as many as received him, to them he gave the right to become God's children, to those who believe in his name: 13 who were born not of blood, nor of the will of the flesh, nor of the will of man, but of God. 14 **The Word became flesh, and lived among us. We saw his glory, such glory as of the only born Son of the Father, full of grace and truth**.)*

A true light, the only born Son of God, full of grace and truth: such a description is not likely to apply to someone who would or even could err, let alone commit sin. And as such, John simply doesn't baptise Jesus. One would assume he does, given everything else that happens, but he doesn't. John simply refuses to have Jesus baptised, he won't have it; it is his gospel and he will have none of such nonsense. The following narrative depicts the first time that John meets Jesus:

*(John 1:29 The next day, he saw Jesus coming to him, and said, "**Behold, the Lamb of God**, who takes away the sin of the world! 30 This is he of whom I said, 'After me comes a man who is preferred before me, for he was before me.' 31 I didn't know him, but for this reason I came baptizing in water: that he would be revealed to Israel." 32 John testified, saying, "**I have seen the Spirit descending like a dove out of heaven, and it remained on him**. 33 I didn't recognize him, but he who sent me to baptize in water said to me, 'On whomever you will see the Spirit descending and remaining on him is he who baptizes in the Holy Spirit.' 34 **I have seen, and have testified that this is the Son of God**.")*

John doesn't have John baptise Jesus - that is an easy way to remember that, isn't it? John the gospel-writer is completely out of the gospel-writers' league, and even Matthew doing what he pleases pales next to him. John couldn't possibly have John baptise Jesus because he explicitly (although not literally) states that Jesus is free of sin, so he just omits the deed - as simple as that. Because he also knew what was the reason behind the baptism of Jesus, as well as the implications of said baptism, and decides to not baptise Jesus but play along nicely and please Mark's legacy by repeating the most significant event - the Holy Spirit descending on him - and bury it all under a ton of words.

John doesn't even suggest that Jesus was baptised by dropping the word 'water': he plays absolutely straight and fair, leaving it all up to the already programmed mind of the reader to read the baptism of Jesus into his words. What John the gospel-writer does truly is just, brave and praiseworthy, it is all very highly commendable; I honestly mean that, no sarcasm intended.

It is all just as very highly commendable as it is shocking

The quest into baptism continues with Matthew, and the statement from John about Jesus baptising him in stead. That helps with the quest into baptism and provides a clarification for his comment just a few verses before:

(Matthew 3:11 "**I indeed baptize you in water for repentance**, but he who comes after me is mightier than I, whose sandals I am not worthy to carry. **He will baptize you in the Holy Spirit**. 12 His winnowing fork is in his hand, and he will thoroughly cleanse his threshing floor. He will gather his wheat into the barn, but the chaff he will burn up with unquenchable fire.")

That is a difference, and a connection between John and Jesus (apart from them being related): John baptises in water, Jesus baptises in the Holy Spirit. Matthew explicitly uses the word 'in' and not 'with'; only Luke baptises 'with' water, all the others baptise 'in'. In Matthew also, Jesus can baptise people with the baptism he has been baptised with:

*(Matthew 20:22 But Jesus answered, "You don't know what you are asking. Are you able to drink the cup that I am about to drink, and be baptized with the baptism that I am baptized with?" They said to him, "We are able." 23 He said to them, "You will indeed drink my cup, and **be baptized with the baptism that I am baptized with**; but to sit on my right hand and on my left hand is not mine to give, but it is for whom it has been prepared by my Father.")*

Whatever that may mean - still no detail whatsoever on it all. The very last mention of baptism by Matthew comes at the very end when Jesus instructs his disciples, and we have another application of baptism: people can be baptised 'in the name of' someone else. Could that be a reference to the baptisms that people have been baptised with, and with which baptisms they can baptise other people, as narrated by Jesus?

*(Matthew 27:19 Go and make disciples of all nations, **baptizing them in the name of the Father and of the Son and of the Holy Spirit**,)*

Jesus will baptise in the Holy Spirit, according to John, and here Jesus tells his disciples to baptise in the name of (the Father and the Son and) the Holy Spirit - those two could be the same, given their strong likeliness, or at least two of a kind.
Baptising 'in the name of'; I can imagine words spoken on such an occasion. By the baptiser? The baptised? Both? Are those words spoken softly, aloud, once or twice or even more often? Are the words spoken, or can they also be words that are sung, or even a poem perhaps? A prayer?
After three whole gospels, we know literally nothing about baptism; except that people have been baptised in the river Jordan and that it involves emerging from water (although only Jesus did that), and that one can be baptised with the baptism that someone else has been baptised with. It seemingly was the calling of a John the

Baptist, a relative of Jesus, who wasn't seen by anyone until he started baptising because he 'was in the desert until the day of his public appearance to Israel' (Luke 1:80). As far as we know John the Baptist was the only person on the face of the earth ever to have baptised anyone.

After three whole gospels, that's the entirety of our truth concerning baptism.

It isn't until John (the gospel-writer) that Jesus performs some baptising of his own:

*(John 3:22 After these things, Jesus came with his disciples into the land of Judea. He stayed there with them and baptized. 23 John also was baptizing in Enon near Salim, **because there was much water there**. They came, and were baptized; 24 for John was not yet thrown into prison.)*

Paranoid people will probably point at verse 24, claiming that it's a smoking gun, but let's move on: apparently a lot of water is needed for baptism.

That can only indicate that more than one person can be baptised by someone at the same time: even if John's disciples would also be baptising, how much (body of) water would be needed for simultaneous baptising? Roughly anything from 1 to 10 square metres of water per baptism or person to be baptised?

I think this is an important clue, and that more than one person can be baptised by a baptiser at the same time. John could have any number of disciples, from a minimum of three (at some point he calls two of them, so there must be more than two) to any number of thousands if you like, although a dozen or more seems more likely - which is a completely random and unfounded number by the way, but so is thousands. With a hundred baptisers and 10 square metres per baptised, would a shallow lake of 25 by 40 metres qualify as "much water"? We can only guess.

There is another interesting fact about baptism:

(John 4:1 Therefore when the Lord knew that the Pharisees had

heard that Jesus was making and baptizing more disciples than John
*2 (**although Jesus himself didn't baptize, but his disciples**), 3 he left*
Judea and departed into Galilee.)

Jesus himself didn't baptise there after all, it appears - only his
disciples. Jesus had twelve disciples, and those twelve could baptise
more than John and his disciples together!
Actually, now we mention it, it says nowhere that John's disciples
did any baptising, John is always the one doing the baptising, and
when John speaks about baptising he never uses the plural, it's
always himself doing all the work.
That's a relief, there is some certainty there. But it is also slightly
complicating the reason for 'much water' being necessary for John's
baptising in John's gospel chapter 3, if it's only John doing the
baptising - although that would decisively indicate that mass-
baptism was practiced by John, with perhaps a maximum of ten
people baptised per baptism, if the twelve disciples of Jesus could
outperform John. That is, of course, entirely assuming that the
disciples of Jesus were baptising only one at a time, that the
disciples of Jesus were just as quick as John in baptising a person,
that the terrain was equal for both parties, with the slope of the hill
as well as the shallowness of the water for both about fairly the
same angle, that the people to be baptised were about the same
age and agility so that one wouldn't for instance have to wait for
ages until that old lady finally got around being baptised, much like
that old lady in front of you at the supermarket who just can't seem
to locate the right coins in her small change, and... - and now I'm
being difficult, and I'll stop it

With these verses being the last of John on baptism, there is
nothing on baptism in the four gospels at all, whatsoever. Baptisms
involves emerging from water, sometimes prayer can follow
afterwards, one's baptism can be reapplied to others so the act or
method of baptism seems to have a reusable property, and baptism
is not one-on-one but multiple people (a guesstimate is a dozen)
can be baptised by a single baptiser at the same time. Lastly, one

can be baptised 'in the name of the Father and of the Son and of the Holy Spirit' and Jesus was said by John to baptise in the Holy Spirit. Known baptisers: John the Baptist himself and the disciples of Jesus - but definitely not Jesus himself. Baptism serves the goal of repentance and causes remission of sins, and most surprisingly even Jesus was baptised although John the gospel-writer disagreed with that idea. Jesus himself anxiously announced his second baptism, possibly indicating that he was going to sin at some point in the future, but that has never been witnessed.

If verily veracious, only Jesus comes up from the water when baptised: in Matthew and Mark alone. The only gospel-writer who has other people being baptised in water is Mark, and that is in his 1:5 when people are baptised in the Jordan river. Is this really all then? Yes it is, absolutely all there's to it in the first four gospels, and that is exactly when and where the whole concept of baptism is birthed

If you forget everything you've always "known" about baptism and go through the four gospels, this is the exact and complete definition of baptism: nothing less, and most certainly nothing more. And at the exact point in time when all four gospels had been written for the first time together (likely somewhere at the end of the 1st century CE), this undoubtedly also must have been the complete definition of baptism.

I will dig deeper then, and make an exception for John the Baptist: I really want to get to the bottom of this, in order to identify all the details of baptism - there must be far more to it than this!

It isn't until the book of Acts that baptism becomes more, starting as a varying ritual with people being baptised in the name of Jesus Christ 'for the forgiveness of sins', upon which people receive the gift of the Holy Spirit (Acts 2:38). Being baptised in the name of Jesus Christ appears to be some primary form of baptism after which another can take place, according to the phrase in Acts 8:16 'only been baptized in the name of Christ Jesus'. Chapter 8 also shows us that walking into or going down into water is used in baptising:

(Acts 8:36 As they went on the way, they came to some water, and the eunuch said, "Behold, here is water. What is keeping me from being baptized?" 37 He commanded the chariot to stand still, and they both went down into the water, both Philip and the eunuch, and he baptized him.)

A requirement, possibly some kind of pre-ceremony, shows up as well:

*(Acts 10:47 "**Can anyone forbid these people from being baptized with water? They have received the Holy Spirit just like us.**" 48 He commanded them to be **baptized in the name of Jesus Christ**. Then they asked him to stay some days.)*

Receive the Holy Spirit and then you can be baptised in the name of Jesus Christ; that sure looks like a requirement, unless it's particular for the Gentiles who are mentioned here. And how it's used here, it seems that one can even insist on baptism in the name of Jesus Christ after one has received said Holy Spirit! Given the scene from Acts 8, it seems that just being in water is good enough for a baptism; it is fair to assume that the two persons just stood in water, although it remains unclear how far they went into it. Insightful information, the lot of it. Chapter 11 once more demonstrates that one can also be baptised in the name of the Holy Spirit, and chapter 12 shows exotic side effects of being baptised:

*(Acts 12:1 While Apollos was at Corinth, Paul, having passed through the upper country, came to Ephesus and found certain disciples. 2 He said to them, "**Did you receive the Holy Spirit** when you believed?" They said to him, "**No, we haven't even heard that there is a Holy Spirit.**" 3 He said, "**Into what then were you baptized?**" They said, "**Into John's baptism.**" 4 Paul said, "John indeed baptized with the baptism of repentance, saying to the people that they should believe in the one who would come after him, that is, in Jesus." 5 **When they heard this, they were baptized***

in the name of the Lord Jesus. 6 When Paul had laid his hands on
them, the Holy Spirit came on them and they spoke with other
languages and prophesied.)

John baptised with the baptism of repentance - that seems to be
the first stage of baptism, after which you apparently don't receive
the Holy Spirit. The next stage is being baptised in the name of the
Lord Jesus, and that presumably can follow immediately after the
first stage.
As Paul demonstrates here, upon being baptised in the name of
Lord Jesus one receives the Holy Spirit. Another extra detail
disclosed is Paul laying his hands on them; is that invoking the Holy
Spirit or just part of the baptism ritual? What is not helping is that a
few chapters earlier:

(Acts 8:14 Now when the apostles who were at Jerusalem heard
that Samaria had received the word of God, they sent Peter and
John to them, 15 who, when they had come down, prayed for them,
that they might receive the Holy Spirit; 16 for as yet he had fallen
on none of them. They had only been baptized in the name of
Christ Jesus. 17 Then they laid their hands on them, and they
received the Holy Spirit.)

Wait - being baptised in the name of Christ Jesus doesn't give you
the Holy Spirit? That seems to be fairly guaranteed, given verse 16.
So we then have baptisms in the name of Jesus Christ, Lord Jesus,
and Christ Jesus - three different baptisms, it appears.
According to Acts 10:47 you can be baptised in the name of Jesus
Christ when you have received the Holy Spirit. Being baptised in the
name of Lord Jesus leads to the Holy Spirit coming on to you (Acts
12:5-6), yet being baptised in the name of Christ Jesus is guaranteed
to not let you receive the Holy Spirit, but that can be fixed by just
laying hands on you (Acts 8:15-17).
After Acts only a few verses mention baptism but its application
remains (this) wide and vague, and utterly confusing.
John the Baptist only performs on a handful of stages in the

gospels, and only during a very limited time, and then is silenced forever. Looking at his initial withdrawal from public for probably three decades he strikingly closely resembles one of those people in books who had their records expunged by the FBI, CIA or another TLA. John appears out of nowhere, strikes once or twice, and disappears for good - he's the ninja of the gospels. Is John the Baptist a figment of Thomas' imagination, thus forming an effective historical fact for the Church just like Thomas did with Thomas, Judas, Simon Peter, Matthew and James the Just - not to forget Jesus himself?

Yes, of course

John the Baptist is the most important prophet ever in the history of Christianity.

The only prophet, actually, ever, to be alive during the life of a Messiah - the Messiah, according to Christianity.

The only prophet ever to be related to a Messiah - the Messiah, according to Christianity.

What's more, this prophet even had direct and indirect contact with said Messiah - the Messiah, according to Christianity.

This John the Baptist truly is "a prophet of the Most High" (Luke 1:76).

And this is all that remains of his legacy, his ministry, his teachings? His entire life? This is the entirety of the role he played as the utmost important prophet of Christianity?

I'm more than willing to argue that John the Baptist came from Thomas and couldn't possibly be ignored given the kind of attention and brightness of spotlight he received from Thomas, being mentioned in the same logion as Adam although both were said to be "born of woman" - was that a joke by Thomas?

Because the Messiah was prophesied to have a forerunner John was cunningly portrayed from the very beginning of Mark as Elijah in disguise: literally clad in Elijah's clothes, and clothed in Malachi's 4:5 and Isaiah's 40:3 prophecies of 'preparing the way of the Lord'. There is no description of anyone else's attire in the four gospels, save for John the Baptist - and the irony of it all is, they're not even his own clothes.

Yet a painful lesson learned by the gospel-writers during copying from Thomas is that combining Thomas with scripture too directly will turn out ugly, and Project Elijah did turn out ugly: only the Jews that didn't care about the Elijah prophecy would have believed in John the Baptist.

Delicately balancing between Elijah and John the Baptist, thus not knowing exactly what to do with John, the gospel-writers turned him into somewhat of a prophet doing his extremely non-descript baptism thing and stashed him away for later. But there never was a later, as he was quickly silenced in a bizarre way: as Herod's prisoner he was beheaded on request of the daughter of Herodias (who merely passed along her mother's wish). That's not all; the request literally was to bring John's head on a platter - all this was granted because Herod swore an oath to her to give her anything she wanted, up to half of his kingdom.

What a tragic and absurd death! Such a cruel, strange, awkward thing - what is the story behind that? The official story is that John was imprisoned by Herod for uttering one sentence, at that same moment incurring the wrath of his brother's wife, Herodias:

(Mark 6:18 For John said to Herod, "It is not lawful for you to have your brother's wife." 19 Herodias set herself against him, and desired to kill him, but she couldn't,)

Matthew shares the same story, Luke doesn't at all, he has virtually nothing on John the Baptist - but adds a detail:

*(Luke 3:18 Then with many other exhortations he preached good news to the people, 19 but Herod the tetrarch, being reproved by him for Herodias, his brother's wife, **and for all the evil things which Herod had done**, 20 added this also to them all, that he shut up John in prison.)*

A slightly better reason for imprisonment, or rather, less bad - but then again Herod really was known - according to the historian Josephus - to be a cruel despot who had a few of his own sons executed. But that would be Herod the Great, who allegedly murdered the newborns in Bethlehem, of which the only historical record is Matthew 2:10 and that same historian Josephus. The Herod who allegedly had John the Baptist beheaded (John's death was put on record by Josephus as well) was Herod Antipas, one of his sons, who came to rule Galilee after his death - and this Herod was unknown for any cruelty of any kind.

Granted, this Herod swore an oath:

*(Matthew 14:6 But when Herod's birthday came, the daughter of Herodias danced among them and pleased Herod. 7 Therefore **he promised with an oath to give her whatever she should ask**. 8 She, being prompted by her mother, said, "Give me here on a platter the head of John the Baptizer." 9 The king was grieved, but for the sake of his oaths and of those who sat at the table with him, he commanded it to be given, 10 and he sent and beheaded John in the prison.)*

An oath - that really is something that can't be broken. But which king is silly enough to promise a young girl whatever she wants, and swear an oath on that? Mark even goes a whole lot further than that:

*(Mark 6:22 When the daughter of Herodias herself came in and danced, she pleased Herod and those sitting with him. The king said to the young lady, **"Ask me whatever you want, and I will give it to you."** 23 He swore to her, **"Whatever you ask of me, I will give you, up to half of my kingdom."**)*

Up to half his kingdom, is what Herod promises, according to Mark. Why does Matthew omit that fact?

*(Esther 5:3 The king said, **"What do you desire, Esther? What is your request? Ask even to the half of my kingdom, and it shall be***

yours.")

A familiar scene, it seems, or is this mere coincidence? Esther is a queen, wagering half of your kingdom to a queen is not unfeasible - but the (probable) teen daughter of your wife? The half of the kingdom from Mark disappears in Matthew, such is certain.
While we're at it, by now we've become well acquainted with the rather loose way in which prophecies sometimes are treated by the gospel-writers: for instance Mark's pointer in 1:2 to Isaiah, which in fact refers to both Malachi and Isaiah. Matthew's false claim to prophecy fulfilled by the Bethlehem massacre when he points to Jeremiah 31:15 which for a change really is a prophecy, but about the people of Israel in exile, and already fulfilled centuries earlier - and about Ramah, not Bethlehem. Matthew's false claim to prophecy fulfilled regarding the flight to Egypt; Matthew's false claim to a non existing prophecy regarding Jesus coming from Nazareth; Matthew's confusion of Zechariah with Jeremiah when Judas returns the 30 silver pieces (which is in the chapter on Judas). In the light of all that, would it be feasible that the so very peculiar beheading of John the Baptist served a purpose? Other than relieving the gospel-writers of their duty to assign him a true role as Jesus' one and only prophet and to thoroughly deepen his character - and have him finally actually do something to 'turn the hearts of the fathers to the children, and the hearts of the children to their fathers' as the real Malachi prophecy foretold?

*2 Kings 2:1 **When Yahweh was about to take Elijah up by a whirlwind into heaven, Elijah went with Elisha** from Gilgal. 2 Elijah said to Elisha, "Please wait here, for Yahweh has sent me as far as Bethel." Elisha said, "As Yahweh lives, and as your soul lives, I will not leave you." So they went down to Bethel. 3 The sons of the prophets who were at Bethel came out to Elisha, and said to him, **"Do you know that Yahweh will take away your master from your head today?"** He said, "Yes, I know it. Hold your peace."*

Laugh if you will, I know I did when I first saw it. Not a prophecy at all yet a historical narrative of Elijah's being taken up into heaven, and even already fulfilled - and it does contain the words 'take...away...master...head' but that's really all about it. The master is taken from the head, it's not saying the reverse, that the head of the master will be taken, and head is naturally used figuratively here.

Is it insane to presume that this "prophecy" instigated Mark's invention to have John the Baptist beheaded? In the light of the loose way in which the prophecies are wielded, I think not. I think that the gospel-writers had been frantically looking from the very start of their gospel for a way to get rid of John the Baptist so Elijah could take his place in the transfiguration: John's entire purpose is to die as fast as he can, so they can use the Elijah in him. They could have dropped John from the stairs but that would have raised suspicion. They could have given him some kind of heroic death but heroes have character, and they were intent on not deepening John's character - John was Elijah and Elijah alone, period. So John's imprisonment was invented, the scene from Esther remembered, and all that was needed was a proper death. Was it bad memory of 2 Kings? It seems absolutely plausible that one would remember Elijah being taken up to heaven in a fiery chariot, rather than him suffering of his head being taken away - this is all getting less feasible by the minute, isn't it?

Absurd idea? Yes. Preposterous? Maybe.

Mark has a pointer:

*(Mark 9:12 He said to them, "Elijah indeed comes first, and restores all things. **How is it written about the Son of Man, that he should suffer many things and be despised**? 13 But I tell you that Elijah has come, and **they have also done to him** whatever they wanted to, **even as it is written about him**.")*

As it is written about him? Is Mark claiming that John met his fate accordingly to what was written about him, in scripture? Prophesied perhaps even, within the very loose context of the gospel-writers? That must mean Elijah of course, as John the Baptist is a Thomas invention and nowhere to be found in the Tanakh. But there is nothing about Elijah in the Tanakh that indicates what would happen to him after he had returned from his presumed death - in theory he could still be living of course, many people in the Tanakh grew to be many hundreds of years old. So this must be about John, but that can't be?! Then John must have suffered something that was "prophesied" in the context of Elijah.

The fate of John the Baptist referred to by Mark in this way, pointing to 'suffer many things and be despised', could hardly be his unjust imprisonment, but must have been that other grand negative event in his life: death by beheading. The Jews have 'also' done to John what they wanted to, similar to the Son of Man. So they have done something to John that they have also done to Jesus at that moment? We know Mark by now, and he almost gets it right, he says almost exactly what he means to say.

Unfortunately, Luke doesn't repeat anything Mark said here . Fortunately, Matthew does:

*(Matthew 17:12 but I tell you that Elijah has come already, and they didn't recognize him, but **did to him whatever they wanted to. Even so the Son of Man will also suffer by them**.")*

Matthew repeats all of Mark, and discloses that the suffering of many things and the being despised that Mark mentions hasn't already happened to Jesus. By using the future tense, Matthew implicitly states here that whatever Jesus has undergone by now, more than half-way through his gospel, is nothing compared to what Jesus will undergo in the future: 'will also suffer by them'.

So what the Jews have done to John is what they will do to Jesus, and what they will do to Jesus is what they have done to John. That can mean only one thing: death.

Matthew repeats Mark, but leaves out the reference to scripture. Wait, what?! Matthew of all people is passing on a chance to quote scripture? That very same Matthew who makes up scripture prophecy from scratch if need be? That very same Matthew indeed doesn't look up Mark's prophecy about the death of John the

Baptist; doesn't quote Mark's prophecy about the death of John the Baptist; doesn't name the prophet of Mark's prophecy about the death of John the Baptist, and doesn't even merely repeat Mark's vague scripture reference about the death of John the Baptist. This seems similar to the baptism of Jesus: a bait of scripture yet nobody bites.

Can John the gospel-writer offer any help? Alas, he mentions nothing about John the Baptist and Herod, no imprisonment or death in his story to be found

Mark thought that he'd be fulfilling scripture by beheading John the Baptist, also known as Elijah - and he even wrote that down. So I wouldn't be surprised if a very old version of a bible were to be found somewhere that contains verses or, more likely, a footnote with a direct or indirect reference to Elijah or the second book of Kings along with the passage of John the Baptist's beheading, with highly likely yet another claim of a prophecy fulfilled.

Killing three birds with one stone it would be: getting rid of (the name and) the character of John the Baptist who Thomas forced onto the gospel-writers just like he did with (the name of) Jesus. It would be undisputedly proving beyond the shadow of a doubt that John in fact was Elijah because he suffered "the same death" as Elijah. The bonus to it would be fulfilling yet another prophecy - gospel-writers' style.

What could be the most likely other explanation for Mark pointing to scripture and no one else copying him? That the scripture in question was actually looked up and judged to be not plausible enough to continue on, perhaps even a mistake - but John the Baptist being beheaded couldn't be undone. So that story simply was repeated and retold, the vague pointer to 'it being written' omitted, and that was that

John the Baptist goes only skin deep, and never developed his character. Even Judas of all people undergoes a major character development in the Church story (there's a chapter on him later on), yet John the Baptist fails to obtain the body required for and deserving of a prophet in the usual Judaic sense of the word. Prophets who love to fill page after page with monologues from God or themselves, full of instructions that are carefully and meticulously quantified and qualified.

It's not as if they forgot to elaborate on John; Luke spends 21 consecutive verses on John in his very first chapter, starting at verse 5; then he takes a break for Mary's birth and continues again at verse 57, ending with verse 80. Forty-five, 45, verses on the birth of John; so there was plenty of space and energy to dedicate to John, and plenty of time and attention to do so.

Yet after Luke's chapter 1 not more than a few handfuls of verses are spent on John in all four gospels together. Eleven verses are spent by Luke on his "preaching", a word which, truth be told, is more than overrated: "share clothes and food which you have in abundance" and "don't be dishonest when exercising your profession as tax collector or soldier" is, loosely translated, the full extent to what John states there - that's all far from exciting or mind-blowing.

The gospel-writers didn't want to elaborate on John, they wanted John to just be Elijah - and they all excused themselves by Luke's spiritless invention:

1:80 The child was growing and becoming strong in spirit, and was in the desert until the day of his public appearance to Israel

John the Baptist fails to become Elijah, fails to get the approval of the Jews, and even John the gospel-writer feels obliged to spend a few verses on Project Elijah - with the stunning result (and thus apparent goal) of letting John the Baptist emphatically deny that he is Elijah:

*(John 1: 21 They asked him, "What then? **Are you Elijah**?" He said, "I am not." "Are you the prophet?" He answered, "No." 22 They said therefore to him, "Who are you? Give us an answer to take back to those who sent us. What do you say about yourself?" 23 He said, "I am the voice of one crying in the wilderness, 'Make straight the*

way of the Lord,' as Isaiah the prophet said.")

Did John the Baptist, blandest of all prophets when it comes to evaluating his own explicitly recorded actions, develop enough character to become a credible Church person in stead of just a name in Thomas? The answer to that can only be unanimous, notwithstanding all my findings and claims in this very chapter. So at least that mission was successful

Mark's legacy continued

Alright. Let's get back to the gospel-writers and see how they deal with the remainder of Mark's legacy.

Luke does a very interesting mash-up of logion 13a and the first parts of 21:

(13a) Jesus said to his disciples, "Compare me to someone and tell me whom I am like."
(21a) Mary said to Jesus, "Whom are your disciples like?"
(21b) He said, "They are like children who have settled in a field which is not theirs.
(21c) When the owners of the field come, they will say, 'Let us have back our field.'
(21d) They (will) undress in their presence in order to let them have back their field and to give it back to them.

*7:31 "To what then should I compare the people of this generation? What are they like? 32 They are like children who sit in the marketplace, and **call to one another**, saying, 'We **piped to you**, and you didn't dance. We mourned, and you didn't **weep**.'*

*(Matthew 11:16 "But to what shall I compare this generation? It is like children sitting in the marketplaces, who **call to their companions** 17 and say, 'We **played the flute for you**, and you didn't dance. We mourned for you, and you didn't **lament**.')*

Matthew copies Luke fairly to the letter and makes it all concise, fluid, and, dare I say it, warm ('companions'). He does not personify the generation and thus removes Luke's 'people' but leaves the first person plural intact in the following sentence - life with Matthew is never boring.

Not counting 13a, I count 3 logia in chapter 7, the grand total now stands at 13. 9 logia in chapters 6 and 7, 90% of those are new...

Luke chapter 8 starts with the parable of the sower. I have copied all three here including the verse before: this is where Mark introduces the parable as a style for the first time, and even has Jesus explain it:

(9a) Jesus said, "Now the sower went out, took a handful (of seeds), and scattered them.
(9b) Some fell on the road; the birds came and gathered them up.
(9c) Others fell on the rock, did not take root in the soil, and did not produce ears.
(9d) And others fell on thorns; they choked the seed(s) and worms ate them.
(9e) And others fell on the good soil and it produced good fruit: it bore sixty per measure and a hundred and twenty per measure."

*(Mark 4:2 He taught them many things in parables, and told them in his teaching, 3 "Listen! Behold, the farmer went out to sow, 4 and as he sowed, some seed fell by the road, and the birds came and devoured it. 5 Others fell on the rocky ground, **where it had little soil**, and immediately **it sprang up**, because it had **no depth of soil**. 6 **When the sun had risen, it was scorched**; and because **it had no root, it withered away**. 7 Others fell among the thorns, and the thorns **grew up, and** choked it, and **it yielded no fruit**. 8 Others fell into the good ground, and yielded fruit, growing up and increasing. Some produced **thirty times, some sixty times, and some one hundred times** as much." 9 He said, "Whoever has ears to hear, let him hear.")*

*8:4 When a great multitude came together, and people from every city were coming to him, he spoke by a parable. 5 "The farmer went out to sow his seed. As he sowed, some fell along the road, and it was **trampled under foot**, and the birds of the sky devoured it. 6 Other seed fell on the rock, and as soon as it grew, it **withered away, because it had no moisture**. 7 Other fell amid the thorns, and the thorns **grew with it**, and choked it. 8 Other fell into the good*

*ground, and grew, and produced **one hundred times** as much fruit."
As he said these things, he called out, "He who has ears to hear, let
him hear!"*

*(Matthew 13:3 He spoke to them many things in parables, saying,
"Behold, a farmer went out to sow. 4 As he sowed, some seeds fell
by the roadside, and the birds came and devoured them. 5 Others
fell on rocky ground, where they didn't have much soil, and
immediately **they sprang up,** because they had **no depth of earth.** 6
When the sun had risen, they were scorched. Because they **had no
root, they withered away**. 7 Others fell among thorns. The thorns
grew up and choked them. 8 Others fell on good soil and yielded
fruit: some **one hundred times as much, some sixty, and some
thirty**. 9 He who has ears to hear, let him hear.")*

Emphasis is on the differences between the three.
All leave out Thomas' worms, and please observe the sandbox
Thomas inadvertently leaves: 9c has an unclear outcome (if they did
not produce ears, what did they produce) and cause (isn't it obvious
that the seeds can't take root in the soil, if they fell on rock?) and
Mark immediately takes off on the (over-)explanation trip. Luke
condenses that part of Mark to the extreme, and Matthew almost
literally follows Mark.
Luke is condensing Mark's numeric twist and only uses 'one
hundred'; where Luke usually moves closer to Thomas, this time he
just goes off in a direction of his own. He expands verse 5 with the
path and 'trampled', uses the odd pleonasm 'of the sky' (similar to
the mustard seed parable but that is yet to come) and swaps the
perfectly logical 'no depth of soil' on the rocks for 'no moisture'.
Perhaps because he sticks to Mark's 'withered' but doesn't want to
copy Mark's invention of the scorching sun? Or Luke was something
of a gardener and it made perfect sense to him that plants on rocks
wither in the sun because the only way to compensate the heat is
by having (access to) moisture, which can only be achieved by
having roots? I'm not being cynical; sometimes knowledge can work
to someone's disadvantage.

Matthew sticks entirely to Mark, not surprisingly this time, and next to the scorching sun also follows up with Mark's numbers, although this time they're reversed. Luke is out of order here but Matthew coming after Mark is undeniable.

Do I have a solid case for Thomas coming first? Well, yes: follow the sandbox. All that the gospel-writers create and change is theirs alone, and I have emphasised that in bold - that which remains and all three share, is the pure content of Thomas

Luke also explains why he explains the parable just as Mark does twice in chapter 4, redirecting logion 62 in order to elevate the disciples above the crowd; the second part is a mere reference to Isaiah 6:9-10, of which Luke uses the briefest form:

(62a) Jesus said, "It is to those who are worthy of my mysteries that I tell my mysteries.
(62b) Do not let your left (hand) know what your right (hand) is doing."

*(Mark 4:10 When he was alone, those who were around him with the twelve asked him about the parables. 11 He said to them, "To you is given **the mystery** of God's Kingdom, but to those who are outside, all things are done in parables, 12 that 'seeing they may see, and **not perceive**; and hearing they may hear, and not understand; lest perhaps they should turn again, and their sins should be forgiven them.'")*

*8:9 Then his disciples asked him, "What does this parable mean?" 10 He said, "To you it is given to know the mysteries of God's Kingdom, but to the rest in parables; that 'seeing they may **not see**, and hearing they may not understand.'*

(Matthew 13:10 The disciples came, and said to him, "Why do you speak to them in parables?" 11 He answered them, "To you it is given to know the mysteries of the Kingdom of Heaven, but it is not given to them. 12 For whoever has, to him will be given, and he will

*have abundance; but whoever doesn't have, from him will be taken away even that which he has. 13 Therefore I speak to them in parables, because seeing they **don't see**, and hearing, they don't hear, neither do they understand. 14 In them the prophecy of Isaiah is fulfilled, which says, 'By hearing you will hear, and will in no way understand; Seeing you will see, and will in no way perceive; 15 for this people's heart has grown callous, their ears are dull of hearing, and they have closed their eyes; or else perhaps they might perceive with their eyes, hear with their ears, understand with their heart, and would turn again, and I would heal them.' 16 "But blessed are your eyes, for they see; and your ears, for they hear. 17 For most certainly I tell you that many prophets and righteous men desired to see the things which you see, and didn't see them; and to hear the things which you hear, and didn't hear them.)*

Mark is very poor again, unwillingly suggesting that there's only one single mystery by using the singular form. Luke fixes that and also swaps Isaiah's perceiving for seeing, both of which Matthew copies. Matthew then gives us the full Monty, explicitly pointing to Isaiah, and that the prophecy is partly fulfilled, and even following up with literally quoting Isaiah 6:10 in verse 15.
Best of all, however, is Matthew fixing both Mark and Luke because they are suggesting that Jesus knowingly and willingly speaks in parables in order to have Isaiah's prophecy fulfilled, by using the word '(so) that'. Matthew notices it and is shrewd enough to turn that around, telling us that Jesus is speaking in parables precisely 'because' of the callous hearts that Isaiah prophesied - it is the Jews' unbelief that is causing him to do so.
More surprisingly, Matthew adds verse 12 which is a literal copy of logion 41. And closes in verse 17 with an altered copy of logion 38a conflated with Jeremiah 5:21, befitting his context (both logia will be discussed later). Matthew oh Matthew, once again you perfect it all!
Thomas, Mark, Luke, Matthew: the order is undeniably clear; one simple part of a logion gets once again turned and twisted in so many Church ways, exploited to serve so many Church goals - and

once more we see its gradual process of growth. The first copier makes a mistake or two, the second fixes one of them, then the third comes in and fixes the last, using the now perfect version to slap on more than a few verses full of literal scripture reference

A literal copy of logion 33b follows (logion 33a is used later):

(33a) Jesus said, "Preach from your housetops that which you will hear in your ear.
(33b) For no one lights a lamp and puts it under a bushel, nor does he put it in a hidden place, but rather he sets it on a lampstand so that everyone who enters and leaves will see its light."

*(Mark 4:21 He said to them, "Is the lamp brought to be put **under a basket** or **under a bed**? Isn't it put on a stand?)*

*8:16 "No one, when he has lit a lamp, covers it **with a container**, or puts it **under a bed**; but puts it on a stand, **that those who enter in may see the light**.*

*(Matthew 5:15 Neither do you light a lamp and put it **under a measuring basket**, but on a stand; and it **shines to all who are in the house**.)*

Luke, as accustomed, reverts to the literal Thomas copy. He undoes the question introduced by Mark and adds the purpose almost literally: giving light to those who enter (and leave). Matthew redacts that last bit and also makes the action concise by naming only one place where not to put the light, copying Mark's 'basket' for that and changing it into a 'measuring basket'. Matthew also copies Luke's lighting of the lamp and beautifully rephrases its purpose into a harmless prop stage, and we've already seen Mark turn the hidden place into a bed in order to prevent the need for interpretation. Thomas, Mark, Luke, Matthew - the order is crystal-clear.
Apparently triggered by these verses, the next verse cites logion 6c:

(6a) His disciples questioned him and said to him, "Do you want us to fast? How shall we pray? Shall we give alms? What diet shall we observe?"
(6b) Jesus said, "Do not tell lies, and do not do what you hate, for all things are plain in the sight of heaven.
(6c) For nothing hidden will not become manifest, and nothing covered will remain without being uncovered."

*(Mark 4:22 For there is nothing **hidden**, except that it should be **made known**; neither was anything made **secret**, but that it should **come to light**.)*

*8:17 For nothing is **hidden** that will not be **revealed**; nor anything **secret** that will not **be known and come to light**.*

*(Matthew 10:26 Therefore don't be afraid of them, for there is nothing **covered** that will not be **revealed**, or **hidden** that will not **be known**.)*

Mark avoids Thomas' '(become) manifest' and struggles, turning it into the tentative '(should be) made known' and he reuses the 'should be' in the second phrase - poor as usual, at the same time implying that secrets are 'made' with the sole purpose of them coming to light.
The double negative of Luke's first phrase is, of course, originally Thomas - but he also repeats that in the second phrase and it becomes confusing with the 'will not' theoretically applying to the 'come to light' as well: "secret that will not come to light".
Matthew fixes it elegantly and eloquently, and puts the second part of the sentence before the first one, which actually is better than Thomas, as hidden is a more advanced and elaborate state of something invisible than covered. And revealed, of course, is a much better Church word than the evident Thomas pointer of 'made manifest'. Luke adds 'will not be known' to Mark's 'come to light' and Matthew happily adopts the result, dropping the 'come to

light' - only good things come to light, of course.
Thomas, Mark, Luke, Matthew - once more.
Quite a bit of Mark is being undone by Luke as well as Matthew. Have you noticed?

And the next one is a literal copy of logion 41 seen just prior in Matthew (logion 62):

(41) Jesus said, "Whoever has something in his hand will receive more, and whoever has nothing will be deprived of even the little he has."

(Mark 4:24 He said to them, "Take heed what you hear. With whatever measure you measure, it will be measured to you, and more will be given to you who hear. 25 For whoever has, to him more will be given, and he who doesn't have, even that which he has will be taken away from him.")

8:18 Be careful therefore how you hear. For whoever has, to him will be given; and whoever doesn't have, from him will be taken away even that which **he thinks** *he has."*

19:26 'For I tell you that to everyone who has, will more be given; but from him who doesn't have, even that which he has will be taken away from him.

(Matthew 13:12 For whoever has, to him will be given, **and he will have abundance***; but whoever doesn't have, from him will be taken away even that which he has.*
(...)
Matthew 25:29 For to everyone who has will be given, **and he will have abundance***, but from him who doesn't have, even that which he has will be taken away.)*

Luke for some reason adds the verb 'think' in his first attempt which (naturally) is rejected as it leaves room for interpretation. The 'more' in Mark is from Thomas and disappears in Luke's first attempt only to resurface in his second, yet Matthew turns it into 'abundance' and beautifully switches to 'but' as correct connective to show contrast.

Given the minute differences and the duplicate use, the order is a challenge here, although just as in the other cases of copying there is a story which unfolds, so perhaps this is a good time to comment on the whole process again.

As concise as Thomas is, Mark is first to copy and suffers the pioneer's fate, trying to change too much: the 'hand' (crucial in Thomas, apparently) disappears and the impersonal act of receiving is changed to giving so that God becomes the main character of this story, not 'whoever' (and likewise so with 'deprived' and 'taken away'. Mark also drops the opposing 'something' and 'nothing' as those also are too specific and might evoke questions (e.g. "something of what?") - but forgets to drop 'more' along with them. On his first attempt Luke fixes the 'more' as well as Mark's crooked sentence that got stuck in the process of swapping 'deprived' for 'taken away', ending up with a very nice juxtaposing of 'whoever has, to him' versus 'whoever doesn't have, from him'. He also adds the 'think' which no one likes, perhaps to compensate for removing the 'little' of Thomas. Matthew seems to do a literal copy of that in his first attempt, keeping everything of Luke but changing the conjunction to the correct 'but' and dropping 'thinks'. As perfect as that is, Matthew can't resist and has to overdo Luke by inserting the 'abundance' phrase.

Is Luke inspired by Matthew on his second attempt? He copies Matthew's 'but' and moves the indirect object to the first phrase: 'will be given' now becomes a hollow phrase so he puts the 'more' back in. Matthew likes the new Luke a lot and does a perfect literal copy although he sticks to his own 'abundance'.

The order is a puzzle as Luke and Matthew each have two versions of which the last ones are identical twins. The interaction between both gospel-writers is evident, but the exact order isn't. Mark being first with his very lengthy version is evident, Thomas could be first or last

Logia 99a and 99b are the last to be found in chapter 8:

(99a) The disciples said to him, "Your brothers and your mother are standing outside."
(99b) He said to them, "Those here who do the will of my father are my brothers and my mother.
(99c) It is they who will enter the kingdom of my father."

*(Mark 3:31 His mother and his brothers came, and standing outside, they sent to him, calling him. 32 A multitude was sitting around him, and they told him, "Behold, your mother, your brothers, and your sisters are outside looking for you." 33 He answered them, "Who are my mother and my brothers?" 34 **Looking around at those who sat around him**, he said, "Behold, my mother and my brothers! 35 For **whoever does the will of God** is my brother, my sister, and mother.")*

*8:19 His mother and brothers came to him, and they could not come near him for the crowd. 20 Some people told him, "Your mother and your brothers stand outside, desiring to see you." 21 But he answered them, "My mother and my brothers are **these who hear the word of God, and do it**."*

*(Matthew 12:46 While he was yet speaking to the multitudes, behold, his mother and his brothers stood outside, seeking to speak to him. 47 One said to him, "Behold, your mother and your brothers stand outside, seeking to speak to you." 48 But he answered him who spoke to him, "Who is my mother? Who are my brothers?" 49 **He stretched out his hand toward his disciples**, and said, "Behold, my mother and my brothers! 50 For **whoever does the will of my Father who is in heaven**, he is my brother, and sister, and mother.")*

Where Mark deviously inserts a comma so he labels all around him as doing the will of God, implying that if you follow Jesus you do the will of God, Luke just sticks to Thomas yet doesn't explicitly refer to anyone present, leaving up to interpretation who he means by 'these'. Matthew prefers all of Mark and perfects it, adding flow and eloquence: the beautiful hand gesture and the 'will of my Father who is in heaven' instead of just 'God'. And explicitly points to the disciples alone, not the crowd or 'those around him' - another affirmation of the special status of his disciples.

Mark suffers the pioneer's fate very well with his elaboration and explanation, sketching the scene perfectly with a crowd between Jesus and his relatives - before starting his verses, maybe that makes a difference.

Either it's a complete coincidence that Matthew addresses his disciples, or the only likely inspiration for that is Thomas. Matthew may or may not have read Luke here (just as Luke may have read only Thomas, yet his 'desiring to see you' seems inspired by Mark's 'looking for you'), but he sure did read Mark, and not the other way around. Luke really entirely goes his own way every now and then. Thomas comes first and has his usual nuanced version, without making a case by implying that his followers do the will of God. And, as usual, is utterly concise

The parts that Luke and Matthew play

It must be clear by now what role Luke and Matthew play.
Luke, by very often reverting to Thomas, seems to have to bend the Church Jesus into the direction of the Thomas supporters. Matthew undoes most of Mark and occasionally completely ignores Luke but creates the best of both worlds out of the two, while adding scripture reference or merely dark and doom whenever befits him. Matthew is the true master of words and comes last, both of which must be blatantly obvious by now. He usually follows Luke over Mark although he always adds a touch of Mark to his own; he's the final redactor of the two gospels and in fact the primary foundation of Jesus, on which firm and solid basis John can mystify away without worrying about a thing.

When it comes to doctrine, Luke once again is the good cop, sticking to either Mark or Thomas, although he always sticks to Thomas and only to Mark when Mark either followed Thomas to the very letter, or just made up something so that there is no Thomas at all to follow for Luke. And Matthew is the very bad cop, really, pointing his finger of repentance and impending doom whenever he can, throwing around implicit or explicit references to the Tanakh and Isaiah's prophecies on each and every occasion.

In a sense, Luke and Matthew are the perfect good cop / bad cop combo against Mark: Luke is the good cop, showing a lot more Thomas leg than Mark, and Matthew is the bad cop sweeping that same evidence under the carpet again. Or is Matthew the good cop from the point of view of the Jews, so closely embedding Jesus in the prophecies and settings of the Tanakh and the Judaic wrath of God, and Luke the bad cop, putting more stress on the benign and new Jesus? It all depends on your point of view and one thing is obvious: Luke and Matthew together accommodate many viewpoints, and certainly throw a lot more Thomas and scripture at it all.

It seems that word on the streets has it that Luke served "the

Gentiles", basically everybody but the Jews, and that Matthew served the Jews. I think that Luke mostly wrote to appease the people who were familiar with and fond of Thomas, and that Matthew had to try hard to convert and convince the truly Judaic Jews that Jesus really was their true Messiah

As someone who's fond of words, style and wordplay, I must admit I greatly admire Matthew's eloquence. Where Mark stutters and stammers and often ends up with poor sentences without properly connecting (in)dependent clauses, and where Luke pays more attention to the literal and exact wording or phrasing of Thomas than the natural flow of the resulting sentence(s), Matthew is a natural with words: he fluently flows through everything Mark and Luke with straight A's.

I'm very much inclined to the idea that even before their parts were played, the order of these three gospels was already fixed in some minds: Luke was to be last so that the most pure Thomas stuff could still be found, safely stashed away in the back. The raw initial work of Mark was to come before that, also because it was the smallest story both in content but most importantly context with simply too many open endings - and beginnings - to the Messiah; and the magnificent prose of Matthew at the very front - naturally - so it gets the most and best attention.

Back to the verses and logia:

*(Mark 6:7 He called to himself the twelve, and began to send them out **two by two**; and he gave them **authority over the unclean spirits**. 8 He commanded them that they should take nothing for their journey, **except a staff only**: no bread, no wallet, no money in their purse, 9 but to wear sandals, and not put on two tunics. 10 He said to them, "Wherever you enter into a house, **stay there until you depart from there**. 11 Whoever **will not receive you** nor hear you, as you depart from there, **shake off the dust** that is under your feet for a testimony against them. Assuredly, I tell you, it will be more tolerable for Sodom and Gomorrah in the day of judgment than for that city!" 12 They went out and preached that people should*

repent. 13 They cast out many demons, and anointed many with oil who were sick, and healed them.)

9:1 He called the twelve together, and gave them power and **authority over all demons**, and to **cure diseases**. 2 He sent them out to preach God's Kingdom and to heal the sick. 3 He said to them, "Take nothing for your journey-**no staffs**, nor wallet, nor bread, nor money. Don't have two coats each. 4 Into whatever house you enter, **stay there, and depart from there**. 5 As many as **don't receive you**, when you depart from that city, **shake off even the dust** from your feet for a testimony against them." 6 They departed and went throughout the villages, preaching the Good News and healing everywhere.

(Matthew 10:1 He called to himself his twelve disciples, and gave them **authority over unclean spirits**, to cast them out, and to **heal every disease and every sickness**. 2 Now the names of the twelve apostles are these. The first, Simon, who is called Peter; Andrew, his brother; James the son of Zebedee; John, his brother; 3 Philip; Bartholomew; Thomas; Matthew the tax collector; James the son of Alphaeus; Lebbaeus, who was also called Thaddaeus; 4 Simon the Zealot; and Judas Iscariot, who also betrayed him. 5 Jesus sent these twelve out and commanded them, saying, "Don't go among the Gentiles, and don't enter into any city of the Samaritans. 6 Rather, go to the lost sheep of the house of Israel. 7 As you go, preach, saying, 'The Kingdom of Heaven is at hand!' 8 **Heal the sick**, cleanse the lepers, and **cast out demons**. Freely you received, so freely give. 9 Don't take any gold, silver, or brass in your money belts. 10 Take no bag for your journey, neither two coats, nor sandals, **nor staff**: for the laborer is worthy of his food. 11 Into whatever city or village you enter, find out who in it is worthy, and **stay there until you go on**. 12 As you enter into the household, greet it. 13 If the household is worthy, let your peace come on it, but if it isn't worthy, let your peace return to you. 14 Whoever **doesn't receive you** or hear your words, as you go out of that house or that city, **shake the dust off your feet**.)

A commentary-free bucket (or rather, bath tub) of words from all three, for a change.
Another self-invented Thomasine riddle, with the same looseness and boundary-free application by Matthew as seen before - although it's evidently a quite lengthy remake of logion 14b:

(14b) When you go into any land and walk about in the districts, if they receive you, eat what they will set before you, and heal the sick among them.

What do we recognise again? The fact that, in the absence of Thomas, Luke follows Mark almost to the letter (although he includes the staff among the excluded travel item, which gets Matthew's blessing). Matthew writes an entire paragraph, adding all the names of all the disciples, the exclusion of Gentiles and Samaritans along with the inclusion of Israelites (prophecy stuff, I think), the proclamation instruction, and so forth: the gospel's sandbox at work.
Even for Matthew there is a lot of poetic freedom in this, and it strikes me as a significantly different approach from what we have seen so far. Although Luke has the story twice, namely also at the start of chapter 10 (the sending out of the seventy two), which bears similarities to some of Matthew but none of his 10:1-14

The epitome of Jesus

Before we continue with the next logion I'm going to take the opportunity to pay proper attention to this very essence of Thomas. It's the revelation of Thomas' revelation for me and the reason why I started reading scripture after I became acquainted with the text of Thomas, trying to find out what happened to this Jesus - and eventually found that he had been almost completely eradicated, submerged in doctrine, subordinated to original sin.

The Jesus of Thomas is just a man, with a thorough understanding of how things work. What the disciple Thomas experiences in logion 13 is nothing magical but just a moment of enlightenment, revelation, that will come to pass in a matter of hours, days or weeks. The disciple Thomas is "alive", right here, only to return to "death" again - albeit slightly less dead and a bit more alive than before. He is momentarily one, and will return to being two.

All of Thomas' teachings and instructions lead to this moment: the perceiving of the world as it is, the observing of that world so you recognise what is in your sight: dead people everywhere, corpses, people wearing other people's clothes: everyone acting in the Grand Play and reading from Script just playing their Roles, blissfully unaware of it all.

This very *Aha Erlebnis* will pass, but nothing will be the same afterwards.

Here is my interpretation of his words:

(13a) Jesus said to his disciples, 'Compare me to someone and tell me whom I am like.'
(exactly those words)
(13b) Simon Peter said to him, 'You are like a righteous angel.'
(exactly those words). Just a flattering projection from Simon, in line with (his) mental models of Judaism or any other religion that employs angels?
(13c) Matthew said to him, 'You are like a wise philosopher.'

(exactly those words). A more sincere projection from Matthew, in line with (his) mental models like Greek or Roman literature?

(13d) Thomas said to him, 'Master, my mouth is wholly incapable of saying whom you are like.'

(exactly those words). Thomas is utterly confused here - words fall short of everything he feels, thinks, experiences - a moment of full awareness

(13e) Jesus said, 'I am not your master.

(exactly those words). Jesus solidly rejects the role of teacher and guru - at least directly to Thomas. And no, he doesn't mean that he's his servant either. Thomas understands and experiences what Jesus has been trying to convey all along and so now they are equals

(13f) Because you have drunk, you have become intoxicated from the bubbling spring which I have measured out.'

Because you've listened - and understood! - you now are utterly confused, confounded by this new view on life

(13g) And he took him and withdrew and told him three things.

(exactly those words). Probably "I am you" or "You are me" or something like that, or maybe Jesus told Thomas "You are God" (which would make perfect sense, as we all are God)

(13h) When Thomas returned to his companions, they asked him, 'What did Jesus say to you?'

(exactly those words)

(13i) Thomas said to them, 'If I tell you one of the things which he told me, you will pick up stones and throw them at me; a fire will come out of the stones and burn you up.'

(exactly those words). The stoning would be because of blasphemy, a proper Jewish habit back then. How would fire come out of the stones? Stoning would spiritually and emotionally backfire, as it would be fuelled by fear and hate. And fear and hate always consume and hurt their bearer far more than who or what they are directed at

How did the disciple Thomas get to this very moment? By continuously seeking almost every minute of the day. And seeking, he has found: that there is nothing to seek; it is what it is and it's already complete and perfect - perfectly balanced. Everything around you is made up of one or more creations of others, figments of their imagination, mental models - and all of yours are copies of other people's, mixed a bit to your own individual liking, "choice". Everything you perceive, all your perceptions: none of them is original, none of them is really yours - it is all hearsay, mental models, mutual agreements - what is called "truths". It is the sum total of the world Thomas writes about, and the disciple Thomas perceives that at this very moment - his seeking has come to an end.

Why do we seek? Because of the separation that occurs to us all. We are all one and as one we come into this world, but at a very young age we identify ourselves and then there's a feeling of disconnect; suddenly we are an individual, separated from the rest. Is it because our Mom or Dad points at us and says "Jack" or "Jill" or any other name that we were given? And then points at her- or himself and says "Dad" or "Mom"? Or is that just a major event in the beginning of the inevitable process of separation? Which reaches its climax when we ourselves utter our very first "Mom" or "Dad"?

The child feels as if it is something separate, the centre of its own universe: a sense of "self" arises, "me" versus "you" - and that feels like a great loss. And from that very moment on the search for that which is lost starts: seeking has begun - the seeking for the oneness that once was.

Why has it been lost? We don't know but we blame ourselves for that, because our self is the first entity we encounter when we come into being, when we identify ourselves. And blaming ourselves, we find - or rather, create - a reason: we caused the separation because we're not enough [...fill in the blanks...].

Fill in the blanks, take your pick: not loved enough, not appreciated enough, not valued enough, not powerful enough, not strong enough, not pretty enough, not skinny enough, not fat enough - the list is endless and every person picks a different item from it. A few items sometimes, but one or two of those make it to the top of the list.

It is completely irrelevant which item you choose, but from that moment on your journey will consist entirely of overcompensation. If one feels not loved enough, he will make sure that the evidence of being loved will pile up in front of his door, that his or her Instagram account will be liked and loved by multitudes, surround him- or herself with animate or inanimate objects that are proof of being loved: cats, children, statues of fairies or garden gnomes - anything will do. Not powerful enough? Hard work will be put into creating a territory, extending it into something bigger, a domain, and maybe it will become a kingdom, a small empire even - perhaps that takes the form of a company, but just being very influential in your own hometown can do the trick as well. Not valued enough? Diplomas will be collected, medals, achievements, and they will not be put away in the attic but hung in plain sight for everyone to see. Most of what we do on our journey is act to feel better about ourselves. The individual seeker is convinced that we have the choice and the ability to act; that out of the action comes consequence, and that things happen as a result of that individual's choice to act - everything that happens, we take personally: as not enough [...] as we feel, we oddly think that we're driving most if not everything in this world, our world. Superstition and jinxing are fine examples of that, but the most apparent sign is guilt - or rather, Guilt.

The concept of original sin perfectly fits that picture.

It reaffirms our thinking that we caused that feeling of great loss, it reaffirms that we are the cause of it, it reaffirms that we have to make amends in order to become whole again, one - but it is just as false as everything else that we invent to clarify our existence, our purpose, our goal.

So why does Thomas stress the fact that we have to seek, if there's nothing to be found? We have to seek in order to find out that there's nothing to be found, nothing to heal, nothing to fix. We already (should!) know that no matter the quantity and quality of overcompensation we apply to our lives, we never feel whole enough, we never feel like an end has come to our efforts and that we have achieved our goal, The Goal. Some of us persist and simply can't stop increasing their efforts, extending their domain: workaholics, drug overdose and alcoholics are clearly visible examples of that, yet it is not like we do only bad on our journey of overcompensation - some of us move mountains and sadly that reaffirms us in the assumption that we're doing the right thing. Some of the most successful people in the world are driven by a deepest feeling of [...fill in the blanks...].

Find the world, your perception of your world, observe your life for what it is: an endless journey of overcompensating for something that never occurred, never has been real - it's a dead thing, a corpse; your mission is destined to fail. You are trying to prove yourself "not guilty" of a crime that never was committed.

Fast as regards the world, abstain from it, renounce that world, stop what you're doing - and you'll find yourself, become superior to that world. By casting fire on that world, continuously critically viewing it, you'll recognise what is in your sight, and what is hidden will become plain to you.

Recognise that you've come into being, have become two: separated from the one that you were. You've started to wear different clothes on every occasion and made yourself one favourite set of clothes that you wear day in, day out. Cast off those clothes, trample them underfoot like the little child you once were, non-dual, one, whole. Have the two make peace in this one house, be solitary and elect, for you are from the kingdom of light.

Cast your net into the sea and you'll drag it up full of small fish; you might find the large fish but you won't be able to pick it unless you first throw back all the small fish - there's only one way how that can be the case.

That's it, that's the message - and in this very logion Thomas really gets it: he becomes troubled, he is astonished, and rules over the All: in this very moment

Alright. The comparison then, logion 13:

(13a) Jesus said to his disciples, "Compare me to someone and tell me whom I am like."

(13b) Simon Peter said to him, "You are like a righteous angel."

(13c) Matthew said to him, "You are like a wise philosopher."

(13d) Thomas said to him, "Master, my mouth is wholly incapable of saying whom you are like."

(13e) Jesus said, "I am not your master.

(13f) Because you have drunk, you have become intoxicated from the bubbling spring which I have measured out."

(13g) And he took him and withdrew and told him three things.

(13h) When Thomas returned to his companions, they asked him, "What did Jesus say to you?"

(13i) Thomas said to them, "If I tell you one of the things which he told me, you will pick up stones and throw them at me; a fire will come out of the stones and burn you up."

*(Mark 8:27 Jesus went out, with his disciples, into the villages of Caesarea Philippi. On the way he asked his disciples, "**Who do men say that I am**?" 28 They told him, "John the Baptizer, and others say Elijah, but others, one of the prophets." 29 He said to them, "But who do you say that I am?" Peter answered, "**You are the Christ**.")*

*9:18 As he was praying alone, the disciples were with him, and he asked them, "**Who do the multitudes say that I am**?" 19 They answered, "'John the Baptizer,' but others say, 'Elijah,' and others, that one of the old prophets has risen again." 20 He said to them, "But who do you say that I am?" Peter answered, "**The Christ of God**."*

*(Matthew 16:13 Now when Jesus came into the parts of Caesarea Philippi, he asked his disciples, saying, "**Who do men say that I, the Son of Man, am**?" 14 They said, "Some say John the Baptizer, some, Elijah, and others, Jeremiah or one of the prophets." 15 He said to them, "But who do you say that I am?" 16 Simon Peter answered, "**You are the Christ, the Son of the living God**." 17 Jesus answered him, "Blessed are you, Simon Bar Jonah, for flesh and blood has not revealed this to you, but my Father who is in heaven. 18 **I also tell you that you are Peter, and on this rock I will build my assembly, and the gates of Hades will not prevail against it.** 19 **I will give to***

you the keys of the Kingdom of Heaven, and whatever you bind on earth will have been bound in heaven; and whatever you release on earth will have been released in heaven.")

All three make the responses and respondents anonymous save for Simon Peter, putting all the spotlights on him - while neatly name-dropping John the Baptist next to Elijah as part of Project Elijah, not to forget.

Luke sticks entirely to Mark - although his 'one of the prophets of old has risen' deserves an extra point there - and again Matthew blows it all completely out of proportions. 'Who do men say that I, the Son of Man, am?' That is more than a rhetorical question; it is a brazen one. Yet the answer - not only the son of God, but of the living God - is a great find and very Thomasine. Matthew cements the future here by explicitly pointing to Peter as his follow-up, and directing all the attention to him instead of Jesus. He couldn't have overdone the theatrical drama any more: 'you are Peter, and on this rock I will build my church'.

It is obvious that Matthew's gospel comes last (John is a mere mystic poet and borders on the same level of riddles as Thomas) and that he must grasp every opportunity to transgress from a Messiah to the establishment of an Institute: the Church's true primary goal of power and control is made manifest here. What happens right here is the Passing of the Deed; Peter is named and made sole heir of Jesus' legacy and all that the Church has to do from this point on is simply point (yes) to this text.

Two verses, 64 words; kicking off close to two millennia of supreme reign and world power - who would have thought or even dared to imagine that it would really work out the way it has?

How unbelievable and implausible is it that Peter gives these three vastly different answers to this most burning question by Jesus? And why is it no surprise at all that Matthew of all people dives so very deep into the gospel sandbox right here?

What are the odds now, really, of Thomas taking all this religious-political prophecy-pushing manipulation and turning it into his

magical logion 13?
Thomas, Mark, Luke, Matthew - most undeniably so

Logion 55b, taking up the cross, is combined with logion 1:

**(55a) Jesus said, "Whoever does not hate his father and his
mother cannot become a disciple to me.
(55b) And whoever does not hate his brothers and sisters and take
up his cross in my way will not be worthy of me."
(1) And he said, "Whoever finds the interpretation of these
sayings will not experience death."**

*(Mark 8:34 He called the multitude to himself with his disciples, and
said to them, "Whoever wants to come after me, **let him deny
himself**, and take up his cross, and follow me. 35 For whoever wants
to save his life will lose it; and whoever will lose his life for my sake
and the sake of the Good News will save it. 36 For what does it
profit a man, to gain the whole world, and forfeit his life? 37 **For
what will a man give in exchange for his life**? 38 For whoever will
be ashamed of me and of my words **in this adulterous and sinful
generation**, the Son of Man also will be ashamed of him, when he
comes in his Father's glory, with the holy angels.")
(...)
9:1 He said to them, "Most certainly I tell you, there are some
standing here who **will in no way taste death until they see God's
Kingdom come with power**.")*

*9:23 He said to all, "If anyone desires to come after me, **let him
deny himself**, take up his cross, and follow me. 24 For whoever
desires to save his life will lose it, but whoever will lose his life for
my sake, will save it. 25 For what does it profit a man if he gains the
whole world, and loses or forfeits his own self? 26 For whoever will
be ashamed of me and of my words, of him will the Son of Man be
ashamed, when he comes in his glory, and the glory of the Father,
and of the holy angels. 27 But I tell you the truth: There are some of
those who stand here who **will in no way taste of death until they***

see God's Kingdom."

*(Matthew 16:24 Then Jesus said to his disciples, "If anyone desires to come after me, let him deny himself, take up his cross, and follow me. 25 For whoever desires to save his life will lose it, and whoever will lose his life for my sake will find it. 26 For what will it profit a man if he gains the whole world and forfeits his life? **Or what will a man give in exchange for his life**? 27 For the Son of Man will come in the glory of his Father with his angels, **and then he will render to everyone according to his deeds**. 28 Most certainly I tell you, there are some standing here who **will in no way taste of death until they see the Son of Man coming in his Kingdom**.")*

Emphasis on the differences; the hate towards brother and sister is turned into 'deny himself' by all three.
Luke does a literal copy of Mark but drops Mark's reference to the gospel, as does Matthew - I'm saving a comment on that for the next paragraph. Luke turns 'to gain' into 'if he gains' and changes 'forfeit his life' to 'loses and forfeits his own self' - Matthew keeps the first, rejects the second.
Luke drops the question about what to exchange for a life but Matthew puts it back in. And of course Matthew adds the reference to the judgment that awaits.
All keep the reference to logion 1 as well with 'taste death' but it changes significantly: Mark's 'God's Kingdom come with power' simply becomes 'God's Kingdom' in Luke, yet Matthew turns it all into 'Son of Man coming in his kingdom'.
Matthew seems to stick to Mark here over Luke, Luke being in between can be argued by him introducing 'desires', 'if he gains', 'taste of death' and Matthew keeping those - thin threads indeed, but all three are astonishingly close to each other. Could Luke come after Matthew? No, Luke keeps the 'ashamed' verse of Mark which Matthew hasn't copied

What is very significant however is Mark's use of the word gospel in his 8:35; Mark mentions the word eight times, Luke only twice, and

Matthew uses it four times - but suffixes it three times with 'of the kingdom'. Where Mark is aiming at writing a gospel as a weapon against Thomas, Luke has dropped the entire notion of one: his first use of 'gospel' is the disciples preaching it after they've been endowed by Jesus with the gift to heal and cure, and Jesus uses it just before he's challenged on his authority - perhaps a mistake. Matthew's only use is when a woman has put ointment on his head, and that gospel is likely referring to Jesus' incarnation.

Mark's ambition was to invent a gospel - that goal has been greatly surpassed by now

This same logion 55 (fairly identical to logion 101) is used only by Luke and Matthew in full, or should I say, brief:

(55a) Jesus said, "Whoever does not hate his father and his mother cannot become a disciple to me.
(55b) And whoever does not hate his brothers and sisters and take up his cross in my way will not be worthy of me."

*14:26 "If anyone comes to me, and **doesn't disregard** his **own** father, mother, **wife, children, brothers, and sisters**, yes, and his **own** life also, he can't **be my disciple**. 27 Whoever doesn't bear his **own** cross, and come after me, can't **be my disciple**.*

*(Matthew 10:37 He who **loves** father or mother more than me is not **worthy of me**; and he who loves **son or daughter** more than me isn't **worthy of me**. 38 He who doesn't take his cross and follow after me isn't **worthy of me**.)*

Luke picks the short straw again and copies the literal Thomas logion, and again his fantasy runs a bit wild, probably also inspired by his earlier copy in 9:23. Trying to end with a short verse that puts emphasis on only 'cross' and 'disciple', he combines all relatives into the first verse yet also adds 'wife and children', perhaps as a warm gesture of inclusion to all. I really like his 'bear' as it emphasises the hardship of following the Church's Christ, and the 'even his own life' point to his earlier copy.

It is interesting to see how Luke added 'own' to 'his own father' (and pretty much everything else) - did he understand what Thomas really meant here? Yet again Matthew ditches it all... and comes up with a very nice and concise version, once again profiting from the struggles of his predecessor.

Comparing Matthew to Thomas, Luke might as well not have done anything in between if it weren't for inspiring Matthew to 'son or daughter' and the structure of his verses, reordering Thomas. Matthew deserves praise for avoiding the word 'hate' and changing that into 'not love (more than me)', surprisingly positive.

Last but not least, it is evident that 'my disciple' must be swapped for 'worthy'; Luke likely got lost during the splitting and recombining of Thomas into his, ended up with the choice between 'disciple' and 'not worthy' and picked the wrong word - twice. There are only twelve disciples in this story Luke, get with the program!

Logion 86: Matthew literally follows Luke, although changing 'God's Kingdom' for 'Follow me' is strong, concise, and in line with the change from God's Kingdom to Matthew's "Jesus is All"-approach. However, it is very surprising that Matthew has one of the disciples object, expressing the wish to bury his father:

(86) Jesus said, "The foxes have their holes and the birds have their nests, but the son of man has no place to lay his head and rest."

9:58 Jesus said to him, "The foxes have holes, and the birds of the sky have nests, but the Son of Man has no place to lay his head." 59 He said to another, "Follow me!" But he said, "Lord, allow me first to go and bury my father." 60 But Jesus said to him, "Leave the dead to bury their own dead, but you go and announce God's Kingdom."

*(Matthew 8:20 Jesus said to him, "The foxes have holes and the birds of the sky have nests, but the Son of Man has nowhere to lay his head." 21 **Another of his disciples said to him**, "Lord, allow me*

first to go and bury my father." 22 But Jesus said to him, "Follow me, and leave the dead to bury their own dead.")

The disciple does raise questions: that which leads Jesus to his answer in 8:20 is a question by a scribe - and then Matthew follows up with 'Another (of his disciples)' speaking to him? Is he suggesting that the scribe is one of his disciples? An oddity, I presume.
With regards to the order: it is unclear why the gospel-writers left out 'and rest', perhaps the Messiah wasn't supposed to rest? Or did they want to stress the idea that he didn't belong? The order could be anything, Thomas could even be last

That concludes chapters 8 and 9, and I count 10 logia in them (logion 14 has been discussed in chapter 5), totalling 23 now. Chapter 10 starts off with a garbled and elaborate copy of the very start of chapter 9; sending out 72 men to heal and cure, prefaced by logion 73a - the same logion which in Matthew prefaces the version that he and Luke had prior. That logion is a literal copy of Thomas although, of course, the Lord has been replaced by the Lord of the harvest:

(73a) Jesus said, "The harvest is great but the laborers are few. (73b) Beseech the Lord, therefore, to send out laborers to the harvest."

*10:2 Then he said to them, "The harvest is indeed plentiful, but the laborers are few. Pray therefore to the Lord **of the harvest**, that he may send out laborers into his harvest.*

*(Matthew 9:37 Then he said to his disciples, "The harvest indeed is plentiful, but the laborers are few. 38 Pray therefore that the Lord **of the harvest** will send out laborers into his harvest.")*

The differences between Thomas and the gospel-writers are subtle but telling: Jesus doesn't worship his Lord, nor is he meek towards him. He uses 'beseech', not 'pray'. Luke even adds 'may' which

Matthew changes to 'will', but Thomas just beseeches his Lord to send, simple as that. His harvest? No, the harvest. And the harvest is just 'great', a fair antonym for 'few', not 'indeed plentiful'.
In theory Thomas could have taken these and turned them into his logion, stripping it of all religious attributes - but it's also telling that Luke uses this immediately preceding his sending out of the 72, whereas Matthew uses it when Jesus observes the multitudes that are awaiting his healing

When sending out the 72, Luke naturally reuses logion 14b. It comprises 10 verses but I'll only show the three that apply:

(14b) When you go into any land and walk about in the districts, if they receive you, eat what they will set before you, and heal the sick among them.

10:7 Remain in that same house, eating and drinking the things they give, for the laborer is worthy of his wages. Don't go from house to house. 8 **Into whatever city you enter, and they receive you, eat the things that are set before you.** *9* **Heal the sick who are there,** *and tell them, 'God's Kingdom has come near to you.'*

What is odd here is that not only Luke is the only one with this strange event, but that it shows great similarities with Matthew's version of the original event in his chapter 10 - save for logion 14b, of course. And Luke's version right here shows a lot more similarity with logion 14b than his other.
That return of the seventy-two is immediately followed by logion 38a, which in Matthew prefaces the sower parable. Luke uses it twice:

(38a) Jesus said, "Many times have you desired to hear these words which I am saying to you, and you have no one else to hear them from.
(38b) There will be days when you will look for me and will not find me."

*10:23 Turning to the disciples, he said privately, "Blessed are **the eyes** which see the things that you see, 24 for I tell you that many prophets **and kings** desired to see the things which you see, and didn't see them, and to hear the things which you hear, and didn't hear them."*

17:22 He said to the disciples, "The days will come when you will desire to see one of the days of the Son of Man, and you will not see it.

*(Matthew 13:16 "But blessed are **your eyes**, for they see; **and your ears, for they hear**. 17 For most certainly I tell you that many prophets **and righteous men** desired to see the things which you see, and didn't see them; and to hear the things which you hear, and didn't hear them.)*

Luke as well as Matthew uses the occasion to elevate the disciples once more yet Matthew expressly directs the verse at them by changing Luke's impersonal 'the' to 'your', and doubles up with 'ears' and 'hear' which matches the logion. Of course that result is inspired by scripture, Isaiah 6:9-10 mentioned earlier. Matthew also changes 'kings' to 'righteous men'. Luke has a second attempt in his chapter 17 where he reverts to a literal copy of 38b but stands alone in doing so.
Love thy neighbour is the last of this chapter. We've seen it in Mark earlier:

(25) Jesus said, "Love your brother like your soul, guard him like the pupil of your eye."

*(Mark 12:28 One of the scribes came, and heard them questioning together, and knowing that he had answered them well, asked him, "Which commandment is the greatest of all?" 29 Jesus answered, "The greatest is, **'Hear, Israel, the Lord our God, the Lord is one**: 30 you shall love the Lord your God with all your heart, and with all*

*your soul, and with **all your mind**, and with **all your strength**.' This is
the first commandment. 31 **The second** is like this, 'You shall love
your neighbor as yourself.' There is no other commandment greater
than these.")*

*10:25 Behold, a certain lawyer stood up and tested him, saying,
"Teacher, what shall I do to inherit eternal life?" 26 He said to him,
"What is written in the law? How do you read it?" 27 He answered,
"You shall love the Lord your God with all your heart, with all your
soul, with **all your strength**, and with **all your mind**; and your
neighbor as yourself." 28 He said to him, "You have answered
correctly. Do this, and you will live." 29 But he, desiring to justify
himself, asked Jesus, "Who is my neighbor?"*

*(Matthew 22:35 One of them, a lawyer, asked him a question,
testing him. 36 "Teacher, which is the greatest commandment in the
law?" 37 Jesus said to him, "'You shall love the Lord your God with
all your heart, with all your soul, and with **all your mind**.' 38 This is
the first and great commandment. 39 **A second** likewise is this, 'You
shall love your neighbor as yourself.' 40 The whole law and the
prophets depend on these two commandments.")*

The very first 'love thy neighbour' is from Leviticus 19:18, so it's
quite impossible to claim that only or mostly Thomas inspired Mark
here. The second part of logion 25 refers to Deuteronomy 32:10:

*(Leviticus 19:18 "'You shall not take vengeance, nor bear any grudge
against the children of your people; but you shall **love your
neighbor as yourself**. I am Yahweh.)*

*(Deuteronomy 32:10 He found him in a desert land, in the waste
howling wilderness. He surrounded him. He cared for him. **He kept
him as the apple of his eye**.)*

Emphasis on the parts that will be commented on. I mentioned
Mark singling out two of the ten commandments, and only these

particular two - what an odd coincidence that is. Mark makes the mistake of explicitly labelling the two as 'the first' and 'the second' commandment, but Luke evades Mark's obvious and painful first and second nomination and just puts them together in one sentence as an answer to his question about the law - that's a great find. Matthew has the finishing touch, introducing the neighbourly love as a command that is 'likewise', at the same time so very carefully wording the first command as 'the greatest' command, and the second as 'a second' command. Both drop Mark's insertion of Deuteronomy 6:4 in his 12:29 preceding the first commandment. Did Matthew purposely ignore Luke? I think Luke's find is by far the best; although he avoids the words 'commandment' he also does avoid the words 'first' and 'second'. I can understand that Mark and Matthew, unlike Luke, do want to stress that they are commandments, and that they must state that the first is the first - but it makes it conspicuous that only these two commandments are singled out.

Luke can be linked to Mark as he also uses 'strength' (and reverses the order of that and 'mind') which Matthew decides to drop.

Once more we see the story unfold: a simple logion from Thomas leads to an elaborate and complex scene as the first gospel-writer incorporates it while adding (too) much detail. Then the second gospel-writer comes along and fixes most if not all mistakes. The third or last gospel-writer applies the finishing touch.

I do realise that my now so oft repeated explanation on the unfolding of this story always involves the same persons in the same order, so it's not much of a generally applied pattern, is it? I could leave out some detail and state that the first copier usually introduces too much detail next to some things left to be desired, and that the last gospel-writer fixes these: that has been proven in chapters 6 and 7, where 8 out of the 9 logia were new and thus started by Luke, not Mark.

The order is partially clear, and Thomas being first is visible once more through the sandbox: scribes or lawyers ask a question about the greatest commandment or how to inherit eternal life. Jesus answers or the man posing the question does. The first commandment shows minor differences every time and Mark precedes it with scripture. The introduction to the second commandment is fairly different or even absent. Then the "second commandment" is identical in all three versions ('You shall love [...] your neighbor as yourself.'), and whatever comes after is, yet again, fairly to completely different.

The gospel sandbox: whatever is shared and perfectly identical comes from Thomas. If it is different, it is directly related but not from Thomas or purposely rewording Thomas. If wildly different, it is indirectly related and serving general Church purpose, usually scripture or doom and gloom

Three additional logia make 26; the next two chapters will add more than half to that total score

Luke chapters 11 and 12: the bulk of logia

Chapter 11 kicks off with a prayer, the next ritual a religion needs: Our Father. Matthew has that in chapter 6, and as usual it is slightly longer and more eloquent than Luke.

Logion 92a and 94 follow, both identical to the letter between Luke and Matthew, and logion 92b undoubtedly inspired them for the mixed up implementation of the asking:

(92a) Jesus said, "Seek and you will find.
(92b) Yet, what you asked me about in former times and which I did not tell you then, now I do desire to tell, but you do not inquire after it."
(94) Jesus said, "He who seeks will find, and he who knocks will be let in."

*11:9 "I tell you, keep **asking**, and it will be **given** you. Keep **seeking**, and you will **find**. Keep **knocking**, and it will be **opened** to you. 10 For everyone who asks receives. He who seeks finds. To him who knocks it will be opened.*

*(Matthew 7:7 "**Ask**, and it will be **given** you. **Seek**, and you will **find**. **Knock**, and it will be **opened** for you. 8 For everyone who asks receives. He who seeks finds. To him who knocks it will be opened.)*

Matthew stays surprisingly close to Luke and literally copies his very first find. The fine difference between Thomas and the gospel-writers is being let in versus being opened to - the threshold is present in the Church version. The order could be anything, really

Logion 35 follows, and this time it's so garbled in Luke that Matthew reverts straight to the original - that's a first, Luke doing a Markan! The issue there probably lies in the fact that logion 35 is to be found in logion 21 as well, namely in e, f and g: the arming of the house owner is in 21f. Luke seems to combine both, tries to say an awful lot with very little words, and ends up with confusion and almost nothing that can be related to logion 35:

(35) Jesus said, "It is not possible for anyone to enter the house of a strong man and take it by force unless he binds his hands; then he will (be able to) ransack his house."
(21e) Therefore I say, if the owner of a house knows that the thief is coming, he will begin his vigil before he comes and will not let him dig through into his house of his domain to carry away his goods.
(21f) You, then, be on your guard against the world.
(21g) Arm yourselves with great strength lest the robbers find a way to come to you, for the difficulty which you expect will (surely) materialize.

(Mark 3:27 But no one can enter into the house of the strong man to plunder unless he first binds the strong man; then he will plunder his house.)

*11:21 "When the strong man, **fully armed**, guards his own dwelling, his goods are safe. 22 But when someone stronger attacks him and overcomes him, he takes from him **his whole armor in which he trusted**, and divides his plunder.*

(Matthew 12:29 Or how can one enter into the house of the strong man and plunder his goods, unless he first bind the strong man? Then he will plunder his house.)

The emphasis is on Luke's words that I couldn't possibly locate elsewhere - that puzzle will remain.
As commented on in Mark the binding of the hands seems significant in Thomas yet both leave it out because binding Satan merely by his hands isn't a strong enough image to fit their context; they miss the point of Thomas whose goal is to plunder the house whereas theirs is to conquer the man (Satan). Thomas points to the

weak point of the strong man that is guarding the house: his hands are all that need to be bound, and with relatively little effort you can achieve a task that seems impossible: take the house of a strong man by force. This is not the only time that the gospel-writers miss a crucial point of Thomas in their zeal to possess his content and turn it into theirs, and it most certainly won't be the last.

The order is dubious although Thomas evidently comes first. Luke could be anywhere and Mark and Matthew are so very close to each other that the both of them could be anywhere too, in any order

Luke stands alone in completing a logion previously touched by Mark but will save 79c for the final chapters, like Mark and Matthew do:

(79a) A woman from the crowd said to him, "Blessed are the womb which bore you and the breasts which nourished you."
(79b) He said to her, "Blessed are those who have heard the word of the father and have truly kept it.
(79c) For there will be days when you will say, 'Blessed are the womb which has not conceived and the breasts which have not given milk.'"

*11:27 It came to pass, as he said these things, a certain woman out of the multitude lifted up her voice, and said to him, "Blessed is the womb that bore you, and the breasts which nursed you!" 28 But he said, "On the contrary, blessed are those who hear the **word of God**, and keep it."*

It doesn't get more literal than that really - 'father' becomes 'God', of course. The order could be anything given the close resemblance, although this is the only scene in Thomas where he's in front of a crowd and Luke gratefully duplicates the occasion; for once the gospel-writers don't create their own scenery and context. Would it make sense for the gospel-writers to copy the past tense of 'keep'?

Most certainly not, you have to work for the Church without pause. Would it make sense for Thomas to take 'keep' and turn it into 'have kept'? If only we were to know his exact meaning - I could give my interpretation but it would miraculously fit, of course: one doesn't come up with theories that don't fit the issue or challenge at hand.

So in stead, it's easier to point to the fact that this logion was available in its completeness but got split up by the gospel-writers; they can handle and use 79a and 79b together, but 79c is out of their league - which they'll prove by inverting it when they use it. Thomas first, then Luke - even if there are doubts at this point they'll disappear when 79c is encountered

Luke introduces yet another new logion, 24c and 24d, but needs to repeat the previously mentioned logion 33b in 8:16 in order to get going. Matthew doesn't, making it nicely concise by removing the careful (over)explaining of Luke:

(24a) His disciples said to him, "Show us the place where you are, since it is necessary for us to seek it."
(24b) He said to them, "Whoever has ears, let him hear.
(24c) There is light within a man of light, and he lights up the whole world.
(24d) If he does not shine, he is darkness."

*11:33 "**No one, when he has lit a lamp, puts it in a cellar or under a basket, but on a stand, that those who come in may see the light**. 34 The lamp of the body is the eye. Therefore when your eye is good, your whole body is also full of light; but when it is evil, your body also is full of darkness. 35 Therefore see whether the light that is in you isn't darkness. 36 **If therefore your whole body is full of light, having no part dark, it will be wholly full of light, as when the lamp with its bright shining gives you light**."*

(Matthew 6:22 "The lamp of the body is the eye. If therefore your eye is sound, your whole body will be full of light. 23 But if your eye

*is evil, your whole body will be full of darkness. If therefore the light that is in you is darkness, **how great is the darkness**!)*

Matthew makes proper use of the future tense here, which Luke does only in his last verse. Following his agenda of stressing doom and gloom, Matthew has no need for Luke's joyful 11:36 focusing entirely on a body full of light, even repeating that while turning it into an allegory. Matthew is perfectly content leaving that out and ending with 'darkness', his favourite theme and mood set. Undeniably, Matthew comes after Luke here - unless Luke specifically chose to ignore Matthew completely and spread his happy message nonetheless, which actually could be fairly plausible given the peculiarities and exceptions we've seen in his prose. Matthew follows a pioneer's copy almost to the letter however and this is not the first time, although Matthew does ignore the parts of Luke that follow Thomas by putting the emphasis on the light and not the dark.
It is out of the question that Thomas is first: 24 perfectly fits his logion 50, his theory of origin ('[...] We came from the light [...]')

Logion 89 is next, another logion that's a bit of a riddle. Both Luke and Matthew take the opportunity to combine the Pharisee bashing of logion 39 with logion 89 in one chapter:

(89) Jesus said, "Why do you wash the outside of the cup? Do you not realize that he who made the inside is the same one who made the outside?"
(39a) Jesus said, "The pharisees and the scribes have taken the keys of knowledge (gnosis) and hidden them.
(39b) They themselves have not entered, nor have they allowed to enter those who wish to.
(39c) You, however, be as wise as serpents and as innocent as doves."

*11:39 The Lord said to him, "Now you Pharisees cleanse the outside of the cup and of the platter, but **your inward part is full of***

extortion and wickedness. 40 You foolish ones, didn't he who made the outside make the inside also? 41 But give for gifts to the needy those things which are within, and behold, all things will be clean to you.
(...)
*52 Woe to you lawyers! For you **took away the key of knowledge**. You didn't enter in yourselves, and those who were entering in, **you hindered**."*

*(Matthew 23:14 "But woe to you, scribes and Pharisees, hypocrites! Because you **shut up the Kingdom of Heaven against men**; for you don't enter in yourselves, **neither do you allow those** who are entering in **to enter**.*
(...)
*25 "Woe to you, scribes and Pharisees, hypocrites! For you clean the outside of the cup and of the platter, but **within they are full of extortion and unrighteousness**. 26 You blind Pharisee, first clean the inside of the cup and of the platter, that its outside may become clean also.)*

Emphasis on the parts that are shared yet different.
Matthew's Pharisee bashing takes up his entire chapter 23 - that on a side-note. Luke does a literal Thomas, copying the creator of the cup in verse 40, which Matthew - again - drops while adopting the 'full of extortion'. Luke addresses lawyers but literally copies Thomas with '(took away) the key of knowledge' albeit with the unfortunate singular form of 'key'; Matthew sticks to Thomas and addresses Pharisees and scribes, adding drama by using the beautiful '(shut up) the Kingdom of Heaven'. While so doing Matthew also avoids uncomfortable questions about those same keys of knowledge (well then what and where are those keys?). Matthew perfectly fixes Luke's indecisive 'hindered' (was the act of hindering successful or not?) with 'not allowing' - changing Thomas' past tense to present. It is telling that Matthew doesn't use the creator of the cup - we've seen it so often now that Luke usually sticks close to Thomas, and that Matthew so often moves away

from that, while both share common wording and phrasing. They most certainly have different agendas.

Last but most certainly not least, whereas it is clear that Thomas' Pharisees and scribes hid the keys, it is not immediately obvious that those keys belong to doors of an edifice containing knowledge that one can enter. With Matthew switching to kingdom, it is: a second time that Matthew outperforms Thomas who is just slightly too brief here.

Once more Luke's pioneer's copy is followed to the letter by Matthew although there's a small sandbox where Luke twists Thomas' 'inside' into an accusation towards the Pharisees' 'inward part' that Matthew again changes to 'within' - it is striking how often the gospel-writers turn the mesmerizing, balanced and unbiased Thomas into a polarising theme befitting their Church goal, although Luke neatly preserves the creator of the cup who made both sides.

Thomas, Luke, Matthew: the order is unmistakably clear.

On a side note, it is clear that the gospel-writers addressed two major themes from Thomas into one: going against Judaic customs and targeting the Pharisees. Where Thomas rejects everything that Judaism came to be, the gospel-writers turn all that towards the Pharisees alone and address praying, fasting and giving alms within that new context, stressing that the Pharisees are hypocrites

8 logia, the grand total now stands at 34. We're halfway Luke and at 94% of the total that Mark achieved

Chapter 12 starts with a repetition of logion 6c found previously in 8:17, where Matthew 10:26 also has been covered, but the combination with logion 33a is new: 6c has already been combined with 33b by Luke 8:16, Matthew used 33b alone in 5:15. The 'inner rooms' is Luke's unfortunate pioneer's invention and dropped once more by Matthew:

(6c) For nothing hidden will not become manifest, and nothing covered will remain without being uncovered."

(33a) Jesus said, "Preach from your housetops that which you will hear in your ear.
(33b) For no one lights a lamp and puts it under a bushel, nor does he put it in a hidden place, but rather he sets it on a lampstand so that everyone who enters and leaves will see its light."

*12:2 But there is nothing covered up that will not be revealed, nor hidden that will not be known. 3 Therefore whatever **you have said in the darkness** will be heard in the light. What you have **spoken in the ear in the inner rooms** will be proclaimed on the housetops.*

*(Matthew 10:26 Therefore don't be afraid of them, for there is nothing covered that will not be revealed, or hidden that will not be known. 27 What **I tell you in the darkness**, speak in the light; and what **you hear whispered in the ear**, proclaim on the housetops.)*

Luke is addressing a crowd, Matthew the disciples - I don't often sketch the differences in context, I believe it's more a rule than an exception that each gospel-writer has Jesus speak fairly the same under quite different circumstances. This time, however, it explains the difference in subject: Luke is warning the crowd to not do anything secret, Matthew is instructing the disciples to spread the word.
Luke suffers the pioneer's fate again and (correctly) translates Thomas' 'hearing in your ear' to words that are spoken in private (inner, hidden) rooms - but keeps both of them; Matthew fixes the unfortunate pleonasm and comes up with 'whispered'. Evidently, Luke was not familiar with the saying.
Luke follows Thomas, Matthew follows his agenda. Thomas, Luke, Matthew: without the slightest doubt.
We see once more two logion parts that together make a perfectly coherent story: shout out loud what is whispered (33a), for no one creates light to hide it in the dark, but puts it on a pedestal to shine for all (33b). The gospel-writers split it and disperse its parts, and it is very difficult to argue that Thomas read Matthew and recognised 33a in 10:27 and 33b in 5:15, yet also used the 33a from Luke 12:3

and the 33b from Luke 8:16. Even with all material digitised and the help of sophisticated analytical search tools it would be more than a monumental task: singling out every single verse, categorising it, labelling it, and organising it all

Next is logion 44 where Thomas names the father, the son and the holy spirit: all three naturally leave out blasphemy against the father or son. Luke has an extremely short version of Thomas but gets full credit from Matthew for his 'Son of Man' introduction - blasphemy against the son is changed into "speaking against", apparently something that can be condoned. Matthew combines them both, swaps 'blaspheme' for 'speak against' and reiterates the sentence. 'Either in this age, or in that which is to come' is just grand:

(44) Jesus said, "Whoever blasphemes against the father will be forgiven, and whoever blasphemes against the son will be forgiven, but whoever blasphemes against the holy spirit will not be forgiven either on earth or in heaven."

*(Mark 3:28 "Most certainly I tell you, all sins of the descendants of man will be forgiven, including their blasphemies with which they may blaspheme; 29 but whoever may blaspheme against the Holy Spirit never has forgiveness, but is subject to **eternal condemnation**.")*

*12:10 **Everyone** who speaks a word against the **Son of Man** will be forgiven, but **those** who blaspheme against the Holy Spirit will not be forgiven.*

*(Matthew 12:31 Therefore I tell you, every sin and blasphemy will be forgiven men, but the blasphemy against the Spirit will not be forgiven men. 32 Whoever speaks a word against the **Son of Man**, it will be forgiven him; but whoever speaks against the Holy Spirit, it will not be forgiven him, **either in this age, or in that which is to come**.)*

Once more we witness the gospel-writers struggle from close-by: the triple blasphemy of Thomas is challenging them; which parts of that can be copied? Starting with the easy part, Mark feels confident to state that blasphemy against the Holy Spirit isn't allowed, and doesn't dare take it any further. Luke feels that he can move closer to Thomas by stating that "speaking against" the Son is to be forgiven, refraining from using the word 'blasphemy' for that. The Father? Not going there. Matthew condones Luke's condoning and also doesn't dare to make any statement of going against the Father, but gratefully accepts Luke's find of 'Son of Man' and 'speaking against' and uses the latter on both occasions, once more avoiding typical Thomas words.

Thomas, Mark, Luke, Matthew: undeniably so

Logion 72 is the second occasion where Luke tries out a new logion that doesn't get a follow-up. And it is an odd one here: Thomas humorously notes that he is a unifier, not a divider (and then verifies that with his disciples), and uses the strength of the word divide for the verb as well as the noun in order to enforce that, yet Luke breaks it all:

(72a) A man said to him, "Tell my brothers to divide my father's possessions with me."
(72b) He said to him, "O man, who has made me a divider?"
(72c) He turned to his disciples and said to them, "I am not a divider, am I?"

*12:13 One of the multitude said to him, "Teacher, tell my brother to divide the inheritance with me." 14 But he said to him, "Man, **who made** me **a judge or an arbitrator over** you?"*

Luke probably refers to Moses, although he swaps the roles because it is Jesus making the comment:

*(Exodus 2:14 He said, "**Who made** you **a prince and a judge over***

us? Do you plan to kill me, as you killed the Egyptian?" Moses was afraid, and said, "Surely this thing is known.")

Another lone logion is 63:

(63a) Jesus said, "There was a rich man who had much money.
(63b) He said, 'I shall put my money to use so that I may sow, reap, plant, and fill my storehouse with produce, with the result that I shall lack nothing.'
(63c) Such were his intentions, but that same night he died.
(63d) Let him who has ears hear."

*12:16 He spoke a parable to them, saying, "The **ground of a certain rich man produced abundantly**. 17 **He** reasoned **within himself, saying**, 'What will I do, because I don't have room to store my crops?' 18 He said, 'This is what I will do. **I will pull down my barns, build bigger ones, and there I will store all my grain and my goods**. 19 I will tell my soul, "Soul, you have many **goods laid up for many years**. Take your ease, eat, drink, and be merry."' 20 "But God said to him, 'You foolish one, **tonight your soul is required of you**. The things which you have prepared-whose will they be?' 21 So is he who lays up treasure for himself, and is not rich toward God."*

The verse is unusually lengthy for Luke, who widely expands the original logion and suffers the pioneer's fate - I have emphasised what he shares with Thomas, trying to match Thomas' content that he so greatly expanded. We have seen it before in Mark: if you're the first to copy a logion, you tend to trip over your own tongue, explaining at length the why and how and whatnot. Of course Luke finds a goal to apply the logion to: verse 21.
Logion 36 is in the next two verses, and the last verse seems inspired by logion 63b (sow, reap, barn):

(36) Jesus said, "Do not be concerned from morning until evening and from evening until morning about what you will wear."

*12:22 He said to his disciples, "Therefore I tell you, don't be anxious for your life, what you will eat, nor yet for your body, what you will wear. 23 Life is more than food, and the body is more than clothing. 24 **Consider the ravens**: they don't sow, they don't reap, they have no warehouse or barn, and **God** feeds them. How much more valuable are you than birds!*

*(Matthew 6:25 Therefore I tell you, don't be anxious for your life: what you will eat, or **what you will drink**; nor yet for your body, what you will wear. Isn't life more than food, and the body more than clothing? 26 **See the birds of the sky**, that they don't sow, neither do they reap, nor gather into barns. **Your heavenly Father** feeds them. Aren't you of much more value than they?)*

And once more Matthew sticks to Luke's first try, and perfects it. Fine finds are the rhetorical questions in the last sentence of verse 25 and verse 26 as well as the action implied by the word 'gather', and of course he has to replace the word 'God' by 'heavenly Father' - thus imposing a warm, human image of a man feeding birds (not ravens of course, that's an odd special from Luke). Ravens are one of the birds that God forbade Moses and the Israelites in Leviticus 11:15 - although it is them who God has bring food to Elijah by the brook in 1 Kings 17:4-6. Eerily close however is the resemblance to Job 38:41 'Who provides for the raven his prey, when his young ones cry to God, and wander for lack of food?').
Why does Matthew substitute 'birds' for 'they'? Because it is the very last word of the sentence and he wants to draw the emphasis away from them towards 'you'.
Why does Matthew change Luke's last phrase into a rhetorical question? Because Luke evokes a question with it, while Matthew provokes a "Yes!" with his - mightily fine nuances is what Matthew is after, and what he manages to achieve.
It is very interesting to see how both Luke and Matthew also quote from Oxyrhynchus (Attridge translation) which has an additional part to this logion:

(36) [Jesus said, "Do not be concerned] from morning [until evening and] from evening [until] morning, neither [about] your [food] and what [you will] eat, [nor] about [your clothing] and what you [will] wear. [You are far] better than the [lilies] which [neither] card nor [spin]. As for you, when you have no garment, what [will you put on]? Who might add to your stature? He it is who will give you your cloak."

*12:25 **Which of you by being anxious can add a cubit to his height? 26 If then you aren't able to do even the least things, why are you anxious about the rest**? 27 Consider the lilies, how they grow. They don't toil, neither do they spin; yet I tell you, even Solomon in all his glory was not arrayed like one of these. 28 But if this is how God clothes the grass in the field, which today exists, and tomorrow is cast into the oven, how much more will he clothe you, O you of little faith?*

*(Matthew 6:27 "**Which of you by being anxious, can add one moment to his lifespan? 28 Why are you anxious about clothing**? Consider the lilies of the field, how they grow. They don't toil, neither do they spin, 29 yet I tell you that even Solomon in all his glory was not dressed like one of these. 30 But if God so clothes the grass of the field, which today exists and tomorrow is thrown into the oven, won't he much more clothe you, you of little faith?)*

Needless to say it all is applied to the general Church context where God provides, and so on. I'm trying to not state that in detail every single time as it would become rather obnoxious and ad nauseam. I reckon it is clear by now that every single occasion that lends itself for a twist of Thomas into Church context is grabbed with both hands.

On Oxyrhynchus: Luke and Matthew have identical copies save for the beginning; Luke has verse 26 as extra and both read Oxyrhynchus, struggled with interpreting the riddling "Who might add to your stature" and came up with different explanations. Yet they also read each other, as they share the rest of which only half is similar to Oxyrhynchus, even considering the order of the sentences in Oxyrhynchus.

The order of gospel-writers is inconclusive here, as the two of them stick together so very closely. They expand Thomas greatly, or Thomas greatly condenses them - I will leave it undecided

Logion 76d (mixed with 21e) is hard to recognise in Luke, but Matthew makes sense of it and implicitly discloses the reason for the copy: instructing people to pay yet more attention to the afterlife than the only life that they know - which is an ongoing theme throughout this chapter:

(76a) Jesus said, "The kingdom of the father is like a merchant who had a consignment of merchandise and who discovered a pearl.
(76b) That merchant was shrewd.
(76c) He sold the merchandise and bought the pearl alone for himself.
(76d) You too, seek his unfailing and enduring treasure where no moth comes near to devour and no worm destroys."

*12:33 Sell what you have and give gifts to the needy. Make for yourselves purses which don't grow old, **a treasure in the heavens that doesn't fail**, where **no thief approaches**, neither **moth destroys**. 34 For where your treasure is, there will your heart be also.*

*(Matthew 6:19 "Don't lay up treasures for yourselves on the earth, **where moth and rust consume**, and where **thieves break through and steal**; 20 but lay up for yourselves treasures in heaven, where **neither moth nor rust consume**, and where **thieves don't break through and steal**; 21 for where your treasure is, there your heart will be also.)*

Is Thomas referring to Isaiah 51:8 with 76d?

*(Isaiah 51:7 "Listen to me, you who know righteousness, the people in whose heart is my law. Don't fear the reproach of men, and don't be dismayed at their insults. 8 **For the moth will eat them up like a garment, and the worm will eat them like wool;** but my righteousness will be forever, and my salvation to all generations.")*

Bodies will be consumed like this when dead, so it's no use hoping that something great will happen after you're dead: seek elsewhere, is what Thomas seems to imply - although 'his treasure' is puzzling. Unaware of the Isaiah reference or not, the gospel-writers revert Thomas' message, pointing to heaven instead of earth - an opportunity that can't be missed out on. Luke swaps the 'moth' for 'thief' and the 'worm' for 'moth'; his 'no thief approaches' is a rewording of 'no moth comes near' and once again Matthew changes that to the natural action of a thief: 'thieves don't break through and steal', highly likely inspired as well by logion 21e, which comes next. Luke is not very fluid with his 'treasure in the heavens that doesn't fail', rewording 76d, and Matthew drops it. Thomas' 'destroys' is copied by Luke and changed to 'consume' by Matthew. Matthew also adds the very unique 'rust', possibly to move away from Thomas and cover his source, and repeats the dependent clause, juxtaposing earth to heaven - a beautiful effect.
If Thomas copied anyone, it could only be Luke, as usual. He would have had access to Mark, Luke and Matthew given the time frame of writing the gospels (although he also shares text with John) but over and over again, every single time, Thomas would have picked Luke over all the others. Why?
It fits perfectly the other way around: 'no moth' and 'no worm' inspire and become 'no thief' and 'neither moth' in Luke, 'neither moth nor rust' and 'thieves don't break through and steal' in Matthew; gradual changing of one word in a phrase to two, gradual disappearance of 'no ...'. That same gradual change would have been perfectly sensible the other way around: Matthew, Luke, Thomas - if Thomas had been one of the gospel-writers.
Thomas, Luke, Matthew - it couldn't be any other way. Even though this also is a logion that gets split and we'll see 76a-c later on, 76d is

too different from 76a-c to argue that they belong together

Logia 103 and / or 21e and 21f are once again shared by all three: Mark's only residue is 'master of the house' who he portrays as the Lord, Luke puts the thief back in, naturally changing the carrying away of goods for breaking in, in order to fit his context (his chapter on possessions). He keeps close to Mark where the master went on a journey, and sticks to the returning master. Matthew reverts completely to Thomas and lets the master stay at home. And magnificently changes Luke's 'hour' to 'part of night' for his usual dramatic effect.

Once more, pay attention to the logion, the cryptic parts in it that are not copied, the part that is used elsewhere (21i), and how each evangelist takes 21e and 21f mostly out of content and entirely out of context; emphasis on what is shared and different:

(103) Jesus said, "Fortunate is the man who knows where the brigands will enter, so that he may get up, muster his domain, and arm himself before they invade."
(21a) Mary said to Jesus, "Whom are your disciples like?"
(21b) He said, "They are like children who have settled in a field which is not theirs.
(21c) When the owners of the field come, they will say, 'Let us have back our field.'
(21d) They (will) undress in their presence in order to let them have back their field and to give it back to them.
(21e) Therefore I say, if the owner of a house knows that the thief is coming, he will begin his vigil before he comes and will not let him dig through into his house of his domain to carry away his goods.
(21f) You, then, be on your guard against the world.
(21g) Arm yourselves with great strength lest the robbers find a way to come to you, for the difficulty which you expect will (surely) materialize.
(21h) Let there be among you a man of understanding.
(21i) When the grain ripened, he came quickly with his sickle in his

hand and reaped it.
(21j) Whoever has ears to hear, let him hear."

*(Mark 13:33 Watch, keep alert, and pray; for you don't know when the time is. 34 "It is like a **man, traveling to another country**, having left his house, and given authority to his servants, and to each one his work, and also **commanded the doorkeeper to keep watch**. 35 **Watch** therefore, for you don't know when the **lord of the house** is coming, whether at evening, or at midnight, or when the rooster crows, or in the morning; 36 lest coming suddenly he might find you sleeping. 37 What I tell you, I tell all: **Watch**.")*

*12:35 "Let your waist be dressed and your lamps burning. 36 Be like men watching for their **lord**, when he **returns from the wedding feast**; that when he comes and knocks, they may immediately open to him. 37 Blessed are those servants **whom the lord will find watching when he comes**. Most certainly I tell you that he will dress himself, make them recline, and will come and serve them. 38 They will be blessed if he comes in the second or third watch, and finds them so. 39 But know this, that if the **master of the house** had known in what hour the thief was coming, he would have watched, and not allowed his house to be broken into. 40 **Therefore be ready also, for the Son of Man is coming in an hour that you don't expect him.**"*

*(Matthew 24:42 Watch therefore, for you don't know in what hour your **Lord** comes. 43 But know this, that if the **master of the house** had known in what watch of the night the thief was coming, he would have watched, and would not have allowed his house to be broken into. 44 **Therefore also be ready, for in an hour that you don't expect, the Son of Man will come.**)*

The order is once again completely clear, but let me work it out. Thomas has an owner of the house, at home, expecting a thief. Mark has a man, away - travelling - commanding the doorkeeper to keep watch. The commanding of the doorkeeper to keep watch for the (suddenly introduced) lord of the house leads to Mark's imperative 'Watch!' This is Mark in his most progressed state, twisting and turning Thomas so hard that nothing remains but a poor allegory in a complicated verse (giving authority to servants while also commanding the doorkeeper to watch) without an easily visible shred of Thomas - there are just too many compromises.

Having no Thomas to revert to, Luke goes off on his own: the sandbox kicks in. He copies Mark's general context and scene, drops the doorkeeper like a hot brick, and has a lord, away - at a wedding feast - returning to find servants watching and opening the door (combining the action(s) of the doorkeeper with the servants as subject), but creates the master of the house serving the servants and also introduces the thief. Be ready! It is still messy, but just a different mess.

Matthew sighs at the complexity, and decides to stick to one action; the watching (of Mark). He has a Lord, naturally with a capital L, and then starts the story with Luke's master of the house, who's not away but just not watching (likely being asleep), and Matthew reuses Luke's thief. Be ready! Matthew ends up with a perfectly sensible and concise metaphor fitting the Church agenda while also fitting Thomas.

Where the gospel-writers confuse means with goals in not binding the strong man's hands, they do the same here and think that the breaking in is the goal, whereas in Thomas it is just a means to an end: carrying away the goods.

I've mentioned before that Mark didn't do a lot of rubbing in, and that it seems as if he took the interpretation of his hints for granted; while his verse 35 is obviously referring to the coming of the Messiah, both Luke as well as Matthew feel the need to explicitly spell out the punch line at the end

Could Mark have written his after Luke or Matthew? Reverting from the general 'Be ready' to the (too) specific 'Watch', throwing away the 'Son of Man', the thief, and most importantly of all the fairly literal copy of logion 21e? Not even in theory - so he comes first. Could Luke follow up on Matthew then? Introducing the servants from scratch, or put them back in from Mark's version? Swapping the perfectly normal act of sleeping for a man returning to his house at night from a wedding feast? Over-explaining the first outcome with the master dressing himself for service and the servants reclining at table, overdoing it quite a bit? Only the first editor over-explains when having an initial go at Thomas, or the second editor when trying to fix a hopeless Mark when there's no Thomas to revert to - never the third

Matthew's eloquence and mastery of words and style alone would be more than enough reason to have him as third gospel-writer each and every time; he almost always has some words of both Luke and Mark for which he has a far better synonym, a better order, a dull statement turned into a powerful rhetorical question, an amateur 'and..and' at the very least turned into an 'and..but'. Content-wise Matthew has the darkest doom and gloom, slamming down his beloved Isaiah implicitly or explicitly whenever he can. Threatening, and focusing on the bad, not the good; almost always choosing to end with the negative, the punishment that awaits the disobedient.
Is that enough proof? No, the best proof comes from the evolution of the story between the first gospel-writer and the last, the subtle changes in the words and scenery, the fixing of mistakes, the omission of superfluous or distracting details, and the continuous honing of the results, ever working towards the Church goals

Logion 10 is a lone one again, and Luke applies its core as the fire of judgment day, not a fire that is already burning and that is meant to burn away the Thomas 'world' - of course Luke uses 'kindle' and directs it not towards the world but the earth, neatly in line with Deuteronomy:

(Deuteronomy 32:22 For a fire is kindled in my anger, that burns to the lowest Sheol, devours the earth with its increase, and sets the foundations of the mountains on fire.)

(10) Jesus said, "I have cast fire upon the world, and see, I am guarding it until it blazes."

12:49 "I came to throw fire on the earth. I wish it were already kindled.

Chapter 12 closes with two more logia, and the completeness of the first is a huge surprise, given its lack of apparent intelligibility in Thomas as well: logion 16. Mark trying to reference it earlier in 3:25 remains unconfirmed, or rather, is disproven - 13:12 seems to be the (difficult to recognise) fit. Luke sticks to the riddling Thomas original! While adding mother and daughter (in-law), completely in line with the mirroring in Thomas of the relative clause.
Matthew dismisses 'division' and opts for one of the other original words ('sword'), and also undoes Luke's addition:

(16a) Jesus said, "Men think, perhaps, that it is peace which I have come to cast upon the world.
(16b) They do not know that it is dissension which I have come to cast upon the earth: fire, sword, and war.
(16c) For there will be five in a house: three will be against two, and two against three, the father against the son, and the son against the father.
(16d) And they will stand solitary."

(Mark 13:12 "Brother will deliver up brother to death, and the father his child. Children will rise up against parents, and cause them to be put to death.)

*12:51 **Do you think that I have come to give peace in the earth?** I tell you, no, **but rather division**. 52 For from now on, there will be five in one house divided, three against two, and two against three. 53 They will be divided, father against son, and **son against father**; mother against daughter, and **daughter against her mother**; mother-in-law against her daughter-in-law, and **daughter-in-law against her mother-in-law**."*

*(Matthew 10:34 "**Don't think that I came to send peace on the earth**. I didn't come to send peace, **but a sword**. 35 For I came to set a **man at odds against his father**, and a **daughter against her mother**, and a **daughter-in-law against her mother-in-law**. 36 A man's foes will be those of his own household.)*

The emphasis stresses what Luke and Matthew share. Matthew undoes most of Luke's Thomas, getting rid of the cryptic numbers game. Matthew is never afraid to completely redo the totality of the verses lying before him and turning them into what he himself deems right, spending great attention to detail and adding action and intimacy.
The passive uses of Thomas he turns to intimate action: for example the passive 'there will be' becomes the so very strong 'For I came to', putting Jesus in the lead and even adding it as a motive for his advent. Matthew also condenses, making it all concise, and frequently connects phrases by a conclusive conjunction such as "therefore", "for", "then".
Extra points to Matthew here for installing fear in people's hearts by finishing with his rather well-fitting conclusion (in his context, of course) that a person's enemies will be in his own household.
And double bonus points to Luke for copying this riddling Thomas logion in full, word by word. His chapter 12 is slightly mysterious so it fits well but he doesn't turn this logion to a real advantage - Matthew does, naturally, by directly following up with Thomas' hating of father and mother.
Thomas, Luke, Matthew - it couldn't be any other way. Mark's version is a shy summary of what all three say and could be anywhere

From this chapter I will give three examples of the perfection Matthew strives for:
Thomas uses 'either on earth or in heaven', Mark swaps that for 'eternal', Matthew rejects both yet combines them into the poetic 'either in this age or in the age to come'.

Luke's 'Of how much more value are you than the birds!' must be changed by Matthew into 'Are you not of more value than they?' because Luke leaves room for an open answer instead of a closed one. Matthew changes the style to a rhetorical question - one which can only elicit a positive 'Yes!'. Finally, Matthew isn't able to bear that the focus on the last word distracts from the subject and the message itself, and thus obscures it by replacing the noun 'birds' by the personal pronoun 'they'.

Finally, in these very verses Luke starts with a question 'Do you think that' that could get answered the wrong way, hence Matthew adjusts it ever so slightly to 'Don't think that'

To such lengths is Matthew prepared to go and invest his time in, and he does ameliorate almost everything he touches this way. He is by far the best stylist and word wizard of the three

Logion 91b:

(91a) They said to him, "Tell us who you are so that we may believe in you."
(91b) He said to them, "You read the face of the sky and of the earth, but you have not recognized the one who is before you, and you do not know how to read this moment."

*12:54 He said to the multitudes also, "When you see a **cloud rising from the west**, immediately you say, 'A **shower is coming**,' and so it happens. 55 When a **south wind blows**, you say, 'There will be a **scorching heat**,' and it happens. 56 You hypocrites! You know how to interpret the **appearance of the earth and the sky**, but how is it that you don't **interpret this time**?*

*(Matthew 16:1 The Pharisees and Sadducees came, and testing him, asked him to show them a sign from heaven. 2 But he answered them, "When it is **evening**, you say, 'It will be **fair weather**, for the **sky is red**.' 3 In the **morning**, 'It will be **foul weather** today, for the **sky is red and threatening**.' Hypocrites! You know how to discern*

*the **appearance of the sky**, but you can't **discern the signs of the
times**! 4 An evil and adulterous generation seeks after a sign, and
there will be no sign given to it, except the sign of the prophet
Jonah." He left them and departed.)*

Emphasis on what is shared yet different, Matthew 16:4 is an
addition.
As usual, Luke sticks to Thomas by mentioning both earth and sky,
and almost literally translates 'reading the moment' to 'interpreting
this time'. Matthew sacrifices earth, and feels obliged once more to
interject a prophecy reference, being the word 'sign' (and then
following up on that with this pointer to his own invention of 'the
sign of Jonah' (in 12:40-41)

Can it be more obvious that the entire reason for Luke as well as
Matthew writing both these significantly dissimilar verses is only
what they have in common? Reading the earth and sky yet not
being able to read this moment, which are the original parts of the
Thomas logion?
Luke addresses a multitude of many thousands, Matthew addresses
the Pharisees.
Both use utterly different kinds and uses of weathers, points of the
winds and times of day: Luke uses a cloud from the west and rain
versus a wind from the south and heat, Matthew uses evening and
fair weather given a red sky versus morning and foul weather given
a red sky.
Now why would they change all that so radically, and how could
they justify that? There is a great difference between tweaking or
swapping a word here and there and smoothing out a sentence by
changing word order or changing a passive imperative to an
affirmative rhetorical, as we've grown accustomed to by now,
thanks to Matthew.
Luke's regular great changes towards Mark are understandable
because we know that when he does that, it is because he then
prefers Thomas over Mark (although the reason for doing so we can
only speculate about).

But why, or rather, how, could we possibly justify these great discrepancies right here? These are the very words of the very Lord that he spoke, aren't they (supposed to be)?

It will probably be argued that in fact these were two separate occasions and that Luke missed out on one just like Matthew did on the other, but in fact this situation is very similar to logion 21 with the master of the house and the servants; this is the gospel sandbox in one of its wildest forms, shared between two gospel-writers

I count 8 logia in chapter 12 that haven't been discussed before, totalling 42

Halfway through Luke, only a dozen more logia to go

Chapter 13 has its first logion, 20, in the parable of the mustard seed. The beautifully concise Thomas is amazingly perfect here and doesn't waste a single word. It is time to shed some light on the way Thomas constructs his parables using five stages:

- the turning into an allegory of the subject, the kingdom of heaven (to a mustard seed);
- the naming of the most distinguishing property of that allegory (the smallest of all): it is the begin state for the parable;
- mentioning the required action and condition for the start of the transformation of the allegory: falling is passive, and anyone or anything could have caused it or undergone it; tilled soil, not necessarily fertile, but soil that is worked upon and has received attention - anyone can meet the conditions for entering the kingdom: together these form the trigger for the transformation;
- mentioning the most distinguishing property of its finished transformation (producing something entirely different and - relatively extremely - great): it is the end state for the parable;
- ... and the result of its completed transformation (attracting higher beings, objects, images): that is the result of the parable, the spin-off from the end state

The requirement forms the trigger for the parable and its transformation; it can be split here in a required action and a required condition but together those form the complete requirement for the parable.
All three gospel-writers ruin at least one of these five:

(20a) The disciples said to Jesus, "Tell us what the kingdom of heaven is like."
(20b) He said to them, "It is like a mustard seed.
(20c) It is the smallest of all seeds.
(20d) But when it falls on tilled soil, it produces a great plant and becomes a shelter for birds of the sky."

*(Mark 4:30 He said, "How will we liken God's Kingdom? Or with what parable will we illustrate it? 31 It's like a grain of mustard seed, which, when it is **sown in the earth**, although it is **less than all the seeds that are on the earth**, 32 yet **when it is sown**, grows up, and becomes greater than all the herbs, and **puts out great branches**, so that the birds of the sky can **lodge under its shadow**.")*

*13:18 He said, "What is God's Kingdom like? To what shall I compare it? 19 It is like a grain of mustard seed which a man took and **put in his own garden**. It grew and **became a large tree**, and the birds of the sky **live in its branches**."*

*(Matthew 13:31 He set another parable before them, saying, "The Kingdom of Heaven is like a grain of mustard seed which a man took, and **sowed in his field**, 32 which indeed is **smaller than all seeds**. But when it is grown, it is greater than the herbs and **becomes a tree**, so that the birds of the air come and **lodge in its branches**.")*

Mark uses the compare phrase again with the word 'liken' and makes sure to drop the word 'parable'; being the first one to copy the concise Thomas he turns to over-explaining. The emphasis on sown, twice, is overdoing it; the mustard seed is the smallest even when it is just lying on a shelf, for instance. Naturally, the gospel-writers feel the need to stress that the seed is sown or put - it is human action that delivers its transformation just like it is the Church that curates its believers. Where Mark uses earth and Luke uses garden, Matthew turns it into field. Mark misses the requirement of tilled soil; I will overlook the odd property of 'smallest when sown' and count it as clue.

Luke remarkably leaves out most clues (the requirement and the begin state; the property of being the smallest) although he removes the stuttering 'sown' and 'greater / great' and substitutes Mark's invention of 'shadow' for 'branches'.

Matthew, naturally, holds the most complete and fluid version, using a relatively significant portion of Mark this time. Like the others, he misses out on the trigger as well and, like Luke, sticks to the so very wondrous mustard tree in stead of plant.

In theory Luke could be anywhere with his (typical) past tense, and majority of clues missing: with Matthew he shares the man taking and sowing the seed as well as the tree and branches, and with Mark he shares the 'compare' and 'It is like': Thomas, Mark, (Luke,) Matthew without a doubt.

Please do note that all leave out 'falling on tilled soil'. I made an extra comment on that in Mark, and will do so once more in the chapter on parables

The leaven and the loaf give us logion 96. The gospel-writers compare the leaven to the kingdom instead of the woman - of course. Highly likely inspired by the mustard seed in their previous verse:

(96a) Jesus said, "The kingdom of the father is like a certain woman.
(96b) She took a little leaven, concealed it in some dough, and made it into large loaves.
(96c) Let him who has ears hear."

*13:20 Again he said, "To what shall I compare God's Kingdom? 21 It is like yeast, which a woman took and hid in **three measures of flour**, until it was all leavened."*

*(Matthew 13:33 He spoke another parable to them. "The Kingdom of Heaven is like yeast which a woman took and hid in **three measures of meal**, until it was all leavened.")*

Luke continues and copies his start of the mustard seed, Matthew does the same and again takes the opportunity to use the word parable like Mark did there. Kingdom of the father naturally must become God's Kingdom in Luke, and as a rule Matthew reverts that to 'Heaven'. In theory the order could be anything.

The three measures seem to be inspired by Genesis when God suddenly appears and Abraham rushes to give him bread:

*(Genesis 18:6 Abraham hurried into the tent to Sarah, and said, "Quickly prepare **three seahs of fine meal**, knead it, and make cakes.")*

Logion 4b concludes this chapter: Unclear why Luke adds 'behold' and 'some' and reverses the order, not surprisingly Matthew undoes that:

(4a) Jesus said, "The man old in days will not hesitate to ask a small child seven days old about the place of life, and he will live. (4b) For many who are first will become last, and they will become one and the same."

(Mark 10:31 But many who are first will be last; and the last first.")

13:30 Behold, there are some who are last who will be first, and there are some who are first who will be last."

(Matthew 19:30 But many will be last who are first, and first who are last.)

No idea why Luke is being different again, with his 'some' instead of 'many' he is almost stating the exact opposite.

Needless to say that 4a as well as the last phrase of 4b isn't much of a bait for the gospel-writers; to them it suffices to take only a part of this logion and put it into their context as we have seen happening over and over again by now. In Oxyrhynchus (Attridge translation) 4b has the same mirrored phrase as the gospel-writers: "first-last last-first". This is the second occasion where the Oxyrhynchus differs from Nag Hammadi, and the second occasion that we find the entire Oxyrhynchus in the gospel-writers' text:

For many who are [first] will become [last, and] the last will be first, and [they will become one and the same].”

It stands to reason that the gospel-writers used a Thomas gospel that contained the text that we see in the Oxyrhynchus papyri, and chapter 14 will give us a shred of Thomas that is neither in Oxyrhynchus nor in the Greek version that we have, thus providing us with a piece of content that as of yet hasn't been found in the wild.

Chapter 14 hands out logion 64, and between the gospel-writers it varies from slightly different to outrageously dissimilar. As it is so very large I'll put the comments in between each version - hope that helps:

(64a) Jesus said, "A man had received visitors.
(64b) And when he had prepared the dinner, he sent his servant to invite the guests.
(64c) He went to the first one and said to him, 'My master invites you.'
(64d) He said, 'I have claims against some merchants.
(64e) They are coming to me this evening.
(64f) I must go and give them my orders.
(64g) I ask to be excused from the dinner.'
(64h) He went to another and said to him, 'My master has invited you.'
(64i) He said to him, 'I have just bought a house and am required for the day.
(64j) I shall not have any spare time.'
(64k) He went to another and said to him, 'My master invites you.'
(64l) He said to him, 'My friend is going to get married, and I am to prepare the banquet.

(64m) I shall not be able to come.

(64n) I ask to be excused from the dinner.

(64o) He went to another and said to him, 'My master invites you.'

(64p) He said to him, 'I have just bought a farm, and I am on my way to collect the rent.

(64q) I shall not be able to come.

(64r) I ask to be excused.'

(64s) The servant returned and said to his master, 'Those whom you invited to the dinner have asked to be excused.'

(64t) The master said to his servant, 'Go outside to the streets and bring back those whom you happen to meet, so that they may dine.'

(64u) Businessmen and merchants will not enter the places of my father.''

14:16 But he said to him, "A certain man made a great supper, and he invited many people. 17 He sent out his servant at supper time to tell those who were invited, 'Come, for everything is ready now.' 18 They all as one began to make excuses. "The first said to him, 'I have bought a field, and I must go and see it. Please have me excused.' 19 "Another said, 'I have bought five yoke of oxen, and I must go try them out. Please have me excused.' 20 "Another said, 'I have married a wife, and therefore I can't come.' 21 "That servant came, and told his lord these things. Then the master of the house, being angry, said to his servant, 'Go out quickly into the streets and lanes of the city, and bring in the poor, maimed, blind, and lame.' 22 "The servant said, 'Lord, it is done as you commanded, and there is still room.' 23 "The lord said to the servant, 'Go out into the highways and hedges, and compel them to come in, that my house may be filled. 24 For I tell you that none of those men who were invited will taste of my supper.'"

Thomas has the servant sent out four times. The four excuses are: claims against merchants, just bought a house, prepare the banquet for a friend's marriage, collect the rent for a farm just bought. Jesus then tells the servant to go out and invite just anyone, as businessmen and merchants will not enter the places of his father. That is all completely coherent - although the friend's banquet doesn't seem to fit, assuming that he doesn't make any money preparing it (but, likely being either a businessman or merchant, he probably does).

It is significant in Thomas that the man has received visitors for whom he 'prepares dinner'. The visitors are probably outside, in the study, or just around the house. Suddenly, when they are notified of the dinner being ready, they start making excuses - of an economical or financial type; a process has started where they have advanced to a certain stage but suddenly they pull out of entering the next. This parable seems to be like one of those occasions on which you find out "who your real friends are".

Luke retains that same starting point yet sends three times, albeit with similarly enough excuses, and then adds the invitation to the poor and disabled - a fairly logical yet unmotivated twist. In the final verse Luke fails to give a reason why the people originally invited aren't welcome anymore, and it ends up as a logion wasted, without a clue - pointless. But there is a message, and the message is that the poor and disabled are invited to the Lord's banquet, which is nice of course - this is the benign Jesus.

Once again we see the first evangelist to copy Thomas, struggle - when he significantly changes content by adding yet another group of people to be brought in: just any people for no reason. The meaning of Luke appears to be that God meant the Jews to receive the kingdom by accepting the Messiah but they decline so Luke invites the poor in stead and then extends the invitation to foreigners, heathen - anyone who isn't a Jew. Yet he doesn't take the opportunity to motivate that; Luke sometimes seems somewhat reluctant to deliver the gospel-writers' message

And then, we witness the third occasion where Matthew goes wild, as one may have anticipated by now, given the wandering off by Luke (and the amount of text spent on that?):

(Matthew 22:2 "The Kingdom of Heaven is like a certain king, who

*made a wedding feast for his son, 3 and sent out his servants to call
those who were invited to the wedding feast, but they would not
come. 4 Again he sent out other servants, saying, 'Tell those who
are invited, "Behold, I have prepared my dinner. My cattle and my
fatlings are killed, and all things are ready. Come to the wedding
feast!"' 5 But they made light of it, and went their ways, **one to his
own farm, another to his merchandise**; 6 and the rest **grabbed his
servants, treated them shamefully, and killed them**. 7 When the
king heard that, he was angry, and sent his armies, **destroyed those
murderers, and burned their city**. 8 "Then he said to his servants,
'The wedding is ready, but those who were invited weren't worthy. 9
**Go therefore to the intersections of the highways, and as many as
you may find, invite** to the wedding feast.' 10 Those servants went
out into the highways and gathered together as many as they
found, both bad and good. The wedding was filled with guests. 11
"But when the king came in to see the guests, he saw there a man
who didn't have on wedding clothing, 12 and he said to him, '**Friend,
how did you come in here not wearing wedding clothing**?' He was
speechless. 13 Then the king said to the servants, '**Bind him hand
and foot, take him away, and throw him into the outer darkness**.
That is where the weeping and grinding of teeth will be.' 14 For
many are called, but few chosen.")*

Man becomes king, servant becomes servants, they are sent out
twice almost as an afterthought and their reasoning is mostly
neglected. The oxen that one of Luke's guests has bought turn into
the oxen the king has prepared. A hint of Thomas returns as invited
guests go to their farm and business, which is not in Luke so
Matthew must have read that in Thomas. And then Matthew loses
it all and has the servants seized and killed, the king destroying the
murderers along with their entire city - and then abruptly returns to
normalcy and continues the inviting.

The remainder, with the king spotting (apparently only) one
wedding guest out of 'as many as they found, both bad and good'
wearing no wedding garment and consequently jailing him into the
-outer - darkness, can best be described as absurd. This is a mad

king who punishes an apparent misdemeanour as if it were a vicious crime. Where Luke portrays the loving Jesus, this Matthew depicts the wrath of the angry God - and theirs are essentially one and the same story

Again we see the reoccurring theme of great deviation: when and where the first gospel-writer creates his own story on top of Thomas, the ones who follow are prone to take that even further, this time into absurdity.
It is, however, apart from everything else, a very interesting logion to take when discussing the order of things. Matthew writing this first and then Luke turning it into his version? Absolutely impossible. Thomas copying any of them could be possible, if he truly were the most supreme of all writers in the history of mankind. As a matter of fact, the three parables vary so extremely wildly that in theory the order could be anything, they have next to nothing in common save for the dining theme: it is hard to argue that even one of them is a copy of another.
Logion 93 is one of those uncomfortable ones. Mark has an awkward attempt at it combining the verb of 93b with the content of 93a. Luke undertakes an entirely new experiment, inspired by Mark 9:50 which is on the next page:

(93a) [Jesus said] "Do not give what is holy to dogs, lest they throw them on the dung-heap.
(93b) Do not throw the pearls to swine, lest they [...] it [...]."

*(Mark 7:27 But Jesus said to her, "Let the children be filled first, for it is not appropriate to take the children's bread and **throw it to the dogs**." 28 But she answered him, "Yes, Lord. **Yet even the dogs under the table eat the children's crumbs**.")*

*14:34 Salt is good, but if the salt becomes flat and tasteless, with what do you season it? 35 It is fit neither for the soil **nor for the manure pile. It is thrown out**. He who has ears to hear, let him hear."*

*(Matthew 15:26 But he answered, "It is not appropriate to take the children's bread and **throw it to the dogs**." 27 But she said, "Yes, Lord, but even the **dogs eat the crumbs which fall from their masters' table**.")*

The scene we have seen before in Mark, it is the Syrophoenician woman, prototype of a non-Jew here. The children are the Jews who are supposed to be the first to be invited to God's kingdom, the heathen indeed are compared to dogs by Jesus himself - highly unusually harsh for a statement that is not targeted at the Pharisees.
Matthew follows Mark to the letter here, turning it all into action (the crumbs fall from the table) and drama: the emphasis is laid on the table, not the children's crumbs; and it is the master's table, not just a table.
On a side-note, Matthew might have the missing logion piece here, especially given the similarities between Matthew 5:13 and 7:6: more on that when Matthew is discussed; it is there that we will see that Thomas is a perfectly coherent logion which the gospel-writers split and disperse across the gospels. Here it is clear that Matthew came after Mark, Luke is on his own, and that Thomas only could have inspired Mark (and Matthew) to turn 'holy' into 'children's bread', and not vice versa

Chapter 13 and 14 together give us 5 logia. And the total now amounts to 47

Chapter 15 gives us the parable of the lost sheep, logion 107 in full. I think that it is irony of Thomas and refers to Isaiah 53:6 6 'All we like sheep have gone astray. Everyone has turned to his own way; and Yahweh has laid on him the iniquity of us all.'. Thomas' goal certainly isn't to return the sheep to the other 99, he just takes "pride" in the fact that it goes astray, deviating from the regular and advertised path (the "world" of Thomas); that is why the "shepherd" cares for it more than for the other 99:

(107a) Jesus said, "The kingdom is like a shepherd who had a hundred sheep.
(107b) One of them, the largest, went astray.
(107c) He left the ninety-nine sheep and looked for that one until he found it.
(107d) When he had gone to such trouble, he said to the sheep, 'I care for you more than the ninety-nine.'"

*15:4 "Which of you men, if you had one hundred sheep, and lost one of them, wouldn't leave the ninety-nine in the wilderness, and go after the one that was lost, until he found it? 5 When he has found it, he carries it on his shoulders, rejoicing. 6 When he comes home, he calls together his friends and his neighbors, saying to them, 'Rejoice with me, for I have found my sheep which was lost!' 7 I tell you that even so there will be **more joy in heaven over one sinner who repents, than over ninety-nine righteous people who need no repentance.***

*(Matthew 18:12 "What do you think? If a man has one hundred sheep, and one of them goes astray, doesn't he leave the ninety-nine, go to the mountains, and seek that which has gone astray? 13 If he finds it, most certainly I tell you, he rejoices over it more than over the ninety-nine which have not gone astray. 14 Even so it **is not the will of your Father who is in heaven that one of these little ones should perish.***)

Luke does a Mark and adds insignificant detail in order to try making a story out of the short, sharp, concise Thomas, distracting from the clue - although Luke's clue is clear in his verse 7. Matthew profits once again from the preliminary work done by his predecessor(s), removes all the extra details yet copies Luke's style and construct, and ends up with something quite similar to the Thomas original. Both omit the clue of the sheep being the largest (like the fish in the net of logion 8, which is copied by Matthew alone, much later) in order to allow for their own moralistic clues.

Matthew evidently considers Luke's moral to be flawed but I'm disappointed with Matthew's bland clue, no matter how clearly he applies this logion in order to satisfy his goal of chapter 18, the importance and significance of little children. The sandbox is very much present again, with Luke bringing back the sheep but Matthew not - not such an insignificant detail, one would think? Thomas, Luke, Matthew - no surprises here

Luke spends the remainder of chapter 15 on his self-invented parables of the lost coin and the prodigal son (and even continues in chapter 16 with his dishonest manager). Devoid of allegories and metaphors they are just moralistic stories filled to the rim with humans interacting with humans, sharply contrasting with Thomas - although the parable of the coin is a proper parable according to the rules of Thomas. Later on I will pay extra attention to the stark differences between the Thomas parables and those which the gospel-writers invented themselves.
Chapter 16 finally delivers logion 47b, thus far missing from the copies all three made (old wine, new wine, patch, remember?). Luke adds his own clue of 'God and money' (Mammon) which is quite limitative and rather unimaginative but perfectly fits the theme of his chapter here. Matthew copies Luke word by word and uses it in his sermon on the mount:

(47a) Jesus said, "It is impossible for a man to mount two horses or to stretch two bows.
(47b) And it is impossible for a servant to serve two masters; otherwise, he will honor the one and treat the other contemptuously.
(47c) No man drinks old wine and immediately desires to drink new wine.
(47d) And new wine is not put into old wineskins, lest they burst; nor is old wine put into a new wineskin, lest it spoil it.
(47e) An old patch is not sewn onto a new garment, because a tear would result."

*16:13 **No servant** can serve two masters, for either he will hate the one, and love the other; or else he will hold to one, and despise the other. **You aren't able to serve God and Mammon.**"*

*(Matthew 6:24 "**No one** can serve two masters, for either he will hate the one and love the other, or else he will be devoted to one and despise the other. **You can't serve both God and Mammon.**)*

Mammon in Hebrew means money. Even here it is evident that Matthew comes after Luke as he drops the Thomas pointer of 'servant' - it's the only word that differs between the two of them. Of course one could make the case that Luke chose to specify 'servant' over the general 'one', possibly also wanting to get closer to Thomas, and came after Matthew.
And that Matthew dropped the Mammon moral entirely out of the blue in his Sermon, and forced Luke to write an entire paragraph on money just to accommodate...
We have the logion complete now, and perhaps with the knowledge gained it now is so very clear that these 5 sentences perfectly fit together? How feasible is it that these really are two separate pieces in the gospels that Thomas more than magically managed to piece together? Luke has the other part in chapter 5, Matthew has it in chapter 9.
Given the fact that Matthew follows Luke to the letter here, could it be that this is what "Oxyrhynchus would have said"? We saw logion 4 in there where the "first and last" phrase was repeated, swapping first with last - what I referred to as "mirroring": the same occurs here with "love and hate". I think it is very likely that such is the case, and that "Oxyrhynchus 47b would read":
(47b) And it is impossible for a servant to serve two masters; he will hate the one and love the other, otherwise, he will honor the one and treat the other contemptuously.

Logion 11a is next, and Luke and Matthew both have two tries at it:

(11a) Jesus said, "This heaven will pass away, and the one above it

will pass away.

(11b) The dead are not alive, and the living will not die.

(11c) In the days when you consumed what is dead, you made it what is alive.

(11d) When you come to dwell in the light, what will you do?

(11e) On the day when you were one you became two.

(11f) But when you become two, what will you do?"

*(Mark 13:30 Most certainly I say to you, this generation will not pass away until all **these things happen**. 31 Heaven and earth will pass away, but my words will not pass away. 32 But of that day or that hour no one knows, not even the angels in heaven, **nor the Son**, but only the Father.)*

16:17 But it is easier for heaven and earth to pass away than for one tiny stroke of a pen in the law to fall.

These verses Matthew copies in 5:18, but Luke also has a fuller version further on, which Matthew also follows up on:

*21:32 Most certainly I tell you, this generation will not pass away until all **things are accomplished**. 33 Heaven and earth will pass away, but my words will **by no means** pass away. 34 "So be careful, or your hearts will be loaded down with carousing, drunkenness, and cares of this life, and that day will come on you suddenly.*

(Matthew 5:18 For most certainly, I tell you, until heaven and earth pass away, not even one smallest letter or one tiny pen stroke shall in any way pass away from the law, until all things are accomplished.

(...)

*24:34 Most certainly I tell you, this generation will not pass away until all **these things are accomplished**. 35 Heaven and earth will pass away, but my words will not pass away. 36 "But no one knows of that day and hour, not even the angels of heaven, but my Father only.)*

Emphasis is on what is shared yet worded differently.

I want to point, once again, to all the cryptic parts in this logion that get completely ignored.

One word does Matthew change, 'nor the Son' - from Mark's version. Luke seems to be on his own, although Matthew will use his first copy in his sermon on the mount. If one looks at the logion and what remains of it, it is scant evidence indeed that the gospel-writers copied from Thomas here - 11a is the only phrase that remains untouched throughout the three.

The order could be anything really, there are very little differences and Matthew following Luke is equally as plausible as Luke following Matthew

Or am I pointing to the wrong logion? Isaiah has strong resemblance to what the gospel-writers say:

(Isaiah 51:6 Lift up your eyes to the heavens, and look at the earth beneath; for the heavens will vanish away like smoke, and the earth will wear out like a garment. Its inhabitants will die in the same way, but my salvation will be forever, and my righteousness will not be abolished.)

'Its inhabitants' points to 'this generation', and 'my righteousness' points to 'my words'. And that very same Isaiah seems to be more identical to another logion:

(111a) Jesus said, "The heavens and the earth will be rolled up in your presence.
(111b) And the one who lives from the living one will not see death."
(111c) Does not Jesus say, "Whoever finds himself is superior to the world?"

This appears to be a much better fit, with 'in your presence' also pointing to 'this generation'; even though logion 111 seems to be a mere summary of logion 11, it is likely that the gospel-writers used this version. It is a puzzle without borders and an endless supply of pieces sometimes.

And indeed, again we see a likeness between Isaiah and Thomas

Chapter 17 starts with either logion 48 or 106 leading Mark to his verse:

(48) Jesus said, "If two make peace with each other in this one house, they will say to the mountain, 'Move Away,' and it will move away."
(106) Jesus said, "When you make the two one, you will become the sons of man, and when you say, 'Mountain, move away,' it will move away."

(Mark 11:23 For most certainly I tell you, whoever may tell this mountain, 'Be taken up and cast into the sea,' and doesn't doubt in his heart, but believes that what he says is happening; he shall have whatever he says.)

17:6 The Lord said, "If you had faith like a grain of mustard seed, you would tell this sycamore tree, 'Be uprooted, and be planted in the sea,' and it would obey you.

(Matthew 17:20 He said to them, "Because of your unbelief. For most certainly I tell you, if you have faith as a grain of mustard seed, you will tell this mountain, 'Move from here to there,' and it will move; and nothing will be impossible for you.
(...)
21:21 Jesus answered them, "Most certainly I tell you, if you have faith and don't doubt, you will not only do what was done to the fig tree, but even if you told this mountain, 'Be taken up and cast into the sea,' it would be done.)

In Mark the mountain moving into the sea is highly likely inspired by Psalms 46:2, but Luke replaces the mountain by a sycamore tree: 7

mentions of those in the Tanakh, and it is apparently a very common tree bearing figs: Kings, Chronicles and Isaiah 9:10 mention it. Matthew copies the logion twice, once coming up with the rather unimaginative 'Move from here to there'.

Speaking to a mountain is unique and mentioned only in Thomas, where obviously the mere action of moving a mountain is the monumental achievement - where it moves to is completely irrelevant. Mark trying yet one more time to combine his two goals (incorporate Thomas and refer to scripture) in one sentence distracts Matthew here, and it is one of the rare occasions on which Matthew disappoints from a semantic point of view. He does get it right in his chapter 21 although he evidently feels like he still has to move the mountain somewhere.

It is a very nice evolution that we see here. Thomas has his own context (if you make the two one you can achieve anything, even far beyond what is deemed possible) and the mere moving of the mountain; Mark wraps only the moving mountain in his context and unfortunately suffixes it with the actions of (not) doubting, and believing. Luke spots the weakness and has the stress on faith precede the commanding of the inanimate object, and comes up with the beautiful find of the phrase 'faith like a grain of mustard seed' - which is a cringing allegory but can be allocated value if we acknowledge the way in which the gospel-writers interpreted the parable of the mustard seed. Does the mustard seed tempt Luke to use the sycamore tree instead of the mountain? Isaiah chapter 9 of course is a very important chapter:

(Isaiah 9:2 The people who walked in darkness have seen a great light. The light has shined on those who lived in the land of the shadow of death.
(...)
6 For a child is born to us. A son is given to us; and the government will be on his shoulders. His name will be called Wonderful Counselor, Mighty God, Everlasting Father, Prince of Peace.
(...)
9 All the people will know, including Ephraim and the inhabitants of

Samaria, who say in pride and in arrogance of heart, 10 "The bricks have fallen, but we will build with cut stone. The sycamore fig trees have been cut down, but we will put cedars in their place.")

It would be surprising to find Luke quoting scripture all by himself, I think?
Matthew puts the mountain back in, opting for the so very poor move phrase, but cherishes Luke's find and keeps the 'faith as a grain'. And in his second attempt combines it all: Luke's 'faith', Mark's 'doubt', his context at that moment which is the cursed fig tree, and the original first copy of Mark

Logion 113 is next, and it's quite a bit of a story. Mark and Matthew use 113c twice, in different context and content; first in response to the Pharisees and later when talking to the disciples:

(113a) His disciples said to him, "When will the kingdom come?"
(113b) [Jesus said] "It will not come by waiting for it.
(113c) It will not be a matter of saying 'here it is' or 'there it is.'
(113d) Rather, the kingdom of the father is spread out upon the earth, and men do not see it."

(Mark 8:11 The Pharisees came out and began to question him, seeking from him a sign from heaven, and testing him. 12 He sighed deeply in his spirit, and said, "Why does this generation seek a sign? Most certainly I tell you, no sign will be given to this generation.")

*17:20 Being asked by the Pharisees when God's Kingdom would come, he answered them, "God's Kingdom doesn't come with observation; 21 neither will they say, 'Look, here!' or, 'Look, there!' for behold, **God's Kingdom is within you**."*

One of the most debated verses, Luke once more reverts to the very literal Thomas copy, composing his verse 21 not from 113d but from the first part of logion 3c - with great repercussions

(3a) Jesus said, "If those who lead you say to you, 'See, the kingdom is in the sky,' then the birds of the sky will precede you.
(3b) If they say to you, 'It is in the sea,' then the fish will precede you.
(3c) Rather, the kingdom is inside of you, and it is outside of you.
(3d) When you come to know yourselves, then you will become known, and you will realize that it is you who are the sons of the living father.
(3e) But if you will not know yourselves, you dwell in poverty and it is you who are that poverty."

The Greek word ἐντός ('entos') has only one meaning: (in)side. Nowadays Luke's verse 17:21 usually gets haphazardly translated to 'in the midst (of you)' (the World English Bible is an exception here) instead of 'in(side)', and even in those bible translations when and where it literally says 'in' it is accompanied by an apologetic explanation from biblical commentators. Supposedly Jesus is referring to himself standing in the midst of the Pharisees, so the word 'in' really must be read as "among": naturally, it doesn't particularly fit the agenda of the Church that the kingdom is already available to everyone, let alone that it resides within themselves. Luke, oh Luke, we know it was the most important part of your mission to revert to Thomas as much as possible, but did you really have to copy all of this logion, and in this way? The word 'entos' occurs only twice in the entire New Testament, the other instance being when Jesus also is in the presence of the Pharisees, and accuses them of (not) washing the 'inside' of the cup. And upon checking century-old versions of bibles, it becomes clear:

man wird auch nicht sagen: Siehe hier! oder: da ist es! Denn sehet, das Reich Gottes ist inwendig in euch (Luther Bible 1912) - inwendig in euch = internal in you (plural)

On ne dira point: Il est ici, ou: Il est là. Car voici, le royaume de Dieu est au milieu de vous (Louis Segonde 1910) - au milieu de vous = in the middle of you (plural)

En men zal niet zeggen: Ziet hier, of ziet daar, want, ziet, het Koninkrijk Gods is binnen ulieden (Statenvertaling 1637) - binnen ulieden = inside you (plural)

E non si dirà: Eccolo qui, o eccolo là; perciocchè ecco, il regno di Dio è dentro di voi (Giovanni Diodati 1649) - dentro di voi = inside of you (plural)

ni dirán: Helo aquí, o helo allí; porque he aquí el Reino de Dios entre vosotros está (Sagradas Escrituras 1569) - entre vosotros está = in between you (plural) is

Nem dirão: Eilo aqui, ou eilo ali; porque eis que o Reyno de Deus entre vos outros está (Bíblia Sagrada Almeida 1681) - entre vos outros está = in between you (plural) is

neque dicent ecce hic aut ecce illic ecce enim regnum Dei intra vos est (Latin Vulgate late 4th century) - intra vos est = inside you (plural) is

Neither shall they say, Loe here, or loe there: for behold, the kingdome of God is within you (King James 1611)

The French uses in the middle, the Spanish and Portuese use (in) between, the rest uses in(side). The debate will continue, I'm afraid - in vain.

Luke does it again, not only copying the literal Thomas as much as he can, but here he even rephrases the very core of Thomas: the kingdom is right here on earth for everyone, in everyone, ready and waiting - for you, and not the other way around. Luke gravely damages the so carefully constructed story of Jesus that the Church is fabricating - with one single word.

But, back to work... Matthew doesn't copy this occurrence (he uses an entirely different logion for the Pharisees testing Jesus) so it's only Mark and Luke here.

All three copy the real occasion (with the disciples asking about the kingdom) further on, and Mark takes the opportunity to insert a whole new story around it, which I've left out as it is two dozen verses. Luke and Matthew follow up on the story but with regards to Thomas this time Luke copies only 113c:

*(Mark 13:3 As he sat on the Mount of Olives opposite the temple, Peter, James, John, and Andrew asked him privately, 4 "Tell us, when will these things be? What is the **sign that these things are all about to be fulfilled**?"*
(...)
*21 Then if anyone tells you, 'Look, here is the Christ!' or, 'Look, there!' **don't believe it**.)*

*21:7 They asked him, "Teacher, so when will these things be? What is the **sign that these things are about to happen**?"*

*(Matthew 24:3 As he sat on the Mount of Olives, the disciples came to him privately, saying, "Tell us, when will these things be? What is the **sign of your coming**, and of the end of the age?"*
(...)
*23 "Then if any man tells you, 'Behold, here is the Christ!' or, 'There!' **don't believe it**.)*

Luke fixes Mark's elaborate phrase about the sign and Matthew magnificently condenses and personalises it with 'your coming'. Matthew gladly accepts Mark's first find of contracting logion 113c and 113d and changing Thomas' 'men do not see it' to 'do not believe it', thereby completely skipping the tricky part of the kingdom being spread out upon the earth. Matthew perfects it, as usual, with the beautifully poetic 'end of the age' used earlier during the parable of the seed and the weeds.
No need to once more explicitly rub in the now so very regular and accustomed order, is there?

Logion 79c is next, completing the full logion, and Mark has put his own Thomasine invention in front of it. Luke copies the invention yet leaves out 79c itself; he will copy that in 21:23. I will insert that here as well and can only wonder why Luke, upon being presented with the opportunity to simply copy all three verses in a row, decided to delay the third until he narrates his version of the Abomination of Desolation.

That foretelling of the abomination is the exact moment when Mark and Matthew use these, so technically speaking Luke expedited the first two topics. Again, 79c is inversed by the gospel-writers, and of course applied completely out of context, and befitting theirs - no surprises there:

(79a) A woman from the crowd said to him, "Blessed are the womb which bore you and the breasts which nourished you."
(79b) He said to her, "Blessed are those who have heard the word of the father and have truly kept it.
(79c) For there will be days when you will say, 'Blessed are the womb which has not conceived and the breasts which have not given milk.'"

*(Mark 13:15 and let him who is on the housetop not go down, nor enter in, **to take anything out of his house**. 16 Let him who is in the field **not return back to take his cloak**. 17 But woe to those who are with child and to those who nurse babies in those days!)*

*17:31 In that day, he who will be on the housetop and his goods in the house, let him not go down **to take them away**. Let him who is in the field likewise **not turn back**.*

21:23 Woe to those who are pregnant and to those who nurse infants in those days! For there will be great distress in the land, and wrath to this people.

*(Matthew 24:17 Let him who is on the housetop not go down **to take out the things that are in his house**. 18 Let him who is in the field **not return back to get his clothes**. 19 But woe to those who*

are with child and to nursing mothers in those days!)

Matthew blindly follows Mark again, on a side-note. That seems to be the rule when Luke's version is absent. The sandbox shows itself again: with child, pregnant, with child; nurse babies, nurse infants, nursing mothers. For such a very small sentence the two crucial subjects certainly do undergo large changes in descriptions. The order could be anything, really

Logion 61a appears in verse 34. Luke opts for the literal copy and then repeats that in a variant of his own, creating the poor phrase 'there will be two grinding (grain) together'. Fortunately, as usual, Matthew once more makes changes fixing that ugliness, switching the scene from the bed to a field, and swapping 'other' for 'one'. Once more it is perfectly clear that Thomas leads Luke who copies some of his significant literal words, and that Matthew is trying to hide that fact

(61a) Jesus said, "Two will rest on a bed: the one will die, and the other will live."
(61b) Salome said, "Who are you, man, that you ... have come up on my couch and eaten from my table?" Jesus said to her, "I am he who exists from the undivided.
(61c) I was given some of the things of my father." [...]

*17:34 I tell you, in that night there will be two people in one **bed**. One will be taken and **the other** will be left. 35 There will be **two grinding grain together**. One will be taken and **the other** will be left."*

*(Matthew 24:40 Then two men will be in the **field**: one will be taken and **one** will be left. 41 Two women will be **grinding at the mill**: one will be taken and **one** will be left.)*

And that concludes chapter 17. 6 previously not discussed logia in the last three chapters, added to the 47 counted so far makes for a grand total of 53 logia

The parables of Thomas compared to the gospel-writers

Chapter 18 is used by Luke to be filled with self-invented alleged parables - they are explicitly labelled parables by Luke himself. Why do I call them self-invented? Because they are created from scratch by the gospel-writers, not based on anything from Thomas at all - and it tells. They are just long stories without much if any allegory or metaphor, purely humans interacting with other humans; no animate or inanimate objects to interact with: it once more points out that parables were absolutely alien to the gospel-writers. Here is the first text of chapter 18, the so-called parable of the widow:

18:1 He also spoke a parable to them that they must always pray, and not give up, 2 saying, "There was a judge in a certain city who didn't fear God, and didn't respect man. 3 A widow was in that city, and she often came to him, saying, 'Defend me from my adversary!' 4 He wouldn't for a while, but afterward he said to himself, 'Although I neither fear God, nor respect man, 5 yet because this widow bothers me, I will defend her, or else she will wear me out by her continual coming.'" 6 The Lord said, "Listen to what the unrighteous judge says. 7 Won't God avenge his chosen ones who are crying out to him day and night, and yet he exercises patience with them? 8 I tell you that he will avenge them quickly. Nevertheless, when the Son of Man comes, will he find faith on the earth?"

A parable? It is just a moralistic story, unlike anything in Thomas. Longwinded sentences, and a story consisting entirely of dialogue, with a questionable punch line. A story which not only has an explicit instruction - a moral Church message of course - of what it is supposed to say, but even starts with that.
Humans interacting with humans: no nature, no objects, no hidden meanings; everything is plain English, just to be taken completely

literally - mundane events, the lot of them.

It is poor in every aspect: content, context, wording, style - this definitely isn't a parable like we've seen until now. A Thomas parable always has allegory and starts with a situation; only when a certain precondition is met by action do we witness a transformation to another state, exactly like the parable of the mustard seed which turns into a great plant, and the end state will also bring about a result

Which parables are there in the four gospels? Ordered by Mark, Luke and Matthew, here they are:

	Thomas	Mark	Luke	Matthew
The parable of the strong man	Logion 35	Mark 3:27	Luke 11:21-22	Matt 12:29
The parable of the sower	Logion 9	Mark 4:3-8	Luke 8:5-15	Matt 13:3-9
The parable of the seed and the weeds	Logion 57	Mark 4:26-29		Matt 13:24-30
The parable of the mustard seed	Logion 20	Mark 4:30-32	Luke 13:18-19	Matt 13:31-32
The parable of the tenants	Logion 65, 66	Mark 12:1-11	Luke 20:9-18	Matt 21:33-44
The parable of the budding fig tree		Mark 13:28-31	Luke 21:29-33	Matt 24:32-35
The parable of the faithful servant	Logion 21, 103	Mark 13:34-37	Luke 12:35-40	Matt 24:42-44
The parable of the two debtors			Luke 7:41-43	
The parable of the good Samaritan			Luke 10:30-35	
The parable of the rich fool	Logion 63		Luke 12:16-21	
The parable of the barren fig tree			Luke 13:6-9	
The parable of the leaven	Logion 96		Luke 13:20-21	Matt 13:33
The parable of the wedding feast	Logion 64		Luke 14:16-24	Matt 22:2-14

The parable of the lost sheep	Logion 107		Luke 15:4-7	Matt 18:12-14
The parable of the lost coin			Luke 15:8-10	
The parable of the prodigal son			Luke 15:11-32	
The parable of the dishonest manager			Luke 16:1-8	
The rich man and the beggar Lazarus			Luke 16:19-31	
The parable of the persistent widow			Luke 18:1-8	
The Pharisee and the tax collector			Luke 18:9-14	
The parable of the ten coins			Luke 19:12-27	Matt 25:14-30
The parable of the hidden treasure	Logion 109			Matt 13:44
The parable of the pearl	Logion 76			Matt 13:45-46
The parable of the net	Logion 8			Matt 13:47-50
The parable of the unforgiving servant				Matt 18:23-35
Labourers in the vineyard				Matt 20:1-16
The parable of the two sons				Matt 21:28-31
The parable of the ten virgins				Matt 25:1-12

Twenty-eight parables, 28. Of which 13 are in Thomas, and 15 aren't. On a side note, we see the vast differences in volume between the gospel-writers with Mark a mere 7, Luke 20 and Matthew 18 parables - it shows that adding more parables to the pile was also one of the tasks of Luke and Matthew.

With regards to the parable of the sower I identified 5 distinct Thomas parable properties or elements:

1. it starts with turning the subject or main "actor" into an allegory, the so familiar 'liking' that Thomas regularly does;

2. which has a most distinguishing property, and that forms the begin state for the parable;
3. there is a required condition and action for the transformation of that allegory;
4. its finished transformation has a new most distinguishing property, and is the end state;
5. and its completed transformation leads to a result, it's a spin-off of that end state

These are the very elements of every single Thomas parable, it is my Thomas parable structure and it is extremely strict. Each element is always explicitly stated in the parable

Going by the Thomas parables first, which are these? Note that the following properties will be based on the real logia from Thomas, not the copies in the gospels:

- The parable of the strong man: 1.anyone, 2. enter the house of a strong man, 3. bind(s) his hands, 4. take it by force, 5. ransack
- The parable of the sower: 1. (handful of) seeds, 2. scattered, 3. fell on good soil, 4. produced good fruit, 5. bearing 60 / 120 per measure
- The parable of the seed and the weeds: 1. man who had good seed, 2. enemy sowed weeds among good seed, 3. not pull up the weeds, 4. weeds plainly visible, 5. weeds pulled up and burned
- The parable of the mustard seed: 1. mustard seed, 2. smallest of all seeds, 3. falls on tilled soil, 4. produces a great plant, 5. becomes a shelter for birds of the sky
- The parable of the tenants: 1. good man, 2. leased vineyard to tenant farmers so that they might work it (and he might collect the produce from them), 3. sent servant, 4. tenants give him produce, 5. heir is killed
- The parable of the faithful servant: 1. owner of a house, 2. begin vigil before thief comes, 3. knows that the thief is coming, 4. will not let thief dig through, 5. (will not let) carry away goods

- The parable of the rich fool: 1. rich man, 2. much money, 3. put money to use, 4. fill storehouse with produce, 5. lack nothing
- The parable of the leaven: 1. a certain woman, 2. took a little leaven, 3. concealed it in some dough, 4. made it, 5. large loaves
- The parable of the wedding feast: 1. man who had received visitors, 2. dinner prepared, 3. sent invite to guests, 4. dine, 5. enter the places of my father
- The parable of the lost sheep is a duo-parable; the main character is the shepherd, the secondary is the sheep: 1. shepherd, 2. had a hundred sheep, 3. left the ninety-nine and looked for that one, 4. found it, 5. cared for sheep more than the ninety-nine - 1. one of them, 2. largest, 3. went astray, 4. found, 5. more cared for than the ninety-nine
- The parable of the hidden treasure: 1. man, 2. had a hidden treasure, 3. (one who bought it) went ploughing, 4. found the treasure, 5. began to lend money at interest to whomever he whished
- The parable of the pearl: 1. merchant, 2. had a consignment of merchandise, 3. discovered a pearl, 4. sold merchandise, 5. bought pearl alone for himself
- The parable of the net is a double parable; the main story can be divided into two sub-stories: (A) 1. wise fisherman, 2. drew net up from the sea full of small fish, 3. found a fine large fish, 4. threw all the small fish back into the sea, 5. chose the large fish without difficulty; (A1) 1. wise fisherman, 2. cast net into the sea, 3. drew it up from the sea, 4. full of small fish, 5. found a fine large fish; (A2) 1. wise fisherman, 2. found a fine large fish, 3. threw all the small fish back into the sea, 4. chose the large fish, 5. without difficulty

The starting and ending properties are related and express a transformation, and the required condition or action generates the result, a spin-off: of every parable 2) becomes 4) and 3) leads to 5) - if, and only if, 3) is fulfilled, met, accomplished.
For instance in the parable of the sower the scattered seeds produce good fruit with the falling on good soil, and will thus

generate 60 / 120 per measure (whatever that last bit may mean). The rich man could have put his much money to use and filled his storehouse with produce, with the result that he would have lacked nothing - if he hadn't died that night.

Beginning the vigil before the thief comes leads to the thief not digging through into the house, but only if the owner of the house knows that the thief is coming, then the result would be that the goods aren't carried away; and so on.

The pivotal point of each parable is in the requirement, without that nothing happens. The required precondition or action is the secret that leads to the clue, the miracle that happens

Thomas plays with these elements as well. In the parable of the sower Thomas plays with the preconditions themselves, and only with the requirement of good soil fulfilled is the grand transformation from seed to good fruit achieved.

The parable of the seed and the weeds, which is so malformed by Mark? The begin state is the (hidden) seed that is sown. The real transformation of the weeds is inevitable and forms the very threat, it is the dreaded real end state that is the problem - and the answer lies in simply allowing for their transformation to fully complete so that the parable end state is reached and they are plainly visible. That is a double pun right there, as the parable action of not pulling up the weeds will lead to the parable (and real) result of the weeds being pulled up - without hurting the crop.

The parable of the sheep is a duo-parable: both the shepherd and the sheep go on a journey. The sheep goes astray and that likely is accidental, yet the shepherd knowingly and willingly leaves the ninety-nine; both leave the flock and get rewarded for that - the riddle at the end is beautiful. The shepherd doesn't say "I care for you more than for the ninety-nine", he says that he cares more for the sheep than the ninety-nine care for the sheep. Leave the flock, go astray, be different, seek. You will probably be despised by the rest of the flock but in the end you'll find something or someone that is all worth it.

The parable of the hidden treasure? Three people own the hidden treasure, and none of them knows about it. The first man who owns the field doesn't do anything with it. His son who inherits it just views it as commodity and sells it. The buyer finally starts to use it, thence fulfilling the precondition and carrying out the required action for the transformation - in this parable Thomas plays with the actors who (do or don't) fulfil the precondition that is present and intact throughout the entire parable but simply isn't fulfilled until the last actor.

The parable of the net is another riddle, with the large fish in a sea full of small fish - how can that be? In the main story that doesn't become clear, until the story starts with the begin state of the net being cast into the sea. The action of drawing it up from the sea leads to it being full of small fish, the result of which is the large fish that is found - that is odd, isn't it? The large fish isn't really found, because if it were, the parable could end right there; it however is the begin state for a new parable and this time the action is the main action: throwing back all the small fish in order to be able to choose the large fish with the result of that happening 'without difficulty'. It is one of the core parables of Thomas and tells us what will happen when you seek. The net is the collection of events that we are confronted with each and every day throughout our life, all of them small and minor no matter how big they seem to be. Disregard all the minor events, throw back the small fish, each and every one of them, and you'll be able to choose the large fish without difficulty, as the net will end up empty: that is the revelation, the great insight, as sobering and ruthless as it may sound. There is nothing to be found, it is what it is... perfectly balanced, the kingdom is inside you and all around you.

Thomas tells us many things with these parables, each from different angles - and indeed "[...] shall give you what no eye has seen and what no ear has heard and what no hand has touched and what has never occurred to the human mind."

Do you see the marvel in these parables? The cunning, the brevity, the awfully simple complexity - or rather, complex simplicity?
Do you then for instance see how blind the gospel-writers were,

when they haphazardly left out the falling on tilled soil in the parable of the mustard seed? It is the required action and condition, its very essence!

There is an issue with one parable: the tenants. The son is killed and the fruit of the harvest not 'produced', yet the son being killed is a result of the action of sending servants for its produce.
The vineyard being 'leased' (begin state) is intended to lead to it being worked, so that 'he might collect the produce from them' (end state), but the parable shows that sending people to request the produce (action) only generates the death of the heir (result) - next to some collateral damage. The death of the heir couldn't possibly be a spin-off from the end state of the (not!) collected produce, but it is.
So we have here one "failed" parable out of a perfectly functioning thirteen - that might make my theory faulty, wrong even, although it concerns only one out of thirteen parables?
Yet if we look at Thomas, we see that the parable of the vineyard, logion 65, is preceded by logion 64, the parable of the wedding feast. What is remarkable about the wedding feast is that its end state isn't reached, and the result neither: 'Businessmen and merchants will not enter the places of my father'. This also is a parable that fails to happen because the visitors don't perform the action of accepting the invitation; they all make up excuses. The parable works fine but because the action of sending invites fails there is no transformation to an end state, the dinner is prepared but no one dines as far as we know - as in the parable of the tenants. And without the dining there will be no result of entering 'the places of my father'.
There is yet one other parable that fails, and that is the parable of the rich fool, where the poor man's sudden death ruins all his shiny future plans: the money isn't put to use and thus, again, there is no end state and no spin-off from it either.
And that last logion that fails is logion 63, which is preceding the other two: and thus Thomas is presenting us with a consecutive trio of failing parables, with all of them having a failed action which

prevents the transformation to the desired end state. Without an end state, naturally there is no achievement of its inherent result - except for the parable of the tenants

The whole ironic, no, sarcastic point and intent of the parable of the tenants is that there isn't a transformation at all - the parable itself fails, is fruitless (pun indeed). It is destined to fail, according to Thomas.

Does Thomas sacrifice two parables here in order to prepare us for him breaking his own parable law, when logion 65 has a result without the end state being reached, without any transformation being accomplished? It seems to me that such is the case, and that this is another stab at Judaic religion with regards to the prophecies about God sending his son to the rescue (Psalms 2, Isaiah 9:6, and the rhetorical Proverbs 30:4). Thomas attacks that prophecy or idea here just like he attacks the concept of heaven and the habitual rituals of fasting, praying and giving alms, and it is highly unlikely that he based his logion on Isaiah chapter 5: the vineyard is a grateful subject and metaphor for God's playground in the Tanakh, with 101 verses containing the word.

Am I suggesting that Thomas created logion 65 to state that the prophecies about God sending his son would lead to nothing? I am. Am I suggesting that Thomas goes further than that and claims that that would lead to nothing but the killing of his son? I am. Do I then see the incredible irony of it all, that according to my theory Thomas made a statement about something that would never happen according to him, yet magically became allegedly fulfilled by the people who abused his work in order to fight his words, and ended up with a world religion that is based solely on the exact fulfilling of the "prophecy" of which I claim that Thomas said it would lead to nothing?
I do

Nonetheless, Thomas' parable model works, its structure is sound - the parable of the tenants is a cunningly prepared "failure" and unequivocally meant by Thomas as an exception to his rule.

Thomas also has three parables that didn't make it into the gospels:

(97a) Jesus said, "The kingdom of the father is like a certain woman who was carrying a jar full of meal.
(97b) While she was walking on the road, still some distance from home, the handle of the jar broke and the meal emptied out behind her on the road.
(97c) She did not realize it; she had noticed no accident.
(97d) When she reached her house, she set the jar down and found it empty."

(98a) Jesus said, "The kingdom of the father is like a certain man who wanted to kill a powerful man.
(98b) In his own house he drew his sword and stuck it into the wall in order to find out whether his hand could carry through.
(98c) Then he slew the powerful man."

(103) Jesus said, "Fortunate is the man who knows where the brigands will enter, so that he may get up, muster his domain, and arm himself before they invade."

I will call these the parable of the jar, the parable of the powerful man, and the parable of the brigands:

- The parable of the jar: 1. woman, 2. carrying jar full of meal, 3. not realising, noticing, 4. set the jar down, 5. found it empty
- The parable of the powerful man: 1. man, 2. wanting to kill powerful man, 3. drew his sword in his own house and stuck it into wall, 4. in order to find out whether his hand could carry through, 5. powerful man slain
- The parable of the brigands: 1. man, 2. get up, 3. knows where the brigands will enter, 4. muster his domain, 5. arm himself before they invade

These three operate in the exact same way - so we have an extremely coherent set of parables that all exhibit the exact same behaviour, or rather, way of operation. Did the gospel-writers perceive all this? Let's make an inventory of all Thomas parables and their elements as those ended up in their writings. The letters between parentheses refer to the gospel-writers who have it, e.g. (MM) refers to Mark and Matthew, (LM) means Luke and Matthew and not Mark and Luke, etcetera. The parable of the tenants is yet to be discussed, as are those of the hidden treasure, the pearl and the net:

- The parable of the strong man (MLM): Mark mistakes the end state for the result, and even repeats it. Luke makes an extreme mess of it all, starting off with using the result as the begin state - hopeless. Matthew copies Mark, with an identical outcome
- The parable of the sower (MLM): Mark and Matthew fail to explicitly name the seeds at the start. The action of scattering is significantly different from just sowing and that eludes all three. All three fail to handle the result adequately with 'produced ... as much' referring to nothing in specific, just like Genesis 26:12
- The parable of the seed and the weed (MM): Matthew gets them all (and let's forget about Mark as his is such an extremely garbled copy)
- The parable of the mustard seed (MLM): Luke misses out on the begin state of smallest of all seeds. All three fail to recognise and name the required precondition of tilled soil. Mark is a bit feeble on the end result and gets stuck in the growth process of the plant
- The parable of the tenants (MLM): all three are so focussed on busying themselves with the addition of the Isaiah pit and fence and tower (and the owner going into another country, the ejection of the son, and so on) that they forget to mention the begin state, the goal with which the vineyard is leased: 'so that they might work it and he might collect the produce from them'

- The parable of the faithful servant (MLM): an extreme remake by all, this logion. The subject is named but Matthew has a 'master of the house', Mark has 'man' and Luke has 'lord'. All three leave out the result
- The parable of the rich fool (L): Luke turns his begin state into the ground producing abundantly, which seems understandable given the end state, but that's not a begin state that fits his action of 'pull down my barns, build bigger ones' - in fact that's not much of an action at all
- The parable of the leaven (LM): both Luke and Matthew omit 'little' from the begin state, and there's no end state nor result - the point is that the leaven must be mixed with the bread, kneaded, you can't just hide some in flour and expect it to work wonders
- The parable of the wedding feast (LM): Luke doesn't mention the begin state until in the first invite, Matthew waits until the second invite - but they're there. Luke omits the result, and Matthew neither has an end state nor result
- The parable of the lost sheep (LM): neither Luke nor Matthew mention the begin state of 'largest' and Luke has 'lost' as begin state. Luke's result is that he returns the sheep but it counts as a result (of his)

Only Matthew has the following three parables:

- The parable of the hidden treasure (M): the man stumbles upon a treasure hidden in any field, hides it, and then sells all that he has so that he can buy the field. It's completely off and there's no result
- The parable of the pearl (M): the begin state is missing, the action is one of actively seeking pearls, in the end state 'all' is sold in stead of the consignment, the result is omitted
- The parable of the net (M): the begin state is off with 'fish of every kind' and is equal to the end state after the action of drawing is completed. Then another action takes place, that of sorting, and the good end up in a container with the bad just thrown away: two end states as such, there's no

consistency between the begin and end state and the result remains unclear

One parable they got right, out of a total of thirteen. Of everything that lacks there is no real pattern as to the type of element that gets omitted, and about half of the gospel-writers' parables misses out on more than one element.
It is more than fair to say that they completely missed the structure of Thomas' parables, and the most enormous error they commit is the omission of the tilled soil in the parable of the mustard seed, although not mentioning the complete begin state of the vineyard is telling as well. I could be awfully vile and point out that in handling the parable of the tenants the gospel-writers unknowingly liken themselves to the tenants, who work the servants coming to the vineyard in stead of its soil and plants, and thus disregard the goals with which the vineyard was leased; they also do not see or perceive that the tilled soil is the ultimate essence of the parable of the mustard seed - which equally points to the inappropriate actions that they undertake. Both examples illustrate how they won't achieve the transformation for themselves

That does beg the question: how could Thomas possibly have taken these thirteen parables, so very dissimilar in parable structure, and turned each and every one of them into a perfectly concise and coherent parable fitting the five element model without the slightest fault? And even masterfully implanting a failed action in three parables, the last of which has an apparently inexplicable and impossible transformation result, given the entire lack of end state of each?

Let's move on to the final phase of the parables: those parables that are not present in Thomas. Do they have a five element structure? That would be a miracle, given these first thirteen, would it not? For the gospel-writers the goal of making up parables of their own naturally is to prevent the notion or idea that all their parables came from Thomas and that thus Thomas was copied, as simple as

that. Parables are alien to the Tanakh and unique to Thomas, and
the only way to refute the claim that parables came from Thomas
was to make believe that they came from (their) Jesus.

It comes as no surprise that the number of Thomas parables copied
is lower than half of the total, the majority coming from Thomas
would be suspect. In order to stress the abundant use of parables
by Jesus, Matthew even uses his special ability again: making up
prophecies that don't exist or aren't prophecies at all, or both:

*(Matthew 13:35 **that it might be fulfilled which was spoken
through the prophet, saying, "I will open my mouth in parables**; I
will utter things hidden from the foundation of the world." 36 Then
Jesus sent the multitudes away, and went into the house. His
disciples came to him, saying, "Explain to us the parable of the
darnel weeds of the field.")*

Quoted by Matthew is Psalms, here is its context:

(Psalms 78 A contemplation by Asaph.
*1 Hear my teaching, my people. Turn your ears to the words of my
mouth. 2 **I will open my mouth in a parable**. I will utter dark sayings
of old, 3 Which we have heard and known, and our fathers have told
us.)*

This is Asaph speaking here, not God or anything the like, so it is
nothing spoken 'through the prophet' - Asaph wasn't a prophet but
just praised God through song and music in Psalms. It also isn't
future tense, but effectively present tense as Asaph will reveal the
words immediately following this statement - and in fact Asaph is
merely narrating the history of Israel right here. If all that weren't
bad enough, Matthew drops the original second half of verse 2 and
fumbles in something of his own - extra points there for mentioning
hidden and world, by the way.

Matthew's bad memory again? Ah yes, that darn memory of him
has acted up a few times, so this must be confirming that fact. For
now, let it suffice that stressing the (apparently not so obvious) fact

that Jesus spoke in parables has become somewhat of an obsession, and that creating a vast quantity of parables to counter those of Thomas is a must for the gospel-writers

The gospel-writers' parables: Mark

Mark invented the parable of the budding fig tree. It is short and simple:

*(Mark 13:28 "Now from the fig tree, learn this parable. When **the branch** has now **become tender, and produces its leaves**, you know that the **summer is near**; 29 even so you also, when you see these things coming to pass, know that it is near, at the doors. 30 Most certainly I say to you, this generation will not pass away until all these things happen. 31 Heaven and earth will pass away, but my words will not pass away. 32 But of that day or that hour no one knows, not even the angels in heaven, nor the Son, but only the Father.)*

This closely resembles a monologue, a preaching almost. The parable seems to confine itself to verse 28: the subject is the branch of the fig tree and there are two consecutive transformations, becoming tender and producing leaves, although the general action there is the unnamed 'budding'. The result is that summer is near, and the unnamed prerequisite is nature itself? The begin state is not mentioned explicitly either, or it is 'become tender' and the action then is 'produces its leaves' - but there is no end state.
It is clear that the metaphor is used in verse 29 and further on where also a logion is used to point to Judgment Day.
Is this anything like Thomas? Not in the least. Anything like a parable? It's a very good first (and last) attempt by Mark with the animate object, the allegory, the action that brings about transformation, and the result. But is there any precondition to be fulfilled, any explicit action to be performed or not in order to bring about the transformation? Having utter patience, perhaps - but there is nothing to be contributed by anyone here

It's Mark's only one and Luke as well as Matthew copy it, practically word for word. Matthew even nitpicks Mark's 'day or hour' and changes it into 'day and hour' so he did pay close attention to it - but didn't change a thing

Luke's unique parables

How does Luke fare? The parable of the two debtors:

*7:41 "A certain lender had two debtors. The **one owed five hundred denarii, and the other fifty**. 42 When **they couldn't pay, he forgave them both**. Which of them therefore will **love him most**?" 43 Simon answered, "He, I suppose, to whom he forgave the most." He said to him, "**You have judged correctly**."*

The spin-off is the loving of the lender by the debtors, the end state is them being forgiven, the begin state is them having debt - and it is interesting to see that there are two actors with different begin states. A bit of play here, like Thomas? Where only the right begin state could lead to an end state? Alas, no, both begin states have the same end state, but the spin-off varies along with the begin state - now that is interesting indeed.

Is that difference brought about by a difference in action? No, not that; the action is 'couldn't pay' and the end state is that the lender just forgives both. There are two begin states, one action, one end state, yet two results that are fully influenced by the begin states. There is no action to be undertaken or not by anyone, the forgiving of the debt just happens, it is a passive event that occurs to the actors.

It is a compelling start by Luke, and it fits the five element structure of Thomas in a complex way. The judgment at the end is particular of the way the gospel-writers portray Jesus, perhaps, and indicates that Simon's answer is part of the parable and correct - a nice angle. I can also imagine that Luke plays with the parable model and has two different begin states, an action that actually is two actions -

given Simon's answer of forgiving 'most' (so the forgiving must have been forgiving 'some' and forgiving 'more than some'). Likewise the single end state of (the debt) being forgiven actually consists of two: one where 'some' debt has been forgiven and one where 'more than some' debt has been forgiven: the two results then perfectly fit with the rest of the elements occurring double. It is certainly unconventional and not bad at all

The parable of the good Samaritan:

*10:30 Jesus answered, "A certain man was going down from Jerusalem to Jericho, and he fell among **robbers, who both stripped him and beat him, and departed, leaving him half dead**. 31 By chance **a certain priest** was going down that way. When he saw him, he **passed by on the other side**. 32 In the same way **a Levite also**, when he came to the place, and saw him, **passed by on the other side**. 33 But **a certain Samaritan**, as he traveled, came where he was. When he saw him, he was moved with compassion, 34 **came to him, and bound up his wounds, pouring on oil and wine. He set him on his own animal, brought him to an inn, and took care of him**. 35 On the next day, when he departed, he took out two denarii, gave them to the host, and said to him, 'Take care of him. Whatever you spend beyond that, I will repay you when I return.' 36 Now which of these three do you think **seemed to be a neighbor to him who fell among the robbers**?" 37 He said, "He who showed mercy on him." Then Jesus said to him, "**Go and do likewise**."*

We have three actors here, much as in the parable of the hidden treasure. The first two fail to act, but the third one does, exactly similar. Helping the poor man is the required action although that is not expressly named - the entire verse 34 could be the action and although that's quite the opposite of concise, it does fit the five element structure. The story continues for a bit and then we find the spin-off: to seem like a neighbour to the poor man. All we need now is a begin state and an end state so the transformation will be revealed. The begin state would be lying half dead on the ground after being stripped, beaten and departed - again a lengthy one but it counts.

Alas, no end state: taking care of the man can't be counted as the Samaritan tells the inn keeper to continue doing so. There is no news on for instance the wounds of the poor man, which could have helped, or words from him expressing his likely gratitude. We find only an identical quiz by Jesus at the end, this time even followed by an instruction.

Close, but not close enough

The parable of the barren fig tree:

*13:6 He spoke this parable. "A certain man had a **fig tree planted in his vineyard**, and he came **seeking fruit on it**, and **found none**. 7 He said to the vine dresser, 'Behold, these three years I have come looking for fruit on this fig tree, and found none. Cut it down! Why does it waste the soil?' 8 He answered, 'Lord, leave it alone this year also, until **I dig around it and fertilize it**. 9 **If it bears fruit, fine; but if not, after that, you can cut it down**.'"*

At first the begin state seems to be the fig tree, planted in his vineyard. The action of seeking fruit brings about none found and leads to the promise of fertilising it - unconventional and a bit odd but the elements could be identified that way. Then the last sentence is puzzling; is it the usual moral message or is it part of the parable transformation? It is likely that the parable will repeat itself the next year and might bring about a different result - but that's not how Thomas works; a parable can never have more than one outcome under unchanged circumstances. It is a nice allegory and the fig tree is a favourite subject for the gospel-writers, but it appears it all is just an obvious moral message about a not so productive tree that is getting one last, final chance before it's put down: be good, or else...

The parable of the lost coin:

*15:8 Or what woman, if she had ten drachma coins, if she **lost one drachma coin**, wouldn't **light a lamp, sweep the house, and seek diligently** until she found it? 9 When **she has found it**, she **calls together her friends and neighbors, saying, 'Rejoice with me**, for I have found the drachma which I had lost.' 10 **Even so, I tell you, there is joy in the presence of the angels of God over one sinner repenting**."*

The begin state is the coin being lost, the action is clear, and the end state is the found coin. The spin-off is also clear (and quite a party) - this also fits the model perfectly! Luke has created a true Thomas parable here with single elements in stead of double ones like that of the two debtors, and if it weren't for the ever-present moral message at the end, the quite mundane character of the story and the complete lack of allegory, it might even be mistaken for one

The parable of the prodigal son - if anything, it is world famous:

*15:11 He said, "A certain man had two sons. 12 The younger of them said to his father, 'Father, give me my share of your property.' **So he divided his livelihood between them**. 13 Not many days after, the younger son gathered all of this together and traveled into a far country. There he **wasted his property** with riotous living. 14 When he had spent all of it, there arose a severe famine in that country, and **he began to be in need**. 15 He went and joined himself to one of the citizens of that country, and **he sent him into his fields to feed pigs**. 16 **He wanted to fill his belly with the husks that the pigs ate, but no one gave him any**. 17 But when he came to himself he said, 'How many hired servants of my father's have bread enough to spare, and I'm dying with hunger! 18 I **will get up and go to my father, and will tell him, "Father, I have sinned against heaven, and in your sight. 19 I am no more worthy to be called your son. Make me as one of your hired servants**."' 20 "He arose, and came to his father. But while he was still far off, his father saw him, and was moved with compassion, and ran, and fell on his neck, and* *kissed him. 21 The son said to him, 'Father, I have sinned against heaven and in your sight. **I am no longer worthy to be called your son**.' 22 "But the father said to his servants, 'Bring out the best robe, and put it on him. Put a ring on his hand, and sandals on his feet. 23 Bring **the fattened calf, kill it**, and let's eat, and celebrate; 24 for this, **my son, was dead, and is alive again. He was lost, and is found**.' Then they began to celebrate. 25 "Now his elder son was in the field. As he came near to the house, he heard music and dancing. 26 He called one of the servants to him, and asked what was going on. 27 He said to him, 'Your brother has come, and your father has killed the fattened calf, because he has received him back safe and healthy.' 28 But he was angry, and would not go in. Therefore his father came out, and begged him. 29 But he answered his father, **'Behold, these many years I have served you, and I never disobeyed a commandment of yours, but you never gave me a goat, that I might celebrate with my friends**. 30 But when this your son came, who has devoured your living with prostitutes, you killed the fattened calf for him.' 31 "He said to him, 'Son, you are always with me, and all that is mine is yours. 32 But it was appropriate to celebrate and be glad, for this, **your brother, was dead, and is alive again. He was lost, and is found**.'"*

It is a similarly moral message, this time about repenting, and a very long story about riotous living, contemplating, and forgiving. If the first part is considered a long introduction, the son sinning could be the begin state, and the act of confessing his sins leading to the end state of sins forgiven, then the father throwing a feast could be the result. The story unfortunately continues at verse 25 with the other son getting miffed for being good and serving his father his entire life yet not receiving even a goat, while the sinning son is honoured with a fattened calf. It seems to suggest that the action is repeated with the father begging the other son in stead of his brother begging his father? That is short-lived, however, and the result of it is just the father repeating his statement about dead and alive, lost and found: even if the brother did trigger a similar but different action, nothing changes.

It is packed with many actions and most serve to fill the story, not a parable - according to the Thomas model

Where the parable of the prodigal son consists of dialogue for the greater part, the remaining four parables of Luke consist entirely of dialogue. The moral message at each end (or even start) clarifies the sometimes convoluted ways in which they unfold.
It suffices to say that none of these comes even close to a parable, let alone to the Thomas parable structure. They are filled with actions and devoid of any allegory whatsoever as they are narratives of purely humans interacting (and continuously dialoguing) with each other and other humans in stead of handling (in)animate objects.
The parables will be presented one after another after which they'll be summarised

The parable of the dishonest manager:

*16:1 He also said to his disciples, "There was a certain rich man who had a manager. An accusation was made to him that this man was wasting his possessions. 2 He called him, and said to him, 'What is this that I hear about you? Give an accounting of your management, for you can no longer be manager.' 3 "The manager said within himself, 'What will I do, seeing that my lord is taking away the management position from me? I don't have strength to dig. I am ashamed to beg. 4 I know what I will do, so that when I am removed from management, they may receive me into their houses.' 5 Calling each one of his lord's debtors to him, he said to the first, 'How much do you owe to my lord?' 6 He said, 'A hundred batos of oil.' He said to him, 'Take your bill, and sit down quickly and write fifty.' 7 Then he said to another, 'How much do you owe?' He said, 'A hundred cors of wheat.' He said to him, 'Take your bill, and write eighty.' 8 "His lord commended the dishonest manager because he had done wisely, for the children of this world are, in their own generation, wiser than the children of the light. 9 **I tell you, make for yourselves friends by means of unrighteous mammon, so that when you fail,*** *they may receive you into the eternal tents*.

The rich man and the beggar Lazarus:

*16:19 "Now there was a certain rich man, and he was clothed in purple and fine linen, living in luxury every day. 20 A certain beggar, named Lazarus, was taken to his gate, full of sores, 21 and desiring to be fed with the crumbs that fell from the rich man's table. Yes, even the dogs came and licked his sores. 22 The beggar died, and he was carried away by the angels to Abraham's bosom. The rich man also died, and was buried. 23 In Hades, he lifted up his eyes, being in torment, and saw Abraham far off, and Lazarus at his bosom. 24 He cried and said, 'Father Abraham, have mercy on me, and send Lazarus, that he may dip the tip of his finger in water, and cool my tongue! For I am in anguish in this flame.' 25 "But Abraham said, 'Son, remember that you, in your lifetime, received your good things, and Lazarus, in the same way, bad things. But here he is now comforted, and you are in anguish. 26 Besides all this, between us and you there is a great gulf fixed, that those who want to pass from here to you are not able, and that no one may cross over from there to us.' 27 "He said, 'I ask you therefore, father, that you would send him to my father's house; 28 for I have five brothers, that he may testify to them, so they won't also come into this place of torment.' 29 "But Abraham said to him, 'They have Moses and the prophets. Let them listen to them.' 30 "He said, 'No, father Abraham, but if one goes to them from the dead, they will repent.' 31 **He said to him, 'If they don't listen to Moses and the prophets, neither will they be persuaded if one rises from the dead.'"***

The parable of the persistent widow:

*18:1 He **also spoke a parable to them that they must always pray, and not give up**, 2 saying, "There was a judge in a certain city who didn't fear God, and didn't respect man. 3 A widow was in that city, and she often came to him, saying, 'Defend me from my adversary!' 4 He wouldn't for a while, but afterward he said to himself,*

'Although I neither fear God, nor respect man, 5 yet because this widow bothers me, I will defend her, or else she will wear me out by her continual coming.'" 6 The Lord said, "Listen to what the unrighteous judge says. 7 Won't God avenge his chosen ones who are crying out to him day and night, and yet he exercises patience with them? 8 I tell you that he will avenge them quickly. **Nevertheless, when the Son of Man comes, will he find faith on the earth?"**

The Pharisee and the tax collector:

18:9 **He also spoke this parable to certain people who were convinced of their own righteousness, and who despised all others.** *10 "Two men went up into the temple to pray; one was a Pharisee, and the other was a tax collector. 11 The Pharisee stood and prayed to himself like this: 'God, I thank you that I am not like the rest of men, extortionists, unrighteous, adulterers, or even like this tax collector. 12 I fast twice a week. I give tithes of all that I get.' 13 But the tax collector, standing far away, wouldn't even lift up his eyes to heaven, but beat his breast, saying, 'God, be merciful to me, a sinner!' 14 I tell you, this man went down to his house justified rather than the other;* **for everyone who exalts himself will be humbled, but he who humbles himself will be exalted."**

The four parables show in bold what they are all about: stories working towards their only goal of justifying and stating a moral Church message. I am truly puzzled about the content of that of the dishonest manager, but it is clear that its message at the end is clearly expressed.

Looking at these last five parables, which patterns can be distinguished? What is significant about their structure?

The prodigal son presents the transformation from sinning to confessing son and then introduces the second son, who compares himself to his brother and complains, after which the father sticks to the original result.

The dishonest manager doesn't offer much to go on, both begin and end states are vague and so is the transformation. At the end there's a comparison between children of the world and children of the light, which appears to be at least part of the awkward moral. If there is a result, it would be the lord commending the dishonest manager.

The rich man and the beggar portrays two actors who are each other's opposite: rich and poor. They transform from living to dead and get equally opposite treatments which then get dragged on; it appears that both have a different begin state (the way they live their lives), an identical end state (death) and that the different results vary along with the begin states: it reminds us of the two debtors in a way.

The persistent widow is as poor a parable as the dishonest manager and exhibits the same issues and defects - I fail to see any structure or consistency in either, and struggle with the intended message and how the stories should drive that.

The Pharisee and the tax collector also show a comparison between two actors, acting very differently and almost opposite to one another; the effect of their prayer seems to be accordingly: here the different results would seem to be connected to the difference in their actions and not their begin state(s)

Five "parables", consisting mostly of dialogue; two of them not very intelligible at all, and three of them compare two actors to one another. There is a true transformation in the prodigal son from sinning to forgiven, achieved by the act of confession although that only occurs in the mind of the son. There is a moralistic and predictable transformation in the beggar where the rich man gets punished after death and Lazarus rewarded - however it is no active action. The Pharisee and tax collector end up with different feelings after their prayer which is influenced by their action.

I fail to see much consistency in these parables, not two of them are the same. None of them are alike the Thomas parables, save two - out of nine parables. What do they all share? They all, without exception, have a moral message at the very end which is the clue of each story; the lesson to be taught and learned. That is the only thing they have in common: none of them save two are a parable in the Thomas sense, none of them have a rigid structure, but all of them are lengthy moral stories with a moral message, explicitly stated at the end. Of the nine parables two interact with (in)animate objects but the other seven are solely about humans interacting and mostly dialoguing with other humans, which is very different from the thirteen Thomas parables.

If we assume a chronological order for their creation by their place in Luke, we see that he started off with two very short stories that do show strong resemblance to Thomas parables in form and structure. Then the stories get longer, become filled with humans interacting with humans, and in the end they consist almost entirely of dialogue between humans. There does seem to be a transformation in the way Luke comes up with his own parables, at first sticking close to Thomas but quickly finding his own way and then sticking to that.

These alleged parables of Luke are little more than simple, longwinded, moral stories - and only two out of nine adhere to Thomas' parable structure model

That would conclude Luke although he has one more that I however would like to show in Matthew. Fortunately, John doesn't make up parables of his own although his writing style is highly promising, so Matthew is last and I must admit that I am anxious to see his style

Matthew's unique parables

Matthew has four unique parables: the parable of the unforgiving servant, labourers in the vineyard, the parable of the two sons and the parable of the ten virgins

The parable of the unforgiving servant:

*18:23 Therefore the Kingdom of Heaven is like **a certain king** who wanted to settle accounts with his servants. 24 When he had begun to settle, **one was brought to him who owed him ten thousand***

talents. *25 But because **he couldn't pay, his lord commanded him to be sold**, with his wife, his children, and all that he had, and payment to be made. 26 The servant therefore fell down and knelt before him, saying, '**Lord, have patience with me, and I will repay you all**!' 27 The lord of that servant, being **moved with compassion, released him and forgave him** the debt. 28 "But **that servant** went out and **found one of his fellow servants who owed him one hundred denarii**, and he grabbed him and took him by the throat, saying, '**Pay me what you owe**!' 29 "So his fellow servant fell down at his feet and begged him, saying, 'Have patience with me, and I will repay you!' 30 He would not, but went and **cast him into prison** until he should pay back that which was due. 31 So when his **fellow servants** saw what was done, they were exceedingly sorry, and came and **told their lord** all that was done. 32 Then his lord called him in and said to him, 'You wicked servant! I forgave you all that debt because you begged me. 33 Shouldn't you also have had mercy on your fellow servant, even as I had mercy on you?' 34 **His lord was angry, and delivered him to the tormentors** until he should pay all that was due to him. 35 **So my heavenly Father will also do to you, if you don't each forgive your brother from your hearts for his misdeeds**.*"

This story repeats itself inside itself, which is interesting. A servant owes ten thousand talents, can't pay and is threatened to be sold but begs for patience and is suddenly forgiven. Not showing gratitude or any other parable result, the servant seeks out others who owe him and threatens one of them. The exact same plea that the servant used with his lord is now used by his debtor, and the end state is that the servant has his debtor thrown in prison.
So we see a dissimilar begin state (10,000 talents versus 100), an entirely different action to get the debt paid yet an identical contra-action or excuse, and an entirely different contra-reaction, so to say - but the result of the first scene seems to be an identical repetition of itself, with the original debtor switching roles from debtor to lender.
That rehearsal of the first scene evokes yet another different result

or reaction; the lord learns about the servant's actions, has the forgiving of his debt cancelled, and the servant submitted to torture. So everything gets undone and the only things that remain changed or transformed are the servant now being with his tormentors and the servant's debtor in prison. An awful lot of actions, begin states, end states and results altogether: a highly complicated tale with a seemingly clear lesson for the first debtor: if you are forgiven a huge debt, also forgive others with an incredibly small debt compared to yours - the usefulness of that lesson certainly is questionable. The other debtor, on the contrary, "did everything right" yet got punished nonetheless - which lesson is to be learned from that? That "life can be unfair sometimes"?

One could argue that the result of the first scene is the second scene, and the result of the second scene the third scene - with the third scene undoing the end state of the first scene and finally introducing a "proper" result. It could be considered a highly complicated parable seemingly in line with the five element model but that would certainly be stretching it.

Does this resemble a straightforward Thomas parable with his five element structure? Absolutely not. Does this resemble a typical self-invented gospel-writer "parable" consisting solely of humans interacting and dialoguing with other humans, ending with an explicit moral message that justifies the sometimes somewhat convoluted unfolding of the story? Undeniably so

Labourers in the vineyard:

*20:1 "For the Kingdom of Heaven is like a man who was the **master of a household**, who went out **early in the morning to hire laborers** for his vineyard. 2 When he had agreed with the laborers for **a denarius a day**, he sent them into his vineyard. 3 He went out **about the third hour**, and saw others standing idle in the marketplace. 4 He said to them, 'You also **go into the vineyard**, and **whatever is right I will give** you.' So they went their way. 5 Again he went out **about the sixth and the ninth hour**, and did likewise. 6 **About the*** *eleventh hour he went out and found others standing idle. He said to them, 'Why do you stand here all day idle?' 7 "They said to him, 'Because no one has hired us.' "He said to them, 'You also go into the vineyard, and you will receive whatever is right.' 8 "When evening had come, the lord of the vineyard said to his manager, 'Call the laborers and pay them their wages, beginning from the last to the first.' 9 "When those who were hired at about the eleventh hour came, they each received a denarius. 10 When the first came, they supposed that they would receive more; and they likewise each received a denarius. 11 When they received it, they murmured against the master of the household, 12 saying, 'These last have spent one hour, and you have made them equal to us who have borne the burden of the day and the scorching heat!' 13 "But he answered one of them, 'Friend, I am doing you no wrong. Didn't you agree with me for a denarius? 14 Take that which is yours, and go your way. It is my desire to give to this last just as much as to you. 15 Isn't it lawful for me to do what I want to with what I own? Or is your eye evil, because I am good?' 16 So the last will be first, and the first last. For many are called, but few are chosen."*

Different begin states again, with the labourers being hired at different times of the day. One single identical action of paying wages to each, and one identical end state for each of the labourers in being paid one denarius. There is a result and that is that the labourers who worked the longest, object to getting the same pay as all the others, which gets addressed and ignored. There are five different begin states with five different occasions on which workers get hired, and given the single action I would expect five different end states or five different results, but there is none of that.

The message is clear: this parable was created with the sole purpose of illustrating verse 16, which is the first parts of logion 4b (going by the Oxyrhynchus paper), and which serves to illustrate the moral message of many being called but few chosen, which naturally is explicitly stated at the end, in the moral message

The parable of the two sons:

21:28 But what do you think? A man had two sons, and he came to **the first***, and said, 'Son,* **go work today** *in my vineyard.' 29 He* **answered, 'I will not***,' but afterward he changed his mind,* **and went***. 30 He came to* **the second***, and said the same thing. He* **answered, 'I'm going***, sir,' but he* **didn't go***. 31* **Which of the two did the will of his father***?" They said to him,* **"The first.***" Jesus said to them, "***Most certainly I tell you that the tax collectors and the prostitutes are entering into God's Kingdom before you.*

A much briefer story this time, once more dealing with different states. If the action is the order to go to work then there are even two end states for each actor: the content of the response to the order, and the actual going (or not). Again, the finish of the parable is brought about by a question from Jesus and his answer is more of a judgment towards those he questions then that it has to do with the story: the result seems to be about doing the will of the father and there are two of those; one doing it, and the other not doing it. Once more a moral story, this one is meant to teach the Pharisees a lesson: "(I know) you are pretending to worship God, yet that won't hand you the kingdom because you are like the second son - and that's why tax collectors and prostitutes are entering before you, because they are like the first son". A slightly different way of bringing about the moral message this time, yet it's still explicitly stated at the end

The parable of the ten virgins:

25:1 "Then the Kingdom of Heaven will be like **ten virgins who took their lamps** *and went out to meet the bridegroom. 2* **Five** *of them were* **foolish***, and* **five** *were* **wise***. 3 Those who were* **foolish***, when they took their lamps,* **took no oil** *with them, 4 but the wise took oil in their vessels with their lamps. 5 Now while the bridegroom delayed, they all slumbered and slept. 6 But at midnight there was a cry, 'Behold! The bridegroom is coming! Come out to meet him!' 7*

*Then all those virgins arose, and **trimmed their lamps**. 8 The **foolish**
said to the wise, 'Give us some of your oil, for our **lamps are going
out**.' 9 But **the wise answered**, saying, 'What if there isn't enough
for us and you? You go rather to those who sell, and **buy for
yourselves**.' 10 **While they went away to buy, the bridegroom
came, and those who were ready went in with him** to the wedding
feast, and the door was shut. 11 Afterward the other virgins also
came, saying, 'Lord, Lord, open to us.' 12 **But he answered, 'Most
certainly I tell you, I don't know you.' 13 Watch therefore, for you
don't know the day nor the hour in which the Son of Man is
coming.***

What could I possibly say? I have withheld comment on Matthew's
"parable" style until now, as it is quite, no, completely
disappointing. Is this Matthew as we know him? As I know him? The
Word Wizard, the Earl of Eloquence, the Prince of Perfection? Now
But Then But While Afterward are some of the starting connectives
of the sentences; even Mark would have created a more fluid story
than this. Content-wise this possibly is the poorest story of all the
four gospels and even a child could grasp its meaning - it is no
wonder that none of the self-invented "parables" ever gets
explained by Jesus, as uncomplicated as they unfold, but this one is
just embarrassingly unimposing.
What are the virgins to do at the wedding feast? They have no
purpose. Their lamps have no purpose, trimming them serves no
purpose. The bridegroom opening the door and denying to know
them serves no purpose; as if he would know the other virgins.
Matthew uses inanimate objects but they contribute nothing to the
story.
It is a lengthy, simple story, it is almost the opposite of a Thomas
parable - yet it gets introduced Thomas-style by the liking to the
kingdom in order to suggest that it's another parable that merits
attention and contemplation

One more "parable" we have. The parable of the ten coins is
invented by Luke (19:12-27) and copied by Matthew

*(Luke 19:12 He said therefore, "A certain nobleman went into a far country to receive for himself a kingdom and to return. 13 **He called ten servants of his and gave them ten mina coins**, and told them, 'Conduct business until I come.' 14 **But his citizens hated him, and sent an envoy after him, saying, 'We don't want this man to reign over us**.' 15 "When he had come back again, having received the kingdom, he commanded these servants, to whom he had given the money, to be called to him, that he might know what they had gained by conducting business. 16 The first came before him, saying, 'Lord, **your mina has made ten more minas**.' 17 "He said to him, 'Well done, you good servant! Because you were found faithful with very little, you shall have **authority over ten cities**.' 18 "The second came, saying, **'Your mina, Lord, has made five minas**.' 19 "So he said to him, 'And you are to **be over five cities**.' 20 Another came, saying, 'Lord, behold, **your mina, which I kept laid away in a handkerchief**, 21 for I feared you, because you are an exacting man. You take up that which you didn't lay down, and reap that which you didn't sow.' 22 "He said to him, 'Out of your own mouth I will judge you, you wicked servant! You knew that I am an exacting man, taking up that which I didn't lay down, and reaping that which I didn't sow. 23 Then why didn't you deposit my money in the bank, and at my coming, I might have earned interest on it?' 24 He said to those who stood by, 'Take the mina away from him and give it to him who has the ten coins.' 25 "They said to him, 'Lord, he has ten coins!' 26 **'For I tell you that to everyone who has, will more be given; but from him who doesn't have, even that which he has will be taken away from him. 27 But bring those enemies of mine who didn't want me to reign over them here, and kill them before me.'"*)*

We have seen verse 26, it's logion 41. And apparently this entire "parable" is written solely in order to justify using it, just as Labourers in the vineyard excuses the use of logion 4b.
A nobleman goes into a far country - a favourite gospel-writers' theme by now: Mark starts it in the vineyard parable and reuses it

in the faithful servant; Luke reuses it in the prodigal son and repeats it here. Instructed to conduct business during his absence, ten servants get one coin each from the nobleman. Luke also discloses that the citizens "hate" the nobleman so much that they travel after him to tell him that they don't want his reign - a surprisingly friendly and harmless action, compared to the fierceness of that very verb. When the nobleman comes back after having received the kingdom he went after, the story unfolds.

The first servant made ten more coins and is rewarded with authority over an equal number of cities for that. The second, five. The next kept the coin in a handkerchief out of fear for the man. The nobleman had expected it to be at least put into a bank and receive interest, and as punishment has the coin given to the first servant.

The story ends with the nobleman ordering the death of the citizens who travelled after him and only said that they don't want his reign, which reminds me of what I labelled as "mad king" in Matthew's so entirely different version of the parable of the wedding feast - but this is Luke

*25:14 "For it is like a man going into another country, who called his own servants and entrusted his goods to them. 15 **To one he gave five talents, to another two, to another one**, to each according to his own ability. Then he went on his journey. 16 Immediately he who received the five talents went and traded with them, and made another five talents. 17 In the same way, he also who got the two gained another two. 18 But he who received the one talent went away and dug in the earth and hid his lord's money. 19 "Now after a long time the lord of those servants came, and settled accounts with them. 20 He who received the five talents came and brought another five talents, saying, '**Lord, you delivered to me five talents**. Behold, I have gained **another five talents in addition** to them.' 21 "His lord said to him, 'Well done, good and faithful servant. You have been faithful over a few things, I will set you over many things. **Enter into the joy of your lord**.' 22 "He also who got the two talents came and said, '**Lord, you delivered to me two talents**. Behold, I* have gained **another two talents in addition** to them.' 23 "His lord said to him, 'Well done, good and faithful servant. You have been faithful over a few things. I will set you over many things. **Enter into the joy of your lord**.' 24 "He also who had received the one talent came and said, 'Lord, I knew you that you are a hard man, reaping where you didn't sow, and gathering where you didn't scatter. 25 I was afraid, and went away and **hid your talent in the earth. Behold, you have what is yours**.' 26 "But his lord answered him, 'You wicked and slothful servant. You knew that I reap where I didn't sow, and gather where I didn't scatter. 27 You ought therefore to have deposited my money with the bankers, and at my coming I should have received back my own with interest. 28 Take away therefore the talent from him and give it to him who has the ten talents. 29 **For to everyone who has will be given, and he will have abundance, but from him who doesn't have, even that which he has will be taken away**. 30 Throw out the unprofitable servant into the outer darkness, where there will be weeping and gnashing of teeth.'

Luke's nobleman becomes a man who just goes into another country with no disgruntled citizens on his tail. The servants number three in stead of ten and respectively receive five, two and one coin in stead of one each. They don't wait for the man's return and immediately develop their actions - the first makes five extra coins (not ten), the second two (not five), and the last buries it in the earth in stead of putting it in a handkerchief. What is the reward for the first two? Not authority over as many cities as coins gained, but 'to be set over many things'.
The last servant does get the same instruction as in Luke and his coin also goes to the first servant yet he is punished "Matthew style": thrown into the outer darkness where the weeping and gnashing is, which is the same fate that awaited the guest at the wedding feast that didn't wear proper attire, as well as 'the children of the Kingdom' in Matthew 8:12; the Jews.

Can a story be changed more than how Matthew edited Luke here (or vice versa, in theory)? The skeleton of the narrative structure survives but nothing else, and even the last line changes completely: from killing a bunch of citizens for apparently no legitimate and certainly no just reason, to throwing one servant into the outer darkness.

We have seen the workings of the gospel sandbox, the unclaimed space of freely editable text that is no direct property of either Thomas or the Tanakh. We have also seen that such text is subject to sometimes even brutal editing - and what we witness here is brutal editing.

How far off can two identical texts be? Is there anyone who believes that these are two completely different stories, both told by Jesus and meant to be this different although greatly identical in general structure and outcome? Whatever it is, it's the last of our gospel-writers' "parables", and again it is not at all like the Thomas parables

What are the similarities between the various gospel-writers' "parables", apart from only two of them following the Thomas structure?

The gospel-writers have created fifteen so-called parables. Five of those share similarities with the Thomas parables: the two debtors, lost coin, the budding fig tree, the barren fig tree and the good Samaritan. The two debtors and the lost coin completely correspond to the five elements of Thomas yet lack allegory; the coin is explicitly made a real coin by stating that it is one out of ten. The barren fig tree figures an animate object as subject and has allegory with the man seeking fruit on it and the promise of fertilising it; the budding fig tree has allegory with the producing of leaves and the liking to the nearing of summer; the Samaritan takes three actors before the desired action is fulfilled. Even though none of the last three stories use all five parable elements they come close to a Thomas parable.

The remainder consist of stories that are filled with humans interacting and mostly dialoguing with other humans.

The prodigal son, the dishonest manager, the rich man and the beggar Lazarus, the Pharisee and the tax collector, the persistent widow, the unforgiving servant, labourers in the vineyard, the two sons, the ten virgins and the ten coins: the vast majority of the gospel-writers parables consists entirely of humans interacting and mostly dialoguing with other humans. Are they parables? In the wider sense perhaps they are, as they each have a didactic lesson, even though that is always a highly moral message. Are they succinct, brief, short, concise? Most of them are not, in fact those are the opposite of that. Are they parables in the original sense of the Greek word? Indeed they are comparisons, analogies - but where a parable usually deploys allegory for the comparison, the gospel-writers simply and continuously compare humans to other humans. They narrow that down even further as they compare humans in almost identical situations and basically resort to stories with multiple actors who all undergo the same action or end up with an identical end state, or both - in spite of their differences in begin state.

The prodigal son is the most awkward story and most remote of a parable: the end result for the prodigal son is a feast with a fat calf, and the brother complains that he's never had that - yet he has an entirely different begin state, hasn't performed any of the actions, and thus hasn't reached a similar end state; he might appear as a second actor but actually has no part in the story at all. What is the didactic lesson of the prodigal son for the brother? None, or at best a negative one.

The dishonest manager is a riddle; the dishonest manager very awkwardly gets recommended by his master for tampering with his master's debts to said master's disadvantage. It is completely unclear what else his actions bring about and it is a very unsatisfactory story altogether, alleged parable or not.

The persistent widow is the last story that doesn't have multiple actors. Its moral instruction at the very beginning fortunately tells us how to interpret it, and is a true spoiler: keep pushing people with your repeated request and you will be rewarded, is what this "parable" seems to say

The remaining six stories each have multiple actors who are compared to each other and they all undergo or perform the exact same action.

The rich man and Lazarus have two actors with greatly different begin states (the way they live their lives), undergo the same action (they die) and have greatly different end states (or results, depending on what one wants to read into it): heaven or hell. Good gets rewarded, bad gets punished.

The unforgiving servant shows similarities with that, where both debtors have a greatly different debt, perform the same action of begging, and end up with greatly different end state: torture for one (who initially ended up with his debt being forgiven), imprisonment for the other. Good gets punished, bad gets punished even more.

Labourers in the vineyard has a slight variation on that; each labourer provides labour but some throughout the whole day and some for only one hour; there are five different sets of labourers who each work less hours than those who got hired before them. If getting paid is the action, they all get equal pay and only the labourers who worked all day complain about that. If providing labour is the action, they provide five different quantities of labour yet all get the same pay (and end result). Good gets rewarded, but the reward doesn't vary along with the amount of good done.

The two sons either perform actions contrary to their begin state statements or magically end up with end states that are contrary to their actions of saying what they will do - but what they share is that they say one thing and do the other. So technically they have the same begin state, perform the same action of making a promise (regardless of its content) and end up with an end state that is the opposite of what they promised. As such, the two debtors are identical to each other with every aspect yet achieve different results - but that is because the content of their promises and actions differs from each other. Good actions get rewarded over good words.

The parable of the ten virgins? It has multiple actors although those can be grouped into two groups of five. Different begin state between groups, different actions, different outcomes; it is not much of a story and it is certainly not much of a parable. The good (those who prepare) are rewarded, the bad get punished

What we have here is similar to what the gospel-writers turned the Thomas parables into: a dissimilar collection of stories that don't share a single structure, a central thought or scheme towards the structure of the narrative. What they do share is that each of them serves a highly moralising lesson that usually precedes it or at least gets summarised at the end via a question, judgmental remark, or an elaborate instruction.

Where the gospel-writers introduced the notion of Jesus explaining parables with regards to the Thomas parables, serving the same purpose of teaching highly moralising lessons, they don't feel the need to do so with their own simple stories. Although a good part of them includes an explicit moral message and sometimes even its explanation, that is never triggered from the outside (for instance by disciples asking for an explanation) but it always directly accompanies it.

The parable of the sower gets explained, the parable of the weeds, the "parable" on the mouth and defiling (logion 14, labelled as a parable by Matthew but not included by me), the parable of the faithful servant - all of those are Thomas. It is telling, or rather, a dead give-away that for none of the so-called parables from the gospel-writers an explanation from Jesus is requested by the disciples. That could be excused by the fact that the gospel-writers start creating parables of their own at a very late point in their gospel, and by that time have spent plenty of explanation on the explaining: Mark has his first "parable" in chapter 13 and Matthew does so in chapter 18. Yet Luke has his first own parable in chapter 7, that of the two debtors. It apparently doesn't need any explanation but ends with a question testing whether it was understood correctly: that is close to the other parables that require an explanation, but not quite. The parable of the sower follows, and that is explained at length. Then Luke has another creation, the good Samaritan - and again there's the question at the end. The rich fool follows, a real Thomas - and it gets summarised in one moral verse that is part of Luke's version of the parable, after which Luke continues to stress the importance of being "rich toward God".

The simple truth is that the parables invented by the gospel-writers themselves are so simple, sometimes bordering on very simple, like the parable of the ten virgins, that none of them need any explanation

There actually are three types of parables when we consider them all: the sixteen Thomas parables (only thirteen of which are incorporated into the gospels) filled with allegory and (in)animate objects, each strictly following a five element structure with an explicitly mentioned action that leads to an explicit result, transforming an explicit begin state into an explicit end state. The thirteen gospel-writers' versions of the Thomas parables - of which only one remained intact, retaining the five element structure of Thomas - and finally the fifteen gospel-writers' own "parables" that are mostly longwinded stories filled with humans interacting and dialoguing with other humans, which contain many actions, begin and end states, of which only two share Thomas' structure.

Where the Thomas parables each have a different message and lesson, one that never is explained by Thomas, all the versions of the gospel-writers serve only one single goal: to affirm moral messages of the Church about good and bad, punishment and reward. Even the parables from Thomas that they incorporate into their work are twisted and turned to serve that same purpose. Most of their parables have a judgment at the end, which often is a repercussion, and it seems that it is intended by the gospel-writers to be the result, the consequence of the action(s)

There are stark differences between the parables in Thomas and its copies in the gospels, as well as the gospel-writers' own alleged parables. One thing is without a doubt: it would have been impossible for Thomas to select, out of the dissimilar mess of 28 parables, those 13 parables that showed the greatest resemblance to parables and turn them into his own parables according to his strict five element structure of explicit subject, begin state, action, end state and result.

Spotting that the parable of the mustard seed would become a true parable if a proper action and condition were added to it, maybe something like "falling on tilled soil"?

Spotting that the hidden treasure also needed a proper action, ploughing for instance, and a result perhaps?

Spotting that the parable of the net could work really well if all the moralistic parts where left out, thus stripping over half of it, and adding something about small, large, and choosing perhaps? And that it would accidentally serve to be a core parable of Thomas where he demonstrates the actual way of seeking, and discloses the clue of its result?

Spotting that the parable of the vineyard consisted of two parts and that it would be a perfect idea to separate the corner stone sentences from it, and turn the two into a parable and a separate logion, and have the logion immediately follow the parable? Not without changing the parable and removing the ejection of the heir from the vineyard? Not without smiling and seeing that the gospel-writers had forgotten to include a complete begin state to the parable, and then introducing that in his own logion? Not without removing the way too obvious references to Isaiah with the pit, the fence, yet still sticking to that same vineyard that is the starting theme of Isaiah chapter 5 - next to being mentioned in a hundred other Tanakh verses?

It was evident that the parables of Thomas had to be incorporated. And it is evident that they have been incorporated into the gospels. And it really should be evident that it couldn't possibly be the other way around.

It became evident that Mark had done a very poor job with copying only six and making up only one of his own. So Luke added four more of Thomas, and ten (!) of himself. Matthew added three more of Thomas, and created four of his own - although his version of the ten coins could very well be considered a new copy.

It was also evident that all Thomas' parables had to be turned and twisted to serve Church goals; and that they sure did.

It is evident that the gospel-writers missed Thomas' beautiful and very strict five element structure and missed out on one or more elements in every single parable they copied, save one.

It is evident that they were poor parable creators themselves, equally neglecting those same five elements or any other structure when they came up with their own moralistic stories and labelled them parables - only two of those fit the Thomas five element structure, and no other single structure can be identified in them. They all are stories with a beginning and an end, and a moralistic message prefixing or suffixing them, and mostly they are about rewarding the good and punishing the bad. Call them parables if you want even though almost none are succinct or contain allegory, or use (in)animate objects that serve as metaphors - only two of the fifteen could be mistaken for a Thomas parable

The remainder of Luke

Having commented on the "parables" that Luke starts chapter 18 with, we find my favourite, logion 22: entering the kingdom when you have become like a child again; unlearned, de-dualised, liberated of all your identities, or rather, them-dentities. You'll have to forgive me my poetic freedom here:

(22a) Jesus saw infants being suckled.
(22b) He said to his disciples, "These infants being suckled are like those who enter the kingdom."
(22c) They said to him, "Shall we then, as children, enter the kingdom?"
(22d) Jesus said to them, "When you make the two one, and when you make the inside like the outside and the outside like the inside, and the above like the below, and when you make the male and the female one and the same, so that the male not be male nor the female female; and when you fashion eyes in the place of an eye, and a hand in place of a hand, and a foot in place of a foot, and a likeness in place of a likeness; then will you enter the kingdom."

*(Mark 10:14 But when Jesus saw it, he was moved with indignation, and said to them, "Allow the little children to come to me! Don't forbid them, for God's Kingdom belongs to such as these. 15 Most certainly I tell you, whoever will not **receive God's Kingdom like a little child**, he will in no way enter into it.")*

*18:16 Jesus summoned them, saying, "Allow the little children to come to me, and don't hinder them, for God's Kingdom belongs to such as these. 17 Most certainly, I tell you, whoever doesn't **receive God's Kingdom like a little child**, he will in no way enter into it."*

(Matthew 19:14 But Jesus said, "Allow the little children, and don't

*forbid them to come to me; for the **Kingdom of Heaven belongs to ones like these**." 15 He laid his hands on them, and departed from there.)*

Luke follows Mark although that order could be reversed as well, in theory, given their close resemblance. Matthew copies Mark but leaves out logion 22c (although he changes the message in stating that the kingdom belongs to children) - because he has put his version in the previous chapter, slightly longer:

*(Matthew 18:1 In that hour the disciples came to Jesus, saying, "Who then is greatest in the Kingdom of Heaven?" 2 Jesus called a little child to himself, and set him in the middle of them 3 and said, "Most certainly I tell you, **unless you turn and become as little children, you will in no way enter into the Kingdom of Heaven**. 4 **Whoever therefore humbles himself as this little child** is the greatest in the Kingdom of Heaven. 5 **Whoever receives one such little child in my name receives me**, 6 but whoever causes one of these little ones who believe in me to stumble, it would be better for him if a huge millstone were hung around his neck and that he were sunk in the depths of the sea.)*

Luke has his version of that story, without entering the kingdom:

*Luke 9:46 An argument arose among them about which of them was the greatest. 47 Jesus, perceiving the reasoning of their hearts, took a little child, and set him by his side, 48 and said to them, "**Whoever receives this little child in my name receives me**. Whoever receives me receives him who sent me. **For whoever is least among you all, this one will be great**."*

And so does Mark:

*(Mark 9:34 But they were silent, for they had disputed with one another on the way about who was the greatest. 35 He sat down, and called the twelve; and he said to them, "**If any man wants to be***

*first, he shall be last of all, and servant of all." 36 He took a little child, and set him in the middle of them. Taking him in his arms, he said to them, 37 "**Whoever receives one such little child in my name, receives me**, and whoever receives me, doesn't receive me, but him who sent me.")*

Matthew wins again. Mark fails to give a reason why receiving (like) a child would lead to the kingdom, Luke manages only once to express the unimpressive statement 'For whoever is least among you all, this one will be great' without explaining that "explanation" any further. Matthew makes one statement and his immediate disappearance on one occasion, and then enters the lion's den: he cites the Thomas original - only to break it entirely, and bend it to his own agenda by explicitly stating that you will have to humble yourself (like a child) in order to enter the kingdom.
Be humble. Be financially poor. Be meek. Serve and believe, just hear and accept the Word. That is the message, and it is consistent; and Matthew now applies it to little children: be humble like a little child. To the best of my knowledge, little children are far from humble: they are outspoken, not shy, they're direct, speak their mind, they're the centre of their universe and act like it, having little to no consideration for all the complexities and intricacies of adult life. Humble? Maybe after the age of 6 to 8 or so a child can be taught to be humble, but no little child is humble by nature.
At the end of Luke and Matthew we will have a look at how the gospel-writers have handled the themes of Thomas, and Matthew's verse right here is guaranteed to be in the chapter on children

Only logion 41 is in chapter 19, which Luke used earlier in 8:18 and it was commented on there, together with all occurrences of Mark and Matthew; nothing changed really - the context here is that it ends Luke's version of the ten coins.
The parable of the vineyard is next in Luke; it is going to be a lot of text with all three so brace yourselves, as I will add the cornerstone too while we're at it. I will be using emphasis and first discuss what the next gospel-writer has changed, then show the text:

(65a) He said, "There was a good man who owned a vineyard.
(65b) He leased it to tenant farmers so that they might work it and he might collect the produce from them.
(65c) He sent his servant so that the tenants might give him the produce of the vineyard.
(65d) They seized his servant and beat him, all but killing him.
(65e) The servant went back and told his master.
(65f) The master said, 'Perhaps he did not recognize them.'
(65g) He sent another servant.
(65h) The tenants beat this one as well.
(65i) Then the owner sent his son and said, 'Perhaps they will show respect to my son.'
(65j) Because the tenants knew that it was he who was the heir to the vineyard, they seized him and killed him.
(65k) Let him who has ears hear."

(66a) Jesus said, "Show me the stone which the builders have rejected.
(66b) That one is the cornerstone."

The hedge, pit and tower are a reference to Isaiah 5:2, and invented by Mark, as is the phrase 'beloved son' - the word 'beloved' occurs twice in the first sentence of Isaiah 5, no doubt inspiring Mark there. Mark sticks to Thomas and sends one servant at a time. Thomas sends two servants and one son, but Mark sends out at least a dozen, by the looks of it. Mark also starts the killing before the son has arrived.

The throwing out of the son after he is killed, his ejection from the vineyard, is inserted in order to make the connection to logion 66, the rejected cornerstone - which of course is supposed to be Jesus, as the builders are supposed to be the leaders of Israel. An oblique reference to Isaiah 28:16, it is a literal copy of Psalms 118:22. Is that the case in Thomas as well? Undoubtedly - but it serves as an instruction that you should do what the official teachers reject, not what they teach and instruct you to do. Don't do what the Pharisees and priests tell you to do, do what they tell you not to do.

Last but not least, Mark finishes with the wrath of God. In Isaiah 5:5-6 the vineyard gets destroyed yet it would make no sense for the owner to destroy his own vineyard as a punishment for the tenants killing his son - now would it.

So we so very evidently have here a Thomas logion, cleverly linked to Isaiah, twisted and turned by the gospel-writers, yet with a completely different conclusion than the verses in Isaiah simply because it is not based on Isaiah, nor spoken by Jesus, nor even invented from scratch by the gospel-writers: it is Thomas' and Thomas' alone

*(Mark 12:1 He began to speak to them in parables. "A man planted a vineyard, put a **hedge** around it, **dug a pit for the wine press**, built a **tower**, rented it out to **a farmer**, and went into another country. 2 When it was time, he **sent a servant** to the farmer to get from the farmer his share of the fruit of the vineyard. 3 They took him, beat him, and sent him away empty. 4 Again, he **sent another servant** to them; and they threw stones at him, wounded him in the head, and sent him away shamefully treated. 5 Again he **sent another; and they killed him; and many others, beating some, and killing some.** 6 Therefore still having one, his **beloved son**, he sent him last to them, saying, 'They will respect my son.' 7 But those farmers said among themselves, 'This is the heir. Come, let's kill him, and the inheritance will be ours.' 8 They took him, **killed him, and cast him out** of the vineyard. 9 What therefore will the lord of the vineyard do? He will come and **destroy the farmers**, and will give the vineyard to others. 10 Haven't you even read this Scripture: 'The stone which the builders rejected was made the head of the corner. 11 This was from the Lord. It is marvelous in our eyes'?")*

Luke plays his usual part: he sticks entirely to Thomas. And undoes almost everything Mark made up, except for the wrath part. It is very interesting to see that even with regards to the servants Luke adds only one, who only gets wounded and cast out(!), not sent away empty-handed... is that sabotage I see there, Luke trying to confuse the third servant with Jesus?

Luke fixes Mark's 'farmer' by using the plural so it can be more easily linked to the Israelites, but sticks to 'beloved son' yet has him thrown out first and then killed: not very pragmatic. Luke finishes with a reference to Isaiah 8:15 in verse 18 - yet another surprise

*20:9 He began to tell the people this parable. "A man planted a vineyard, and rented it out to **some farmers**, and went into another country for a long time. 10 At the proper season, he **sent a servant** to the farmers to collect his share of the fruit of the vineyard. But the farmers beat him, and sent him away empty. 11 He **sent yet another servant**, and they also beat him, and treated him shamefully, and sent him away empty. 12 He **sent yet a third**, and they also **wounded him, and threw him out**. 13 The lord of the vineyard said, 'What shall I do? I will send my **beloved son**. It may be that seeing him, they will respect him.' 14 "But when the farmers saw him, they reasoned among themselves, saying, 'This is the heir. Come, let's kill him, that the inheritance may be ours.' 15 Then they **threw him out of the vineyard and killed him**. What therefore will the lord of the vineyard do to them? 16 He will come and **destroy these farmers**, and will give the vineyard to others." When they heard that, they said, "May that never be!" 17 But he looked at them and said, "Then what is this that is written, 'The stone which the builders rejected was made the chief cornerstone?' 18 **Everyone who falls on that stone will be broken to pieces, but it will crush whomever it falls on to dust**."*

Matthew copies Mark and changes the man to master of the house - now there is a neat metaphor used before. He changes servant to servants so the likeness to the prophets (sent out by God to the people of Israel) is easier to make. Where the first servant only gets a beating in Thomas, Mark and Luke, these ones get beaten, killed and stoned - Matthew naturally has to overdo it. He highly likely recognised Thomas' three-act-structure and reverts to it, which is now possible because he sends lots of servants the first two times before he sends in the son (dropping the 'beloved' of Mark and

Luke) who also gets thrown out first and then killed, as in Luke, yet Matthew adds that he is taken before that.

Presumably Jesus is still in the presence of the chief priests and the elders and narrating this story. Where Mark has a monologue and Luke just people who say only two words, Matthew has the priests and elders give him the correct answer to the question what will happen to the tenants, and then rubs it in that they are the tenants in the story, to fall on Luke's stone:

*(Matthew 21:33 "Hear another parable. There was a man who was a **master of a household** who planted a vineyard, set a **hedge** about it, **dug a wine press in it**, built a **tower**, leased it out to farmers, and went into another country. 34 When the season for the fruit came near, he **sent his servants** to the farmers to receive his fruit. 35 The farmers took his servants, **beat one, killed another, and stoned another**. 36 Again, he **sent other servants** more than the first; and they **treated them the same way**. 37 But afterward he **sent to them his son**, saying, 'They will respect my son.' 38 But the farmers, when they saw the son, said among themselves, 'This is the heir. Come, let's kill him and seize his inheritance.' 39 So they took him and **threw him out of the vineyard, then killed him**. 40 When therefore the lord of the vineyard comes, what will he do to those farmers?" 41 They told him, "He will **miserably destroy those miserable men**, and will lease out the vineyard to other farmers who will give him the fruit in its season." 42 Jesus said to them, "Did you never read in the Scriptures, 'The stone which the builders rejected was made the head of the corner. This was from the Lord. It is marvelous in our eyes'? 43 "Therefore I tell you, God's Kingdom will be taken away from you and will be given to a nation producing its fruit. 44 **He who falls on this stone will be broken to pieces, but on whomever it will fall, it will scatter him as dust**.")*

A perfect Matthean ending, as usual - if you ask the Church. Thomas, Mark, Luke, Matthew - it couldn't possibly be any other way, with the gradual transformation, the subtle changes. The by far most important gospel sandbox here is the ejecting of the son, the throwing out of the vineyard of him, in an attempt to mirror the rejection of the cornerstone. The best evidence for it being invented by Mark is the fact that it is toyed with by the gospel-writers; Mark has the son first killed and then thrown out, Luke has him first thrown out and then killed - Luke even has a servant thrown out (!). Matthew has him taken, thrown out, and then killed. Now how can that possibly be, if this entire story serves only one goal for the gospel-writers, namely the narrative of God sending all the prophets to the people of Israel in vain and then, finally, in a desperate last move, sending his one and only son in the certain knowledge (of course, as God knows all) that he will be killed? Isn't the entire and only truth, the grand finale of this small play here, that Jesus will get killed by the Jews?

Then how on earth can it be that each gospel-writer has a more than significantly different version on that so very small act, that tiny mini play of essentially only (one or) two verbs, one subject and one object?

Logion 100, Caesar's coin. How extraordinarily concise Thomas is. Such a simple and short logion and so very essential in its core, juxtaposing Caesar next to God as just another deity that is required by society to be glorified or divinised by its own means, while reserving the primary position in life for the one and only: me - give me what is mine:

(100a) They showed Jesus a gold coin and said to him, "Caesar's men demand taxes from us."
(100b) He said to them, "Give Caesar what belongs to Caesar, give God what belongs to God, and give me what is mine."

*(Mark 12:13 They sent some of the Pharisees and the Herodians to him, that they might trap him with words. 14 When they had come, they asked him, "Teacher, we know that you are honest, and don't defer to anyone; for you aren't partial to anyone, but **truly teach the way of God**. Is it **lawful to pay taxes** to Caesar, or not? 15 Shall we give, or shall we not give?" But he, knowing their **hypocrisy**, said to*

them, *"Why do you test me? Bring me a denarius, that I may see it."*
16 They brought it. He said to them, "Whose is this image and
inscription?" They said to him, "Caesar's." 17 Jesus answered them,
***"Render to Caesar** the things that are Caesar's, and to God the*
things that are God's." ***They marveled greatly at him.***)

20:21 They asked him, "Teacher, we know that you say and teach
*what is right, and aren't partial to anyone, but **truly teach the way***
***of God.** 22 Is it **lawful for us to pay taxes to Caesar**, or not?" 23 But*
*he perceived their **craftiness**, and said to them, "Why do you test*
me? 24 Show me a denarius. Whose image and inscription are on
*it?" They answered, "Caesar's." 25 He said to them, "**Then give to***
***Caesar** the things that are Caesar's, and to God the things that are*
God's." 26 They weren't able to trap him in his words before the
people. ***They marveled at his answer and were silent.***

(Matthew 22:16 They sent their disciples to him, along with the
Herodians, saying, "Teacher, we know that you are honest, and
***teach the way of God in truth**, no matter whom you teach; for you*
aren't partial to anyone. 17 Tell us therefore, what do you think? Is
*it **lawful to pay taxes** to Caesar, or not?" 18 But Jesus perceived*
*their **wickedness**, and said, "Why do you test me, you hypocrites?*
*19 **Show me the tax money**." They brought to him a denarius. 20 He*
asked them, "Whose is this image and inscription?" 21 They said to
*him, "Caesar's." Then he said to them, "**Give therefore to Caesar** the*
things that are Caesar's, and to God the things that are God's." 22
When they heard it, ***they marveled, and left him and went away.***)

Luke swaps 'honest' for 'right' but sticks to 'truly teach the way of
God'. Matthew undoes his first change and nudges up the other to
'teach the way of God in truth'.
With regards to the story: praising Jesus for his particular ability to
teach God's way and then questioning him about something so
trivial, mundane and worldly as paying taxes strikes me as a
wondrous pretext, but the Pharisees probably are supposed to play
with the word Law.

I commented before that the gospel-writers once more miss the point of Thomas and go to extreme lengths in order to link the image on the coin to the punch line, thus introducing a silver coin (the denarius) in stead of a gold one - most people would know that a denarius bears his image, and most people would have almost never even seen a gold coin. In Thomas it is unclear whether or not Caesar's image is on the coin and it is a trivial detail: who cares who you pay taxes to, it is part of the rules of society that you do so: this Caesar will die but he will just be replaced by another Caesar. Likewise it is part of the rules of society that you give to God, and that is equally as insignificant; this God might be replaced by another God but that won't change the System, you will still always be required to give to (a) God just as you're always required to give to (a) Caesar. Only one thing is most significant in your entire life, and that is you yourself: me - give me what is mine.

Yet both Luke as well as Matthew follow Mark's scene almost to the letter; where I labelled Mark as longwinded earlier, apparently his verses perfectly serve the gospel-writers' goal. Praising Jesus, putting down the tricky Pharisees (and Herodians) and showing Jesus' marvellous cunning (and hostile attitude towards them) all at once: that is how they want it.

Given their close similarity, what about the order? The threads I have for Mark-Luke-Matthew are merely two. The end result in Mark is marvelled Pharisees, in Luke they marvel and become silent, in Matthew they marvel, leave him and go away; Luke expands Mark and Matthew expands Luke there. Similarly 'hypocrisy', 'craftiness' and 'wickedness' show a gradual change from just slightly evil and hiding it to outright evil.

Matthew's utmost accomplishment naturally is the fact that Jesus demands to see a tax coin, presumably unprepared, and on apparently suddenly seeing that it bears Caesar's face instantly creates the cunning one-liner - a perfection like that is highly unlikely to come from a first strike. Matthew certainly is last, Mark certainly comes before him, and Luke probably is in between. And Thomas undeniably is first with his beautifully concise version lacking any and all Church motive, directed solely at the true punch line of 'give me what is mine'

I count 4 logia in chapters 18 through 20, totalling 57.
Chapter 21 foretells the destruction of the temple, logion 71:

(71) Jesus said, "I shall destroy this house, and no one will be able to build it [...]."

*(Mark 13:1 As he went out of the temple, one of his disciples said to him, "**Teacher, see what kind of stones and what kind of buildings**!" 2 Jesus said to him, "Do you see **these great buildings**? There will not be left here one stone on another, which will not be thrown down.")*

*21:5 As **some were talking about the temple** and how it was **decorated with beautiful stones and gifts**, he said, 6 "As for **these things** which you see, the days will come, in which there will not be left here one stone on another that will not be thrown down."*

*(Matthew 24:1 Jesus went out from the temple, and was going on his way. **His disciples came to him to show him the buildings of the temple**. 2 But he answered them, "You see all of **these things**, don't you? Most certainly I tell you, there will not be left here one stone on another, that will not be thrown down.")*

Mark's description (and certainly the pretext) of the temple is odd, with Jesus even using the word great - the translation is correct but using high or tall would have been less associative - one can't state anything good about the Temple of course. Luke handles Mark's awkward disciple comment very nicely by turning it into a passive form and also swaps 'great buildings' for the pejorative 'these things' but at the cost of the question. Matthew accepts Luke's finds yet puts the question back in, beautifully turning it into a rhetorical one. Where Luke makes the commentators anonymous, Matthew retains the disciples but has them merely show the buildings, thereby avoiding any and all description of the temple. Thomas,

Mark, Luke, Matthew - unquestionably

Logion 68 is used in full, and Matthew is the best pointer there:

(68a) Jesus said, "Blessed are you when you are hated and persecuted.
(68b) Wherever you have been persecuted they will find no place."

(Mark 13:13 You will be hated by all men for my name's sake, but he who endures to the end will be saved. 14 But when you see the **abomination of desolation, spoken of by Daniel the prophet, standing where it ought not**" *(let the reader understand), "then let those who are in Judea flee to the mountains,)*

21:17 You will be hated by all men for my name's sake. 18 And not a hair of your head will perish. 19 "By your endurance you will win your lives. 20 "But when you see **Jerusalem surrounded by armies, then know that its desolation is at hand**. *21 Then let those who are in Judea flee to the mountains. Let those who are in the middle of her depart. Let those who are in the country not enter therein.*

(Matthew 10:22 You will be hated by all men for my name's sake, but he who endures to the end will be saved. 23 **But when they persecute you in this city, flee into the next**, *for most certainly I tell you, you will not have gone through the cities of Israel until the Son of Man has come.)*

(Matthew 24:15 "When, therefore, you see the **abomination of desolation, which was spoken of through Daniel the prophet, standing in the holy place** *(let the reader understand), 16 then let those who are in Judea flee to the mountains.)*

The abomination of desolation is from Daniel 9:27 (and 11:31 and 12:11) and interpretations of what it has been in the first century CE seem to point to the destruction of Jerusalem's Temple in 70 CE.

Matthew mentions his in chapter 24 yet uses chapter 10 to copy and elaborate on Mark and Luke, and Thomas. Mark's cryptic 'standing where he ought not to be' is changed by Matthew to 'standing in the holy place' yet left out completely by Luke. What all three have in common is the desolation which is directly followed by the fleeing to the mountains by those who are in Judea.

So why did Matthew insert his 10:23? Is that not a fine variation on logion 68b? If so, the preceding verse can only be inspired by logion 68a.

Granted, it is a thin thread - but I think it is thick enough

Logion 79 we have seen earlier in 17:31, Luke once more uses it in 21:23 (and 23:29).

Logion 11a in 21:32-33 has been commented on earlier, regarding its sibling in chapter 16.

The last three chapters of Luke are free of Thomas. What is left are the logia that are unique to each gospel-writer. We have covered all of Mark, we have covered all of Luke with all the versions of his verses that Mark and / or Matthew shared: we will now cover Matthew and see what he did or did not share with Mark. The count of logia will be continued, with the last 2 it currently stands at 59 unique logia

Matthew's Thomas

Matthew tackles some cryptic logia alone, and rightfully so; I wouldn't trust Mark or Luke with them either. John perhaps? Just wait and see...

Matthew's first logion not shared with Luke is found in chapter 5, his sermon on the mount. It combines 24c with 32:

(24a) His disciples said to him, "Show us the place where you are, since it is necessary for us to seek it."
(24b) He said to them, "Whoever has ears, let him hear.
(24c) There is light within a man of light, and he lights up the whole world.
(24d) If he does not shine, he is darkness."
(32) Jesus said, "A city being built on a high mountain and fortified cannot fall, nor can it be hidden."

5:14 You are the light of the world. A city located on a hill can't be hidden.

It is the very best find by far, if you ask John: he will use it as a unique description of Jesus, and John will use it six times. Honestly, it is magnificent. Matthew has Jesus use it here to describe the people but credits go to him for inventing it.

Why no one else used logion 32 before remains a puzzle; it is perfectly innocent yet strong and very intelligible

Logion 22d is next, the grand remake of it - it is one of the Thomas logia impossible to incorporate without grave change. Matthew has a relatively short copy of Mark in his sermon on the mount, and an identical yet slightly different one afterwards:

(22a) Jesus saw infants being suckled.
(22b) He said to his disciples, "These infants being suckled are like those who enter the kingdom."
(22c) They said to him, "Shall we then, as children, enter the

kingdom?"

(22d) Jesus said to them, "When you make the two one, and when you make the inside like the outside and the outside like the inside, and the above like the below, and when you make the male and the female one and the same, so that the male not be male nor the female female; and when you fashion eyes in the place of an eye, and a hand in place of a hand, and a foot in place of a foot, and a likeness in place of a likeness; then will you enter the kingdom."

*(Mark 9:42 Whoever will cause one of these little ones who believe in me to stumble, it would be better for him if he were thrown into the sea with a millstone hung around his neck. 43 **If your hand causes you to stumble**, cut it off. It is better for you to enter into life maimed, rather than having your two hands to go into Gehenna, into the unquenchable fire, 44 'where their worm doesn't die, and the fire is not quenched.' 45 **If your foot causes you to stumble**, cut it off. It is better for you to enter into life lame, rather than having your two feet to be cast into Gehenna, into the fire that will never be quenched- 46 'where their worm doesn't die, and the fire is not quenched.' 47 **If your eye causes you to stumble**, cast it out. It is better for you to **enter into God's Kingdom with one eye**, rather than **having two eyes to be cast into the Gehenna of fire**, 48 'where their worm doesn't die, and the fire is not quenched.')*

*5:29 **If your right eye causes you to stumble**, pluck it out and throw it away from you. For it is more profitable for you that one of your members should perish than for your whole body to be cast into Gehenna. 30 **If your right hand causes you to stumble**, cut it off, and throw it away from you. For it is more profitable for you that **one of your members should perish**, than for your **whole body to be cast into Gehenna**.*

18:5 Whoever receives one such little child in my name receives me, 6 but whoever causes one of these little ones who believe in me to stumble, it would be better for him if a huge millstone were hung around his neck and that he were sunk in the depths of the sea. 7 "Woe to the world because of occasions of stumbling! For it must be that the occasions come, but woe to that person through whom the occasion comes! 8 **If your hand or your foot causes you to stumble**, *cut it off and cast it from you. It is better for you to* **enter into life maimed or crippled**, *rather than* **having two hands or two feet to be cast into the eternal fire**. *9* **If your eye causes you to stumble**, *pluck it out and cast it from you. It is better for you to* **enter into life with one eye**, *rather than* **having two eyes to be cast into the Gehenna of fire**. *10 See that you don't despise one of these little ones, for I tell you that in heaven their angels always see the face of my Father who is in heaven.*

Luke has the millstone verse (18:6) in 17:2 in his Temptations to Sin, by the way - just as one single verse. He doesn't have the rest. Matthew uses 'right eye' and 'right hand' in his sermon - only those, and in that order, yet Matthew's longer version basically is a copy of Mark. The first verse is identical but then Matthew interjects his woes to temptations and condenses the hand and foot verses into one. The only occurrence of Mark's 'God's Kingdom' is replaced by a simple 'life'; apparently the two are interchangeable? The odds of Matthew executing such a brutal edit on Mark are immensely higher than vice versa

In logion 62b there is the mention of a left hand and a right hand. Could it be referring to Genesis chapter 48, where Israel blesses Ephraim over the firstborn Manasseh, Joseph protesting that in vain? The more likely assumption is that it is a common enough saying (for which I have no proof whatsoever), and in the context here its meaning is clear: not everything is to be handed out alike. Logion 62a we have seen applied many times, with Jesus singling out his disciples and elevating them above the crowd.

(62a) Jesus said, "It is to those who are worthy of my mysteries that I tell my mysteries.
(62b) Do not let your left (hand) know what your right (hand) is

doing."

6:3 But when you do merciful deeds, don't let your left hand know what your right hand does,

Logion 93b has been mentioned before and slightly commented on, it is the missing piece in what has been used from the logion thus far. Where 93a underwent great reconstruction, this one is intact. In fact, it is more complete than Thomas and chances are highly likely that it is an exact copy: this is the first (and only) copy by the gospel-writers and it is short; no chance of this addition being a longwinded elaboration by Matthew. Harmless enough in both forms as it is, pigs can't do much more with pearls than crush them, either in their mouth or underfoot.

Turning and attacking might be an addition by Matthew put probably isn't; the object simply going to waste in both occasions wouldn't be befitting in Thomas. Stressing an identical outcome under (slightly) different circumstances would be a waste of words, yet it would be valuable to distinguish between the two kinds of recipients: some might simply waste what is valued (by you), others may even destroy it and be offended by your action. There is, however, a highly likely Church edit in 'trample underfoot' and in the turning: the original wording is probably different but the action is one of destroying and highly likely to mirror the action towards you; my guess is that the original states:

'Do not throw the pearls to swine, lest they grind it and rip you'

The pearls go to pieces or bits, and so do you. The ripping would be too cryptic and specific for Matthew's taste and he'd likely have also added the 'turn to' in order to clarify that the two actions don't take place simultaneously

(93a) [Jesus said] "Do not give what is holy to dogs, lest they throw them on the dung-heap.
(93b) Do not throw the pearls to swine, lest they [...] it [...]."

7:6 "Don't give that which is holy to the dogs, neither throw your pearls before the pigs, lest perhaps they trample them under their feet, and turn and tear you to pieces.

Logion 39 has been commented before yet 39c we haven't encountered yet

(39a) Jesus said, "The pharisees and the scribes have taken the keys of knowledge (gnosis) and hidden them.
(39b) They themselves have not entered, nor have they allowed to enter those who wish to.
(39c) You, however, be as wise as serpents and as innocent as doves."

10:16 "Behold, I send you out as sheep among wolves. Therefore be wise as serpents and harmless as doves.

It is yet another occasion where a logion gets split and we find the various parts in very different places. The sheep and wolves are a great find of course, and Matthew has those prepped in 7:15 where he compares false prophets to wolves in sheep's clothing - adding the (awkward) serpents and doves here fits like a glove.
Of course it is perfectly logical for Thomas to take 39a from Luke 11:52, the only place in the gospels where the keys of knowledge appear, and combine that with 39c from Matthew 10:16, the only place where the serpents and doves are mentioned - or is it? Much more logical than only Matthew daring to lay his hands on this riddling and vague logion part?

Logion 90 is a double surprise. Not only does it come from Matthew here (I would have expected Luke, to be honest) but it is also a quite literal copy:

(90) Jesus said, "Come unto me, for my yoke is easy and my lordship is mild, and you will find repose for yourselves."

*11:28 "Come to me, **all you who labor and are heavily burdened, and I will give you rest**. 29 **Take my yoke upon you and learn from me, for I am gentle and humble in heart**; and you will find rest for your **souls**. 30 For my yoke is easy, and my **burden** is light."*

I am puzzled and confused - no idea what that does here or how it would fit in. Matthew of all people claiming that Jesus' yoke is easy? Matthew precedes the logion with basically the same message, addressing his flock and reinforcing the teacher-student paradigm. And he throws in 'souls' in another attempt to steer his version of this logion into the right direction.
Matthew evidently can't use 'lordship', so he replaces it with 'burden'

Mark has copied logion 57 in combination with 21i but I saved the comment for now:

(57a) Jesus said, "The kingdom of the father is like a man who had good seed.
(57b) His enemy came by night and sowed weeds among the good seed.
(57c) The man did not allow them to pull up the weeds; he said to them, 'I am afraid that you will go intending to pull up the weeds and pull up the wheat along with them.'
(57d) For on the day of the harvest the weeds will be plainly visible, and they will be pulled up and burned."
(21i) When the grain ripened, he came quickly with his sickle in his hand and reaped it.

*(Mark 4:26 He said, "God's Kingdom is as if a **man should cast seed on the earth**, 27 and should **sleep** and rise night and day, and the **seed should spring up and grow**, although he doesn't know how. 28 For **the earth bears fruit by itself: first the blade, then the ear, then the full grain in the ear**. 29 But when the fruit is ripe, immediately he puts in the sickle, because the harvest has come.")*

*13:24 He set another parable before them, saying, "The Kingdom of Heaven is like a **man who sowed good seed in his field**, 25 but while **people slept**, his enemy came and sowed darnel weeds also among the wheat, and went away. 26 But when **the blade sprang up and produced grain**, then the darnel weeds appeared also. 27 The servants of the householder came and said to him, 'Sir, **didn't you sow good seed** in your field? **Where did these darnel weeds come from**?' 28 "He said to them, 'An enemy has done this.' "The servants asked him, 'Do you want us to go and gather them up?' 29 "But he said, 'No, lest perhaps while you gather up the darnel weeds, you root up the wheat with them. 30 Let both grow together until the harvest, and in the harvest time I will tell the reapers, "First, gather up the darnel weeds, and bind them in bundles to burn them; but gather the wheat into my barn."'"*

The similarities between Mark and Matthew are hard to find, equally as hard as the similarities between Mark and Thomas; Mark contributes next to nothing with his version of the logion. Yet Matthew helps to prove that Mark used the logion: the 'sleep', 'springing up' and the wondering about the origin of the plants is what they have in common - and it is clear that Matthew does use the logion.

Matthew leaves out the part of logion 21 and sticks to Thomas fairly closely; he even preserves the clue yet ruins it at the end in order to fit his zealous goal: of course the wicked must be punished first before the good are praised and saved.

Matthew being practically the first copier makes the usual mistakes: he becomes longwinded and over-explains, introducing verses 26-28 (which of course have to have servants in it), whereas Thomas just needs anyone so he can voice his thoughts. Whether those are servants, slaves, sons or daughters, friends or foes is completely irrelevant - it is personnel that receives instructions regarding the way to handle the sowing of the weeds, with the sole purpose that the man doesn't have to talk to himself in order to voice the action of the parable.

Matthew spends too much eye on detail: the bearing of grain, his sleeping men, the enemy going away again - those are all irrelevant details without cause and effect, contributing nothing to the story. Thomas is completely comfortable with merely mentioning that the enemy came by night and sowed the seed; no need to explain how someone could know that without having stopped the enemy - that is simply how short stories, parables, work. Matthew tries enormously hard to "make it intelligible" by letting the weeds first grow so they become visible and can become noticed, upon which the servants have a pretext to question their appearance (naturally stressing the dogma that the dear God brought forth only good "seeds").

So then their master can tell that an enemy has done it, but is that any better than what Thomas does? No, it's futile and useless, because now the master is theoretically still tasked with explaining how he could know without having stopped the enemy - did the enemy just leave a note?

Matthew also tries hard to put the spotlight on the man whom he wants to appear to be in power and wise - but a parable can have only one main character or subject, and here that is the single observation that the enemy's sowing of the weeds will have a negligible effect on the harvest. Under one simple condition: the weeds and seeds now might be equal (in size and / or appearance), but when the process of growth has completed they will be very easy to distinguish from one another - so just let it be, the enemy's action won't have any consequences, if only your action regarding this "threat" is inaction.

Thomas' perfectly sensible burning of the weeds (you can't throw away weeds nor e.g. drown them nor hammer them to a pulp, they will just persist and keep spreading and growing) inspires Matthew to his first gathering up the weeds and (of course) binding and burning them, on which he elaborates in 13:37-43, ending with 'furnace of fire. There will be weeping and gnashing of teeth'. Matthew really is fond of stressing the impending Judgment Day punishment while flogging his much beloved theme of weeping and gnashing of teeth

Matthew next combines the only convenient parts of three logia into one cluster, with the purpose to twist and turn the outcome into his customary message of dark doom again, ending with his beloved "weeping and gnashing of teeth"; 109a, 76a and 76c, and 8a:

(109a) Jesus said, "The kingdom is like a man who had a hidden treasure in his field without knowing it.
(109b) And after he died, he left it to his son.
(109c) The son did not know (about the treasure).
(109d) He inherited the field and sold it.
(109e) And the one who bought it went plowing and found the treasure.
(109f) He began to lend money at interest to whomever he wished."
(76a) Jesus said, "The kingdom of the father is like a merchant who had a consignment of merchandise and who discovered a pearl.
(76b) That merchant was shrewd.
(76c) He sold the merchandise and bought the pearl alone for himself.
(76d) You too, seek his unfailing and enduring treasure where no moth comes near to devour and no worm destroys."
(8a) And he said, "The man is like a wise fisherman who cast his net into the sea and drew it up from the sea full of small fish.
(8b) Among them the wise fisherman found a fine large fish.
(8c) He threw all the small fish back into the sea and chose the large fish without difficulty.
(8d) Whoever has ears to hear, let him hear."

13:44 "Again, the Kingdom of Heaven is like treasure hidden in the field, which a man found and hid. In his joy, he goes and sells all that he has and buys that field. 45 "Again, the Kingdom of Heaven is like a man who is a merchant seeking fine pearls, 46 who having found one pearl of great price, he went and sold all that he had and bought it. 47 "Again, the Kingdom of Heaven is like a dragnet that was cast into the sea and gathered some fish of every kind, 48 which, when it was filled, fishermen drew up on the beach. They sat down and gathered the good into containers, but the bad they threw away. 49 So it will be in the end of the world. The angels will come and separate the wicked from among the righteous, 50 and will cast them into the furnace of fire. There will be weeping and gnashing of teeth." 51 Jesus said to them, "Have you understood all these things?" They answered him, "Yes, Lord."

Apart from completely breaking the first and the last logion, Matthew compares the kingdom not to the people but to the objects, save for the merchant with the pearl. The most polite word to describe verse 48 is "direct", yet it does pave the way for the conclusions of verse 49 and 50.

Matthew is the only one to copy these - what are the chances of Thomas taking these very verses 44 through 48 and turning them into his three logia as they stand? These are quickies, only used to up the logia score and nothing else - there's no connection, no content to either three that leads up to the only one inevitable Matthean conclusion of dark and doom.

Even in the parable of the pearl Matthew misses the clue of the merchandise being a consignment; it is not his: he is shrewd because he sells or uses something that doesn't belong to him

Matthew also stands alone in copying logion 40. Apart from his make-over it basically means the same here, even though Thomas' father and Matthew's Father are utterly different concepts:

(40) Jesus said, "A grapevine has been planted outside of the father, but being unsound, it will be pulled up by its roots and destroyed."

*15:12 Then the disciples came and said to him, "Do you know that the Pharisees were offended when they heard this saying?" 13 But he answered, "**Every plant which my heavenly Father didn't plant***

will be uprooted.

Matthew certainly doesn't shy away from the more cryptic ones, here is logion 30:

(30a) Jesus said, "Where there are three gods, they are gods. (30b) Where there are two or one, I am with him."

*18:19 Again, assuredly I tell you, that if two of you will agree on earth concerning anything that they will ask, it will be done for them by my Father who is in heaven. 20 **For where two or three are gathered together in my name, there I am in the middle of them**."*

One last time we see a fairly different logion on papyrus (Attridge translation):

[Jesus said], "Where there are [three], they are without God, and where there is but [a single one], I say that I am with [him]. Lift up the stone, and you will find me there. Split the piece of wood, and I am there."

An even more puzzling logion, although it seems to point to the solitary and elect as only those who can find (the) God (in themselves) - all other Gods are mere deities and have little to nothing to do with finding revelations.
On a side note, it has become utterly clear by now that the gospel-writers used (something like) the text of Thomas as it is in Oxyrhynchus, not the complete Greek text that we have today. The last two sentences here, with the stone and the wood, appear in reversed order in logion 77 but aren't to be found in logion 30.
The next chapter is chapter 19 and we are presented with Matthew's take on Mark's interpretation of making the two one - I will address that in a few pages from now but will first finish Matthew.
Logion 108 is next:

(108a) Jesus said, "He who will drink from my mouth will become like me.
(108b) I myself shall become he, and the things that are hidden will be revealed to him."

*(Mark 10:38 But Jesus said to them, "You don't know what you are asking. Are you able to **drink the cup that I drink, and to be baptized with the baptism that I am baptized with**?" 39 They said to him, "We are able." Jesus said to them, "You shall indeed **drink the cup that I drink, and you shall be baptized with the baptism that I am baptized with**; 40 but to sit at my right hand and at my left hand is not mine to give, but for whom it has been prepared.")*

*(Luke 12:50 **But I have a baptism to be baptized with**, and how distressed I am until it is accomplished!)*

*20:22 But Jesus answered, "You don't know what you are asking. Are you able to **drink the cup that I am about to drink, and be baptized with the baptism that I am baptized with**?" They said to him, "We are able." 23 He said to them, "You will indeed **drink my cup, and be baptized with the baptism that I am baptized with**; but to sit on my right hand and on my left hand is not mine to give, but it is for whom it has been prepared by my Father."*

Luke is mentioned on the side here; his is the only mention of the baptism to be baptised with - but that is not part of this logion anyway. Matthew follows Mark to the letter, only adding 'by my Father'.

15 logia in this Matthew chapter, 6 of which were already commented on. 9 logia to add to the total, which now stands at 69. What remains are Mark's lone logia, and it will be a very brief chapter

Mark's solos

Mark has only a handful of logia that haven't been adopted by Luke or Matthew. They won't be repeated here, for reasons that will become clear during this very small chapter. As there are no copies of these verses that I suspected to be inspired by Thomas yet didn't count, the verdict is easy.

As stated before, Mark 15:21 could refer to logion 42 - the passer-by phrase, but it's dubious and very thin.

Mark 6:31 (the deserted place where to find rest) could refer to logion 60f but it's equally thin, and besides Mark there are no takers. The deserted place itself is used by Luke while referring to the place where Jesus feeds 5,000, and by Matthew to refer to the place where Jesus feeds 4,000. It is a perfect pretext for being in need of a miracle in order to feed thousands, as there is nowhere else to get food from, and as such it is merely likely that logion 60 is used to include on this occasion. There is also little to nothing to gain by copying this part of the logion, certainly not without putting it to use.

Mark 6:50 then? That is when Jesus shows himself walking on the sea and tells the disciples to not be afraid - I am afraid that is equally as thin and hard to trace back to Thomas' last part of 37b.

Mark 8:11 is where the Pharisees are testing Jesus and seeking a sign - that could be 51a or 113a where the disciples pose the same question to Jesus; but it is so common to test a Messiah and seek a sign from him that it is impossible to build any case

So, apart from these four supposedly copied logia, Luke and Matthew incorporated all of Mark that he copied from Thomas. Before the last of the four gospel-writers is discussed, which will be a relatively brief chapter, it is time to handle the themes of Thomas. The anti-Pharisee attitude and the rejection of Jewish customs has been briefly discussed and there are ample examples of the fact that those two themes have very successfully become combined by the gospel-writers into one: rebuking the Pharisees for numerous reasons, among others stressing that they are hypocrites and show that in the way they pray, fast and give alms. It is a brilliant find really, and indeed killing two birds with one stone - there is nothing further to say on it, it is very well elaborated and makes perfect sense. The next theme: making the two one

Making the two one

'Making the two one' is the most important theme in Thomas and the gospel-writers haven't managed to come up with a lot of text on it - in fact, awfully little. However, this is a proverbial case of quantity versus quality: the direction that the theme is steered in leaves next to nothing to discuss, really. Given the brevity of content from the gospel-writers an unusual amount of context will be copied along:

*Mark 10:1 He arose from there and came into the borders of Judea and beyond the Jordan. Multitudes came together to him again. As he usually did, he was again teaching them. 2 **Pharisees came to him testing him, and asked him, "Is it lawful for a man to divorce his wife**?" 3 He answered, "What did Moses command you?" 4 They said, "Moses allowed a certificate of divorce to be written, and to divorce her." 5 But Jesus said to them, "For your hardness of heart, he wrote you this commandment. 6 But from the beginning of the creation, **God made them male and female**. 7 For this cause **a man** will leave his father and mother, and **will join to his wife**, 8 **and the two will become one flesh**, so that **they are no longer two, but one flesh**. 9 **What therefore God has joined together, let no man separate**." 10 In the house, his disciples asked him again about the same matter. 11 He said to them, "**Whoever divorces his wife and marries another commits adultery against her. 12 If a woman herself divorces her husband and marries another, she commits adultery**."*

*Luke 16:18 **Everyone who divorces his wife and marries another commits adultery. He who marries one who is divorced from a husband commits adultery**.*

*Matthew 19:3 **Pharisees came to him, testing him and saying, "Is it lawful for a man to divorce his wife for any reason**?" 4 He answered, "Haven't you read that **he who made them from the beginning made them male and female**, 5 **and said**, 'For this cause* *a man shall leave his father and mother, and shall be joined to his wife; and **the two shall become one flesh**?' 6 **So that they are no more two, but one flesh. What therefore God has joined together, don't let man tear apart**." 7 They asked him, "Why then did Moses command us to give her a certificate of divorce and divorce her?" 8 He said to them, "Moses, because of the hardness of your hearts, allowed you to divorce your wives, but from the beginning it has not been so. 9 I tell you that whoever divorces his wife, except for sexual immorality, and marries another, commits adultery; and he who marries her when she is divorced commits adultery." 10 His disciples said to him, "If this is the case of the man with his wife, it is not expedient to marry." 11 But he said to them, "**Not all men can receive this saying, but those to whom it is given**. 12 For there are eunuchs who were born that way from their mother's womb, and there are eunuchs who were made eunuchs by men; and there are eunuchs who made themselves eunuchs for the Kingdom of Heaven's sake. He who is able to receive it, let him receive it."*

This is the part where Matthew elaborately comments on Mark's find of 'making the two one', but as mentioned before he didn't want to imitate Mark who dropped the topic of divorce like a brick, and thus prepares his view on divorce in his sermon on the mount:

Matthew 5:31 "It was also said, 'Whoever shall put away his wife, let him give her a writing of divorce,' 32 but I tell you that whoever puts away his wife, except for the cause of sexual immorality, makes her an adulteress; and whoever marries her when she is put away commits adultery.

First things first. Luke spends one meagre verse on it all, and has nothing further on the theme save his verses 17:34-35 on the two in the field or grinding at the mill, of which one will be taken and one will be left - which indeed come from Thomas but have nothing to do with the application of this theme by the gospel-writers. It is clear that on the matter of divorce he very briefly copies Mark in full and leaves it at that: just one small verse - Luke is just not interested in the theme. Matthew builds in the escape clauses Mark omitted: divorce is valid on the basis of adultery, and people can abstain from marriage if they do so desire - it is not an obligation to marry. Why Matthew feels that it could be assumed to be an obligation will become clear in a few minutes.

Starting with Mark, it is evident that he uses Genesis to support his cause. However, there is a double creation story in Genesis:

*(Genesis 1:26 God said, "**Let's make man in our image, after our likeness**. Let them have dominion over the fish of the sea, and over the birds of the sky, and over the livestock, and over all the earth, and over every creeping thing that creeps on the earth." 27 **God created man in his own image**. In God's image he created him; **male and female he created them**. 28 **God blessed them. God said to them**, "Be fruitful, multiply, fill the earth, and subdue it. Have dominion over the fish of the sea, over the birds of the sky, and over every living thing that moves on the earth."*

(...)

*2:21 Yahweh God caused the man to fall into a deep sleep. As the man slept, he took one of his ribs, and closed up the flesh in its place. 22 **Yahweh God made a woman from the rib which he had taken from the man, and brought her to the man**. 23 The man said, "This is now bone of my bones, and flesh of my flesh. She will be called 'woman,' because she was taken out of Man." 24 **Therefore a man will leave his father and his mother, and will join with his wife, and they will be one flesh**.)*

It is clear that in Genesis 1 God creates both man and woman, even speaking to them - on the fifth day. Genesis 2 starts with wrapping up Genesis 1 and the seventh day, and from verse 2:4 on another creation story starts from a different perspective, where the female is created from a part of the man; the narrator concludes that story with his comment in verse 24 that '... join with his wife, and they will be one flesh'.

Mark copies that exact same comment in 10:7-8 and adds to it 'so that they are no longer two, but one flesh' - the phrase of which I said that it was an extra explanation and giving Mark away: he suffers the pioneers' fate and over explains, making it evident that he is trying something out here. And he is, because Mark is cunningly combining the act of creation from the first chapter of Genesis, 'male and female he created them' (Genesis 1:27), with the conclusion from the second chapter of Genesis: man 'will join with his wife' (Genesis 2:24) 'called woman, because she was taken out of Man' (Genesis 2:23).

Another deliberate act of misquoting the Tanakh in order to justify a Church goal - by now, that shouldn't surprise anyone. Why wasn't just everything quoted from chapter 2, would that hurt their case of male and female being two? Apparently, or perhaps - God creating male and female most certainly leaves nothing to the imagination. Matthew even adds to that and does something else entirely - he gratefully copies Mark and deviously inserts the words 'and said', suggesting that Genesis 2:24 isn't spoken by the narrator but by God himself: God himself is suggested to have said that man will join with his wife.

That evidently is an outright lie, and just another manifestation of Mattheanism as we've grown accustomed to by now: the extremely loose wielding of scripture in order to justify words and deeds concerning Jesus in general.

Is it perhaps an accident to ascribe words to God that were spoken by the writer of Genesis? No, the consecutive 'What therefore God has joined together, don't let man tear apart' leaves no room for interpretation at all: again Matthew is (knowingly and willingly?) bending and breaking scripture, and technically speaking this looks to me to be the most serious form of blasphemy possible: putting words into God's mouth.

Now what would be important enough to risk being stoned to death? What on earth could compel a man to put something in writing that would incriminate him beyond the slightest doubt of a crime of which the only possible punishment was certain death, in whichever horrible form it were to be inflicted?

To mitigate things, it was Mark's fault. One of Mark's many faults, the legacy he left to the Church when making up the first version of their Jesus: at the same time of creating the gospel he created the legacy. It was Mark who started it while claiming the highly illogical:

*Mark 10:6 But from the beginning of the creation, God made them male and female. 7 For this cause a man will leave his father and mother, and will join to his wife, 8 and the two will become one flesh, so that they are no longer two, but one flesh. 9 **What therefore God has joined together, let no man separate**.'*

Emphasis is on the parts that are not derived from Genesis but created by Mark: Mark started the story that God joined man and wife. It nonetheless doesn't make sense, the way he prepares that statement: God creates two separate beings yet man decides to "become one" again by joining with a wife - isn't that going against God in some way?

The error lies with Mark combining the first chapter of Genesis with the second: in Genesis 2 it makes absolutely perfect sense that man will join with his wife because woman was created out of man: they originally were one, so it's perfectly logical that they should become one again. But Mark chose, for whatever reason, to start his case with the creation act of Genesis 1 where man and woman are created separately - by God himself.

Mark started the insinuation and Matthew, oh Matthew, breaks scripture again; changing words when and where he deems fit, resulting in blasphemy against God this time - putting words in God's mouth that definitely are not in the scripture that way, scripture that he even literally quotes, proving that he read the exact words. Words that clearly are spoken and can only, must most certainly, unequivocally and definitely be attributed to the narrator of Genesis alone - not God.

Again, what could possibly be worth that? The very least Matthew can be accused of is thoroughly neglecting to verify his hazy memory before falsely attributing words to God himself, which won't change a thing about the very act itself.

Could it be that this right here was done by Matthew solely in order to address Mark's complete contradictory solution to the theme of

Thomas' 'making the two one' in an utterly desperate effort to fix it? Truth be told, poor Matthew is not to be envied here; Mark literally states that God created man and woman as two, and Mark also literally states that man will be making the two one.

Mark is, highly likely unwillingly and unconsciously, very clearly implying that - or rather, leaving enormous room for interpretation for - man will take that concept of man and woman being made two by God and will change it, man will change what God has done, even undo what God has done, by making the two one.

That must most certainly have lead to at least someone going completely out of his mind

Mark says only once to make the two one and implies that God did the same, although Mark's reasoning for that is contradictory. Matthew also says only once to make the two one and fixes Mark's contradictory reasoning by putting words in God's mouth so it seems that God actually did instruct man to make the two one. Yet Matthew also has Jesus condone divorce under a given circumstance, and Matthew also states that those who make 'themselves eunuchs for the Kingdom of Heaven's sake' are exempt from making the two one.

Then Thomas comes along, reads their gospels and decides to create his own Jesus, and also says to make the two one, in overwhelming ways and frequencies - just to only imply that the Jesus of Matthew didn't allow divorce and celibacy?

By now we've become well acquainted with Mark's but most definitely Matthew's exceptionally loose wielding of prophecy and scripture, and as prone as Matthew is to throw scripture at anything, upon seeing Mark's mistake he should just have abstained and merely repeated Mark, or added the authentic part of Genesis 2. Only a cornered cat would resort to the gravest kind of blasphemy just to repeat a point - unless it's not just a point of course, but the utmost important point: setting in concrete the fix for the devastatingly contradictory reasoning that was created to solve the riddle of making the two one

The children will enter the kingdom

In chapter 18 Matthew gave his final twist to Thomas' theme of children; since the beginning the gospel-writers have struggled to put it to use. Let's consider all verses about children, little ones, and so on, and witness the gradual progression.

Here are the parts of Thomas logia that mention children, with a bit of context where useful:

(4a) Jesus said, "The man old in days will not hesitate to ask a small child seven days old about the place of life, and he will live.
(21a) Mary said to Jesus, "Whom are your disciples like?"
(21b) He said, "They are like children who have settled in a field which is not theirs.
(22a) Jesus saw infants being suckled.
(22b) He said to his disciples, "These infants being suckled are like those who enter the kingdom."
(22c) They said to him, "Shall we then, as children, enter the kingdom?"
(37b) Jesus said, "When you disrobe without being ashamed and take up your garments and place them under your feet like little children and tread on them, then will you see the son of the living one, and you will not be afraid"
(46b) Yet I have said, whichever one of you comes to be a child will be acquainted with the kingdom and will become superior to John."
(50b) If they say to you, 'Is it you?', say, 'We are its children, we are the elect of the living father.'

22b and 46b get the most attention, where children enter or become acquainted with the kingdom; logia 4 and 50 are carefully avoided by the gospel-writers

(Mark
Chapter 9
*35 He sat down, and called the twelve; and he said to them, "**If any***

man wants to be first, he shall be last of all, and servant of all." 36
He took a little child, and set him in the middle of them. Taking him
in his arms, he said to them, 37 "Whoever receives one such little
child in my name, receives me, and whoever receives me, doesn't
receive me, but him who sent me."
(...)
42 Whoever will cause one of these little ones who believe in me to
stumble, it would be better for him if he were thrown into the sea
with a millstone hung around his neck.
Chapter 10
14 But when Jesus saw it, he was moved with indignation, and said
to them, "Allow the little children to come to me! Don't forbid
them, for God's Kingdom belongs to such as these. 15 Most
certainly I tell you, whoever will not receive God's Kingdom like a
little child, he will in no way enter into it."
(...)
24 The disciples were amazed at his words. But Jesus answered
again, "Children, how hard it is for those who trust in riches to enter
into God's Kingdom!)

That is all Mark has to say, and it is very little: six verses - and all of those are in his chapters 9 and 10.

Mark starts off with receiving children in Jesus' name, linking that to the logion of the first being last and vice versa, which is quite mysterious. He follows up with the statement that children believe in him and that they thus should not be caused to sin.

Mark then mentions that the kingdom belongs to children, and advances to 'receiving the kingdom like a little child' in order to enter the kingdom - both without any further explanation. He ends with addressing his disciples with 'children' which perhaps suggests that he believes that they will enter the kingdom.

Mark has very little text on the theme and seems to be struggling with turning it into solid content. Luke has a lot more text and a few tries at it as well:

(Luke

Chapter 7
*31 "**To what then should I compare the people of this generation**? What are they like? 32 **They are like children who sit in the marketplace**, and call to one another, saying, 'We piped to you, and you didn't dance. We mourned, and you didn't weep.'*
Chapter 9
*47 Jesus, perceiving the reasoning of their hearts, **took a little child**, and set him by his side, 48 and said to them, "**Whoever receives this little child in my name receives me**. Whoever receives me receives him who sent me. For whoever is least among you all, this one will be great."*
Chapter 10
*21 In that same hour Jesus rejoiced in the Holy Spirit, and said, "**I thank you, O Father**, Lord of heaven and earth, **that you have** hidden these things from the wise and understanding, and **revealed them to little children**. Yes, Father, for so it was well-pleasing in your sight."*
Chapter 12
*32 **Don't be afraid, little flock**, for it is your Father's good pleasure to give you the Kingdom.*
Chapter 16
*8 "His lord commended the dishonest manager because he had done wisely, for **the children of this world** are, in their own generation, wiser than **the children of the light**.*
Chapter 17
*2 It would be better for him if a millstone were hung around his neck, and he were thrown into the sea, rather than that he should **cause one of these little ones to stumble**.*
Chapter 18
*16 Jesus summoned them, saying, "Allow the little children to come to me, and don't hinder them, for God's Kingdom belongs to such as these. 17 Most certainly, I tell you, whoever doesn't **receive God's Kingdom like a little child**, he will in no way **enter into it**."*
Chapter 20
*34 Jesus said to them, "**The children of this age marry, and are given in marriage**.*

(...)
*36 **For they can't die any more, for they are like the angels, and are children of God, being children of the resurrection**.)*

Luke has a lot more to say, it seems - but his 12 verses comprise relatively the exact same quantity, given his much longer gospel. He does spread his throughout his gospel, however. What are the differences between him and Mark? Luke adds the comparison of 'this generation' to children in chapter 7 and copies Mark's manner of referring to people as children in chapter 16 and 20. He copies Mark in chapter 9, 17 and 18, and slightly elaborates on Mark's address by calling people 'little flock' in chapter 12 next to 'little children' in chapter 10, but doesn't progress any further. He does however use the phrase many more times to refer to adults than to real children, and that is quite the opposite of what Mark does. Luke's best finds are 'children of this world', 'children of the light', and last but definitely not least the poetic 'children of God'. Matthew, naturally, elaborates most on the theme of children:

(Matthew
Chapter 5
*9 Blessed are the peacemakers, for they shall be called **children of God**.*
(...)
*45 **that you may be children of your Father who is in heaven**. For he makes his sun to rise on the evil and the good, and sends rain on the just and the unjust.*
Chapter 8
*12 but **the children of the Kingdom will be thrown out into the outer darkness**. There will be weeping and gnashing of teeth."*
Chapter 10
*42 **Whoever gives one of these little ones just a cup of cold water to drink in the name of a disciple, most certainly I tell you, he will in no way lose his reward**."*
Chapter 11
*16 "But to what shall I compare this generation? It is **like children***

sitting in the marketplaces, who call to their companions
Chapter 13
*38 the field is the world, **the good seeds are the children of the Kingdom**, and the darnel weeds are the children of the evil one.*
Chapter 17
*25 He said, "Yes." When he came into the house, Jesus anticipated him, saying, "What do you think, Simon? From whom do the kings of the earth receive toll or tribute? **From their children, or from strangers**?" 26 Peter said to him, "From strangers." Jesus said to him, "**Therefore the children are exempt**.*
Chapter 18
*2 Jesus called a **little child** to himself, and set him in the middle of them 3 and said, "Most certainly I tell you, **unless you turn and become as little children, you will in no way enter into the Kingdom of Heaven. 4 Whoever therefore humbles himself as this little child** is the greatest in the Kingdom of Heaven. 5 **Whoever receives one such little child in my name receives me, 6 but whoever causes one of these little ones who believe in me to stumble, it would be better for him if a huge millstone were hung around his neck** and that he were sunk in the depths of the sea.*
(...)
*10 See that you **don't despise one of these little ones**, for I tell you that **in heaven their angels always see the face of my Father** who is in heaven.*
(...)
*14 Even so it is not the will of your Father who is in heaven that **one of these little ones should perish**.*
Chapter 19
*14 But Jesus said, "Allow the little children, and don't forbid them to come to me; for the **Kingdom of Heaven belongs to ones like these**."*
Chapter 21
*15 But when the chief priests and the scribes saw the wonderful things that he did, **and the children who were crying in the temple** and saying, "Hosanna to the son of David!" they were indignant, 16 and said to him, "Do you hear what these are saying?" Jesus said to*

them, "Yes. Did you never read, **'Out of the mouth of children and nursing babies, you have perfected praise**?'"
Chapter 23
37 "Jerusalem, Jerusalem, who kills the prophets and stones those who are sent to her! How often **I would have gathered your children** together, even as a hen gathers her chicks under her wings, and you would not!
Chapter 27
9 Then that which was spoken through Jeremiah the prophet was fulfilled, saying, "They took the thirty pieces of silver, the price of him upon whom a price had been set, whom **some of the children of Israel** priced,)

Matthew has 20 verses on the theme, and that is almost double the amount of Luke. He starts off in his sermon on the mount with addressing a part of the audience as children of God, Luke's last find. That is quite an entry, and Matthew quickly follows up with 'children of your Father' and, in chapter 8, 'children of the Kingdom'. The last clearly refer to the Jews and Matthew indicates that they won't receive the kingdom; in chapter 13 Matthew utterly confuses this newly found term when he uses it another time, indicating that those are the good seeds (when explaining the parable of the weeds and the seed) - suddenly the children of the Kingdom no longer are the Jews, but Christians?
Matthew copies Luke in chapter 11 and Mark in chapters 18 and 19 and, as is to be expected, throws scripture at it: he cites Psalms 8:2 in 21:16 (where the real children in his preceding verse are an obvious pretext to do so). Will it surprise anyone that there are differences between his quote and the one in Psalms?

*Matthew 21:16 and said to him, "Do you hear what these are saying?" Jesus said to them, "Yes. Did you never read, **'Out of the mouth of children and nursing babies, you have** perfected **praise**?'"*

*(Psalms 8:1 Yahweh, our Lord, how majestic is your name in all the earth! You have set your glory above the heavens! 2 **From the lips of***

babes and infants you have established **strength**, *because of your adversaries, that you might silence the enemy and the avenger.)*

Praise? Strength - strength to defeat the enemy. Yet another Mattheanism; I have lost count and it is just disheartening to see these being repeated over and over, with Matthew now beyond the slightest doubt willingly, knowingly and carelessly bending and breaking, malevolently mutilating scripture in order to fit his goal - and I don't even consider these to be the words of God

Finally, Matthew extends the domain of children even more by using 'children of Israel'.
Matthew doesn't contribute much more than referring more often to people as children, just like Luke, but his most important work is in chapter 18 where he is the first (and only) gospel-writer to elaborate on how and why exactly children receive or enter the kingdom:

*Matthew 18:3 and said, "Most certainly I tell you, unless you turn and become as little children, you will in no way enter into the Kingdom of Heaven. 4 **Whoever therefore humbles himself as this little child is the greatest in the Kingdom of Heaven***

It is mildly amusing that in 18:3 Matthew starts his explanation with a fairly literal copy of logion 46b; twisting Thomas to 'receiving the kingdom like a child' simply hasn't brought about any progression in handling the children theme - they are obviously stuck there. Addressing and labelling (some) people as children has been the only creation so far, and no light has been shed on exactly how children would receive the kingdom - but then at last here it is. 'Humble yourself as this little child' is Matthew's solution, and indirectly it also addresses the riddle that remained about being greater than John the Baptist. Humility is what people should show, a familiar concept by now: be meek, be lowly, be humble: hear the word and accept it, and believe, without question.
As good a find as it may seem, it raises a lot of questions: little

children aren't known for being humble at all. Children have no shame, no tact, children are outspoken, open, direct. Have you ever heard a mother telling her child to speak up? I wouldn't think so, the default instruction is to "be quiet". Children are inquisitive, curious, and the very opposite of humble: confident, bold, audacious.

The definition of 'child' is very broad, however. Infant, toddler, child, adolescent are the four main words used to describe a child, and those show very different behaviour - but regrettably the gospel-writers don't specify exactly what their definition is. What is their most important pointer to a definition? The children that lead Jesus to his very first statement about them entering the kingdom:

Mark 10:13 **They were bringing to him little children**, *that he should touch them, but the disciples rebuked those who were bringing them. 14 But when Jesus saw it, he was moved with indignation, and said to them, "Allow the **little children** to come to me! Don't forbid them, for God's Kingdom belongs to such as these. 15 Most certainly I tell you, whoever will not receive God's Kingdom like a **little child**, he will in no way enter into it."*

Luke 18:15 **They were also bringing their babies to him**, *that he might touch them. But when the disciples saw it, they rebuked them. 16 Jesus summoned them, saying, "Allow the **little children** to come to me, and don't hinder them, for God's Kingdom belongs to such as these. 17 Most certainly, I tell you, whoever doesn't receive God's Kingdom like a **little child**, he will in no way enter into it."*

Matthew 19:13 **Then little children were brought to him** *that he should lay his hands on them and pray; and the disciples rebuked them. 14 But Jesus said, "Allow the **little children**, and don't forbid them to come to me; for the Kingdom of Heaven belongs to ones like these." 15 He laid his hands on them, and departed from there.*

Little children, babies: those are the ones that evoke Jesus' statement. Age zero to six perhaps, given the unique inclusion of 'babies'? Certainly not age twelve to eighteen, when and where children enter adolescence and rebel, putting most if not everything to the test what they have been taught so far. Probably not age six to twelve, given the fact that the Jewish rites of Bar and Bat Mitzvah take place at age 13 for boys and 12 for girls, and make children fully accountable for their actions: about halfway that age seems to sound good for a maximum age range of 'little children'. Age zero to six then is the most likely age range for the children when the gospel-writers sketch the very first scene where Jesus declares that children will enter the kingdom.

What is the definition of humble? 'Having or showing a modest or low estimate of one's importance' and 'of low social, administrative, or political rank' are the two main ones. Humility requires interaction with others, one can't be humble all by himself. Quiet, introvert, scared even - or outgoing, curious, confident: those are character traits that are self sustaining and can show or be expressed in perfect isolation. Humility? One can only be humble towards others.

Humility is not a dominant character property that resides in people by nature; evolution wouldn't have happened if that were the case. Large organisations and institutions, hierarchy itself wouldn't have come into being, nor would fights and wars be likely to occur as awfully frequently as they do. Humility is something that is taught, usually fairly harshly - and the incessant instructions of the gospel-writers to be(come) meek and humble are perhaps the best example and proof of the fact that humans aren't humble by nature.

Children between age zero and six are the centre of their own universe. They cross the street without looking left and right, want to play with animals even when some of those are vicious dogs or feral cats. They climb stairs, balconies and trees without thinking of the way back. They put all kinds of objects into their mouth to experience what it tastes like, regardless where they find it and what those are. They take toys from other kids just as easily as they leave their own toys littering about, all over the place. They cry and scream out loud when they're hungry, tired or just dissatisfied.

Bring them with you into a restaurant, a cinema, a church or any other place where there are strict rules about sound and silence and you will tire yourself trying to keep them quiet on the right occasions. Children of that age do what they want and when they want it, whether it is convenient to those around them or not.

Why then did Matthew state that you have to become humble like children? The answer to that is obvious - it is one more example of the catastrophe that can arise when the two main goals of the gospel-writers are combined too directly and suddenly; selectively quoting Thomas on the one hand and selling the Church Jesus on the other hand.

Children will enter the kingdom; at least that is something that both Thomas and the gospel-writers seem to agree on, superficially. Humble is how the Church wants its flock, such is beyond a doubt. Hence children have to be humble. How many children between age zero and six are in fact humble? Go to the nearest kindergarten and check for yourself; I reckon you might find one or two out of thirty - if you get lucky

John

The last gospel-writer to check for Thomas is John; the count of Thomas logia used so far stands at 67.

John is without a doubt different from the other three; he narrates a continuous story that is fairly close to prose, very different from the others. A great part of it is Jesus repeatedly equating himself to the Father and vice versa, in lengthy monologues and filled with allegories, claiming that Jesus is the bread, the drink, the shepherd, the door, the resurrection and the life, and so on - in a way it resembles some of Thomas; for instance:

14:23 Jesus answered him, "If a man loves me, he will keep my word. My Father will love him, and we will come to him, and make our home with him. 24 He who doesn't love me doesn't keep my words. The word which you hear isn't mine, but the Father's who sent me.

This starts off one continuous monologue by Jesus and lasts until 16:16: two full chapters. Two verses of interaction with his disciples follow, and then the monologue continues until the start of chapter 18, his betrayal - only to be interrupted by another interaction with his disciples in 16:29-30. Such form does the work of John take; there are 75 verses containing the phrase "I am" in his entire gospel (compare Mark, Luke and Matthew with respectively 10, 22 and 20).

John finishes off what his three predecessors started and builds upon their foundation, and uses very little of Thomas - but it is not the quantity, it is the quality that counts, as we will see. And John will also help in other ways, next to copying logia, to build a more than solid case for the creation of Jesus by the Church

If I were to describe the gospel of John in one word, the word would be "absolute". John is resolute in every statement he has his Jesus make, who is speaking absolute "truths". This Jesus is not of the inclusive kind, he is absolutely exclusive. I will quote two parts and leave it at that, for a flying start into a relatively short discussion of John's gospel:

10:7 Jesus therefore said to them again, "Most certainly, I tell you, I am the sheep's door. 8 All who came before me are thieves and robbers, but the sheep didn't listen to them. 9 I am the door. If anyone enters in by me, he will be saved, and will go in and go out, and will find pasture.

*14:5 **Thomas** said to him, "Lord, we don't know where you are going. How can we know the way?" 6 Jesus said to him, "I am the way, the truth, and the life. No one comes to the Father, except through me. 7 If you had known me, you would have known my Father also. From now on, you know him, and have seen him."*

John starts off with logion 28a:

(28a) Jesus said, "I took my place in the midst of the world, and I appeared to them in flesh.
(28b) I found all of them intoxicated; I found none of them thirsty.
(28c) And my soul became afflicted for the sons of men, because they are blind in their hearts and do not have sight; for empty they came into the world, and empty too they seek to leave the world.
(28d) But for the moment they are intoxicated.
(28e) When they shake off their wine, then they will repent."

1:14 The Word became flesh, and lived among us. We saw his glory, such glory as of the only born Son of the Father, full of grace and truth.

John stands alone in copying this one, as he does with most. Hard to build a solid case here as he leaves out the other four sentences and only has a few words from 28a. Is that because his verse has got nothing to do with the entire logion? Could well be; John won't get any points from any Thomas followers for copying it this way even if he did, but he does get many points for this introduction of Jesus: it is just magnificent

John moves the Temple scene (Jesus chasing out the sellers) all the way up to the front, in chapter 2, and we see logion 71: this is the first logion copy by all four

(71) Jesus said, "I shall destroy this house, and no one will be able to build it [...]."

2:19 Jesus answered them, "Destroy this temple, and in three days I will raise it up."

However, John is the first to use it in an entirely different context: Jesus himself. And that's the reason why he adds the phrase about raising it up again in three days. The gospel-writers seem to have a hard time agreeing on the exact time in between Jesus' death and resurrection: Mark said 'after three days', Luke and Matthew said 'on the third day' and now John uses 'in three days' - which is essentially the same as Luke and Matthew, but still: why does John have to be different?
John likely got the inspiration for this verse from one of the false witnesses of Mark and Matthew:

(Matthew 26:61 and said, "This man said, 'I am able to destroy the temple of God, and to build it in three days.'")

Chapter 3 starts off with a highly interesting take on entering the kingdom as a child:

*3:1 Now there was a man of the Pharisees named Nicodemus, a ruler of the Jews. 2 The same came to him by night, and said to him, "Rabbi, we know that you are a teacher come from God, for no one can do these signs that you do, unless God is with him." 3 Jesus answered him, "Most certainly, I tell you, **unless one is born anew, he can't see God's Kingdom**." 4 Nicodemus said to him, "How can a* *man be born when he is old? Can he enter a second time into his mother's womb, and be born?" 5 Jesus answered, "Most certainly I tell you, **unless one is born of water and spirit, he can't enter into God's Kingdom. 6 That which is born of the flesh is flesh. That which is born of the Spirit is spirit.** 7 Don't marvel that I said to you, 'You must be born anew.' 8 The wind blows where it wants to, and you hear its sound, but don't know where it comes from and where it is going. So is everyone who is born of the Spirit."*

Born anew - as simple as that. Be born anew, and you will enter the kingdom. We have just seen the other three gospel-writers struggle clumsily with this theme, clutching at straws, ending up with little more than nothing, pathetically nothing given all their time and efforts. And then, suddenly, there's John.
John doesn't even use the word 'child', only once before has he done so:

John 1:12 But as many as received him, to them he gave the right to become God's children, to those who believe in his name:

John doesn't have the scenes with children and the quizzes by everyone as the three others do, he just has this - and it is mighty strong, and powerful. And not far from the truth, of course - verse 8 is beautiful! John is very cunningly combining the true meaning of Thomas with baptism; not only that, he links to the baptism of John the Baptist (with water) and fortifies the baptism during which the Holy Spirit is received.
John has nothing on children entering the kingdom, nothing on the kingdom, nothing on entering, nothing on children: he just has this. With a simple brief stroke of the pen, seemingly effortlessly, his very first try on the theme, he wipes everything off the table, all the blunt and crude and rudimentary efforts of his predecessors - gone, obliterated.
This is mesmerising. It is mystical yet clear, it is logical, decisive; it is poetry that most if not all can understand. It is a perfect fit for Thomas' children entering the kingdom, born again - this is a fatal

strike, right through the heart. Is this John, or is this Thomas? I can't tell when just looking at 'born anew'

While we are at it, what does John have to say about making the two one? The word 'two' isn't used by John within the context of the theme of making the two one, but he does say plenty about it:

*10:30 **I and the Father are one.***"

*17:20 Not for these only do I pray, but for those also who will believe in me through their word, 21 **that they may all be one; even as you, Father, are in me, and I in you, that they also may be one in us**; that the world may believe that you sent me. 22 The glory which you have given me, I have given to them; **that they may be one, even as we are one**; 23 **I in them, and you in me, that they may be perfected into one**; that the world may know that you sent me and loved them, even as you loved me.*

Mere words these are, without reasoning, arguments, without explanation - but somehow it just seems that there is none needed. Jesus and God, the Father, are one and the same, and if you believe in Jesus you believe in the Father and become one in them. Not only that, those who believe become one with those who believe - one for all, all for one. This is dizzying, it is beautiful, it is beyond anything and everything, it is fulfilling the most innate need and burning desire of all. It is not only solving Thomas' riddle of becoming one, it is magnificently surpassing it.

Magical and mystical answers to Thomas, every single word right here, and appealing to every human being on a fundamentally core and subconscious level.

The Jesus of John also doesn't lower himself, he doesn't make his hands dirty with Pharisee-bashing, he isn't condescending towards them - granted, that is a luxury he can afford because the other three put in the hard work. He is harsh towards them, but polite. This Jesus knows all, he is completely aware of how every single event will unfold, and why, and he is in absolute control. He knows all the cards in his and everyone else's hands and he plays them all. So, with that, all Thomas themes are tackled. Done and dusted, so to say: it takes three gospel-writers to brood two of the biggest themes on Thomas and hatch nothing, then John comes along and the story suddenly has ended, taking everyone by surprise.

Back to reality, alas: there is another side of John. I can't pass on the occasion, a few verses further is Christianity in a nutshell, by John:

*3:16 **For God so loved the world, that he gave his only born Son**, that **whoever believes in him should not perish, but have eternal life**. 17 For God didn't send his Son into the world to judge the world, but **that the world should be saved through him**. 18 **He who believes in him is not judged**. He who doesn't believe has been judged already, because he has not believed in the name of the only born Son of God. 19 This is the judgment, that the light has come into the world, and men loved the darkness rather than the light; for their works were evil. 20 For everyone who does evil hates the light, and doesn't come to the light, lest his works would be exposed. 21 But he who does the truth comes to the light, that his works may be revealed, that they have been done in God."*

God created the world and (evil) people. He sacrificed his son for them; not to judge them but to save them - but only those who believe in his son can be saved. But if you do believe in Jesus, you won't be judged; you will even do the truth, and receive eternal life. Small print to follow, sign here please.

Luke played the good cop and portrayed the benign Jesus, perhaps to attract the people who believed in the Jesus of Thomas, and Matthew played the bad cop portraying the wrathful god of Judaism, perhaps to attract the Jews to Christianity. John plays both roles and his mindboggling logic became the core message of the Church; in John the Baptist's words:

*3:36 One who believes in the Son has eternal life, but **one who disobeys the Son won't see life, but the wrath of God remains on*** *him."*

As enigmatically enchanting as John's previous words were, John still holds the knife to everyone's throat: "believe or be damned for eternity"; let's not forget he plays on the Church's team

Alright, logion 31 follows, thus cited by all four:

(31) Jesus said, "No prophet is accepted in his own village; no physician heals those who know him."

*4:43 After the two days he went out from there and **went into Galilee**. 44 For Jesus himself testified that a prophet has no honor in his own country.*

John seemingly wants to place Jesus' home country in Galilee and Judea (see 7:41-42) at the same time, perhaps trying to follow Matthew, who in his endeavour to fulfil as many prophecies as possible came up with the convoluted story about Jesus originating from Judea (Bethlehem) and from Egypt (on the run from Herod) and from Galilee (Nazareth). But there's more to that in just one page from now

The logia continue in chapter 7:

**(38a) Jesus said, "Many times have you desired to hear these words which I am saying to you, and you have no one else to hear them from.
(38b) There will be days when you will look for me and will not find me."**

7:33 Then Jesus said, "I will be with you a little while longer, then I go to him who sent me. 34 You will seek me, and won't find me. You can't come where I am."

John shares this logion with Luke and Matthew. As mystic and cryptic as John is, this is as close as it gets to this logion. Throwing in the word 'seek' is brilliant of course - or is John inspired by logion 59?

(59) Jesus said, "Take heed of the living one while you are alive, lest you die and seek to see him and be unable to do so."

Of course it is Jesus who's doing the dying here, but John's verses are possibly a conflation of the two logia.
Logion 13 is barely recognisable, and John seems to use it to address Jesus' origin - it really does seem that he wants Jesus to originate from Judea, not Galilee. I will copy only the first parts of logion 13, that has been presented enough by now:

(13a) Jesus said to his disciples, "Compare me to someone and tell me whom I am like."
(13b) Simon Peter said to him, "You are like a righteous angel."
(13c) Matthew said to him, "You are like a wise philosopher."
(13d) Thomas said to him, "Master, my mouth is wholly incapable of saying whom you are like."

*7:40 Many of the multitude therefore, when they heard these words, said, "This is truly the prophet." 41 Others said, "This is the Christ." But some said, "**What, does the Christ come out of Galilee?** 42 Hasn't the Scripture said that the Christ comes of the offspring of David, and from Bethlehem, the village where David was?" 43 **So a division arose in the multitude because of him**.*
(...)
*52 They answered him, "Are you also from Galilee? Search, and see that **no prophet has arisen out of Galilee**."*

Jesus the Nazarene

After the odd hick-up with logion 31 with Jesus going into Galilee exactly because a prophet has no honour in his hometown, it now seems as if John wants to undo Matthew's Nazarene "prophecy fulfilment". As we know Mark didn't manage to address anything else but the last year or so of Jesus, a void which Luke and Matthew (must) fill. Luke comes up with the enrolment story in Bethlehem (fulfilling Micah 5:2) but Matthew introduces Egypt, highly likely with Hosea 11:1 in mind - which is nothing of a prophecy, just a historical notation ('11:1 "When Israel was a child, then I loved him, and called my son out of Egypt.'). The Nazarene "prophecy" of Matthew is even more farfetched, as it can't be located in the entire Tanakh at all - he probably mixed up his words as he's done before. So, after Luke but especially Matthew, John must have remained with a highly contested Jesus origin: Judea was fine, good Tanakh reference, solid prophecy. Egypt was dodgy, to be found in the Tanakh, but not a prophecy. Galilee prophecy, Nazareth? Unheard of.

John is very happy to avoid the entire issue by taking advantage of his beautiful poetic style: he repeats Mark's brusque entry and lets Jesus just enter the scene (with skipping his baptism by John). But, naturally, he does have to address the issue of Jesus' origin and does it this way. Not very convincing but an open end is an end indeed, and, let's face it, poor John did not have much choice. Mark has Jesus come from Nazareth:

(Mark 1:9 In those days, Jesus came from Nazareth of Galilee, and was baptized by John in the Jordan.)

And Matthew jumps to the occasion, pointing to scripture:

(Matthew 2: 23 and came and lived in a city called Nazareth; **that it might be fulfilled which was spoken through the prophets** *that he*

*will be **called a Nazarene**.)*

Mark fortunately doesn't state that Jesus was actually born in Nazareth, and Luke and Matthew use that to have him born in the proper town, Bethlehem, according to Micah's prophecy. Yet Mark does really make a point of naming Jesus of Nazareth 'Jesus the Nazarene' - four times in his gospel is not a coincident.
And one thing lead to another; Luke has the angel visit the virgin in Nazareth, has Joseph and Mary come from Nazareth and travel to Bethlehem in order to fulfil a real prophecy, but explicitly names Nazareth as Jesus' hometown in his copy of logion 31, and history really is written and fixed at that point: Jesus wasn't born in Nazareth, but he did grow up there. Matthew however, always so prone and proud to fulfil as much prophecies as he possibly can, shoots himself in the foot with his Egypt story but certainly with his careless Nazarene prophecy, and his fellow gospel-writers along with it

Or - is there something else?

There is a story in the Tanakh about Nazirite, not Nazareth. What is remarkable about that story is that it bears strong resemblance to a story that we are quite familiar with. Strong? I think that's an understatement. The story has a few players in it: a man, his wife and an angel - and it starts with telling us that the wife is barren, childless: not a virgin indeed, but the result is the same. Sounds familiar?
The angel visits the wife, and tells her that she is (barren and) childless but that she will conceive a son. Sounds familiar?
The last thing the angel tells her is that he shall begin to save Israel (...). Sounds familiar?
And the penultimate sentence the angel speaks is that the child will be a Nazirite to God from the womb. A Nazirite?
It is the story about (the birth of) Samson, whose name may sound familiar because he killed a thousand Philistines single-handedly:

*(Judges 13:3 Yahweh's angel appeared to the woman, and said to her, "See now, you are barren and childless; but you shall conceive and bear a son. 4 Now therefore please beware and drink no wine nor strong drink, and don't eat any unclean thing; 5 for, **behold, you shall conceive and give birth to a son**. No razor shall come on his head, for the child shall be a Nazirite to God from the womb. He shall begin to save Israel out of the hand of the Philistines.")*

The emphasis in verse 5 is there for a very good reason:

*(Luke 1:31 **Behold, you will conceive** in your womb **and give birth to a son**, and shall name him 'Jesus.')*

*(Matthew 1:23 "**Behold, the virgin shall be with child, and shall give birth to a son**. They shall call his name Immanuel," which is, being interpreted, "God with us.")*

There are no other verses in the entire Tanakh that contain the words 'behold' and 'conceive' in that order, nor 'behold' and 'birth', nor 'conceive' and 'birth' - it is plausible that Luke and Matthew even meant this to be a pointer to Judges 13:5.
A Nazirite was someone who made a vow to separate him- or herself from God, and would forever abstain from consuming anything coming from or made out of the grapevine, would never cut the hair on his or her head, and not go near dead bodies. Nazirite means consecrated, separated - a perfect word for a Messiah.
Nazirite, Nazareth - those two words are identical but not quite the same, now are they? That's correct - a bit of history is in place here. The Tanakh was translated from Hebrew into Greek around 250 BCE; a gigantic operation that took approximately two centuries - two hundred years indeed. Very highly likely it was that Greek Tanakh, called Septuagint, that was used by the gospel-writers. Translating is a difficult job - I have had my fair share and am looking at doing probably an equal share in the years to come. It is tedious, repetitive, draining, and demands utmost concentration

and flexibility, while at the same time requiring intuitivism. Even if you're perfect you'll make errors, especially after being at it for hours. And that is when you are translating printed letters, which are guaranteed to always be exactly equal, identical, legible - imagine if it is all handwritten. To complicate matters, Hebrew doesn't contain vowels so it requires either a mammoth brain and vocabulary in order to be perfect, or a hell of a lot of creativity - possibly both.

The Hebrew words for Nazirite and Nazareth look familiar and, needless to say, share 3 of the 4 characters. When consulting the Septuagint, book of Judges chapter 13, verse 5, this is the representation for the word Nazirite:

ναζιραῖον

'nasiraion' is what that says. The 'n' at the end is there because syntactically it is an object ('called a Nazirite') and in Greek then requires a different end form; if it were a subject that would look like (e.g. he is a Nazirite):

ναζιραῖος

That clearly doesn't equal Nazarene as it is to be found in the Greek New Testament:

ναζαρηνος

Yet (only) in Mark chapter 5 we also see:

ναζωραιος

This is 'Nazarene', the word Mark uses four out of the five times that he refers to Jesus 'from Nazareth':

'Jesus, you Nazarene' (1:24); Jesus the Nazarene (10:47); 'with the Nazarene, Jesus' (14:67); Jesus, the Nazarene (16:6).

Does the Septuagint version of 'Nazirite' closely resemble the new Greek version of 'Nazarene'? Very closely, yes - only one letter difference there, but it is still a stretch. Is it possible that it was translated wrongly and that it read "Nazareth" to Mark? That is equally as possible as it is impossible: either-or, fifty-fifty, yes or no. However, it is evident that to Mark, Jesus was Jesus the Nazarene, not Jesus from Nazareth. Luke uses Nazareth seven times, Nazarene only one time - yet it was Luke who introduced the virgin conception by intervention from God - exactly identical to that of

Samson, the Nazirite from birth. Matthew closes the book on it all by having three occurrences of Nazareth, and only one of Nazarene:

*(Matthew 2:23 and came and lived in a city called Nazareth; **that it might be fulfilled** which was **spoken through the prophets** that he will be **called a Nazarene**.)*

Matthew's prophecies again - well at least it's solved now, isn't it? There is no prophecy about a Nazarene, yet there was something close to a prediction about someone about to be born and that involved the word Nazirite: an angel appeared to a childless woman and told her she was pregnant of a son - that is not anything like a prophecy of course, and it was already fulfilled. Yet knowing Matthew, the words about the fulfilled birth of Samson are more than enough to loudly and proudly claim a true prophecy about Jesus.
Is it plausible that Matthew used Samson's birth to justify the word 'Nazarene'? By now, that is not just plausible, likely, or even highly likely; that just is pretty much guaranteed, given the minute difference between the two words. We know Matthew by now, and it is absolutely certain that he wouldn't have hesitated a split second in this case

The question is not 'who got it wrong' - the question is what did Mark have in mind when he called Jesus "the Nazarene". Could he have misread the word, or was he just familiar with the concept of a Nazirite, when a man or woman would make a special vow, the vow of a Nazirite, to separate himself or herself to Yahweh? "Consecrated", "separated to God" is what Nazirite means - a really tempting description to attribute to Jesus.
If anything, it remains unclear why Mark stated that Jesus came from Nazareth, but he certainly didn't state that he was born there. Samson's birth undeniably inspired Luke's birth narrative as well as Matthew's prophecy and we will never know which of the two was first, but the prophecy dug their grave deeper and deeper and raised questions that remain unanswered until today.

It is clear that John rejects the baptism of Jesus; it is also clear that he has the Jews reject a prophet being from Galilee. With John having Jesus go to Galilee while stating that a prophet isn't honoured in his own country, John sows even more doubt about his true origin without actually denying that Jesus was from Nazareth - he masterfully serves both masters by doing so, exactly as he did with the baptism of Jesus

One logion, a minor deviation, many hours of research and over three pages of text on it. I do try hard to not get distracted but it certainly isn't always easy. Does this all add weight to the case that Thomas 31 lead to John's 4:44? Not a whole lot indeed, but it does show that although historical facts can't be undone, they certainly can be unbalanced.
Back to work again, a few more logia of John and then we will get to Judas and Thomas: John has a few surprises for us there as well

*8:12 Again, therefore, Jesus spoke to them, saying, "**I am the light of the world**. He who follows me will not walk in the darkness, but will have the light of life."*

I thought I'd just drop that in there, to abruptly get back on track again. I certainly didn't expect parts of logion 77 to be copied by the gospel-writers, but John dares to do so:

(77a) Jesus said, "It is I who am the light which is above them all.
(77b) It is I who am the all.
(77c) From me did the all come forth, and unto me did the all extend.
(77d) Split a piece of wood, and I am there.
(77e) Lift up the stone, and you will find me there."

I - the Self. It is above all other selves, it drives all perceptions and it is the centre of its own universe. And it is All - everything comes forth from it, and it is inside everything.
Naturally, Jesus is talking not only about himself, but about us all:

we view everything from our own perception, we each view our own world through our own eyes and mind. Whatever it is that we look at, we perceive it through our own lens: ask ten people to describe an object with two words, and no description will be the same.

That is what Thomas means, and it is not what John intends to say here, yet it is highly unlikely that many would disagree with his interpretation. John is Thomas in disguise; he takes Jesus and makes him divine. Given the difference in time Thomas could never have written John, but if he had been challenged to do so, just to see if he could play the devil's advocate, I think his content wouldn't have been far off from what we read in John

Credit is due to Matthew for using '(you are) the light of the world' first, but the application by John is magnificent. I am not counting it, solely because Matthew invented it; John coming up with this mostly by his own would have been very plausible otherwise.
Still, it befits John to use it and it is a worthy beginning of his chapter 8 that he so magnificently concludes with:

8:58 Jesus said to them, "Most certainly, I tell you, before Abraham came into existence, I AM."

I AM. Is John really getting Thomas? Where Luke seems to have to address Thomas believers and Matthew the traditional Jews, John goes an entirely new way and combines both in an unprecedented manner, mystifying the deeper meaning of Thomas. Bluntly counting only the sentences containing the words 'fulfil', 'prophe' and 'written' in the four gospels (and verifying that those indeed all do contain only direct references to fulfilment of scripture), Mark only has 13 verses, Luke has 21, Matthew a grand 28. John? A mere 17.
John doesn't need scripture, he is simply writing his own.
Chapter 8 is full of Thomas, logion 59 is also new:

(59) Jesus said, "Take heed of the living one while you are alive,

lest you die and seek to see him and be unable to do so."

*8:21 Jesus said therefore again to them, "I am going away, **and you will seek me**, and **you will die** in your sins. **Where I go, you can't come.***"

Where Thomas means oneself with the living one and stresses to cherish a momentary "enlightenment", John couldn't have made a more literal copy given his own context.
Logion 43 is new, and Thomas' answer is a typical one. John makes a slip of the tongue here, contradicting his earlier statement in 3:17: 'For God didn't send his Son into the world to judge the world, but that the world should be saved through him.'

(43a) His disciples said to him, "Who are you, that you should say these things to us?"
(43b) [Jesus said to them] "You do not realize who I am from what I say to you, but you have become like the Jews, for they (either) love the tree and hate its fruit (or) love the fruit and hate the tree."

*8:25 They said therefore to him, "**Who are you**?" Jesus said to them, "Just what I have been saying to you from the beginning. 26 I have many things to speak **and to judge** concerning you. However he who sent me is true; and the things which I heard from him, these I say to the world." 27 **They didn't understand** that he spoke to them about the Father.*

Verse 51 uses logion 1, which is now mentioned by all four gospel-writers.

*8:51 Most certainly, I tell you, if a person keeps my word, **he will never see death**."*

Logion 108 is in chapter 10, yet quite different and fairly literally used, quite in line with the bubbling spring used by Thomas in logion 13:

(108a) Jesus said, "He who will drink from my mouth will become like me.
(108b) I myself shall become he, and the things that are hidden will be revealed to him."

*10:37 Now on the last and greatest day of the feast, Jesus stood and cried out, "**If anyone is thirsty, let him come to me and drink**! 38 He who believes in me, as the Scripture has said, **from within him will flow rivers of living water**."*

Chapter 11 has logion 111b, and its theme is similar to the previous logion:

(111a) Jesus said, "The heavens and the earth will be rolled up in your presence.
(111b) And the one who lives from the living one will not see death."
(111c) Does not Jesus say, "Whoever finds himself is superior to the world?"

*11:23 Jesus said to her, "Your brother will rise again." 24 Martha said to him, "I know that he will rise again in the resurrection at the last day." 25 Jesus said to her, "I am the resurrection and the life. **He who believes in me will still live, even if he dies**. 26 **Whoever lives and believes in me will never die**. Do you believe this?"*

The last sentence of verse 26 is an echo of 111c. Another mystic logion, and John again is the only one to copy it. It certainly isn't an obvious copy, and I find myself reluctantly reusing my previous argument of it being as close a copy as it could possibly have been. Unexpectedly, John has a big surprise: all of a sudden, a prime scene for Caiaphas:

11:47 The chief priests therefore and the Pharisees gathered a *council, and said, "What are we doing? For this man does many signs. 48 If we leave him alone like this, everyone will believe in him, and the Romans will come and take away both our place and our nation." 49 **But a certain one of them, Caiaphas**, being high priest that year, said to them, "You know nothing at all, 50 nor do you consider that it **is advantageous for us that one man should die for the people**, and that the whole nation not perish." 51 Now he didn't say this of himself, but **being high priest that year, he prophesied that Jesus would die for the nation**, 52 and not for the nation only, but that he **might also gather together into one the children of God** who are scattered abroad. 53 So from that day forward they took counsel that they might put him to death.*

Five mentions of Caiaphas in John, against zero, one and two in respectively Mark, Luke and Matthew. Caiaphas as an oracle of God - that is quite more than a surprise. Was Caiaphas a sponsor of this text? This is a case of 'shoot first then ask' with Caiaphas acting out a prophecy before it is revealed. It is almost as if the author had already written down verse 50 and then realised he should have come up with an excuse first. Not opting for the removal or change of verse 50 he just added verse 51 and 52?

This is totally unexpected, to include Caiaphas of all people into the grand scheme of God; it is almost turning the Jews into instruments of God as well, with Caiaphas apparently pushing them to kill Jesus. Caiaphas suddenly gets his own stage here, and a very major act and script. Is this an attempt to reconcile with the Jews, excusing them for what they allegedly have done? Is there a need to do so, at the time of this writing? Was there something contemporary going on that made John do this? Perhaps Christians coming from the Gentiles (basically everyone but the Jews, thus also including the Thomas believers who aren't Jewish) numbering less than expected or desired, or is this merely opening a door? It undeniably must have purpose, this is everything but an insignificant turn.

That is not all, Caiaphas has another very significant part in John's gospel; that of a stage prop:

*18:24 **Annas sent him bound to Caiaphas, the high priest**. 25 Now Simon Peter was standing and warming himself. They said therefore to him, "You aren't also one of his disciples, are you?" He denied it and said, "I am not." 26 One of the servants of the high priest, being a relative of him whose ear Peter had cut off, said, "Didn't I see you in the garden with him?" 27 Peter therefore denied it again, and immediately the rooster crowed. 28 **They led Jesus therefore from Caiaphas into the Praetorium**. It was early, and they themselves didn't enter into the Praetorium, that they might not be defiled, but might eat the Passover.*

Once more I am puzzled, baffled even - Caiaphas and Jesus face each other and nothing happens. Jesus is sent to Caiaphas, and immediately the spotlights turn to Peter who denies Jesus a second and third time, the rooster crows and immediately the spotlights turn to Jesus being led away from Caiaphas. What?! That is impossible: the high priest has been in this scene since Mark, using false witnesses to try and get him to confess, and then tearing Jesus' clothes and striking and insulting him (all in order to fulfil prophecies, most from Isaiah chapter 53) - only Luke has a different scene without false witnesses, but with everything else in it. In Matthew the high priest received a name, and it was Caiaphas - that name remains in John but any and all action vanishes in thin air: simply because Annas is his proxy; Caiaphas gets completely off the hook.
It is a marvel of marvels:

*18:12 So the detachment, the commanding officer, and the officers of the Jews seized Jesus and bound him, 13 and **led him to Annas first, for he was father-in-law to Caiaphas, who was high priest that year**. 14 Now it was Caiaphas who advised the Jews that it was expedient that one man should perish for the people.*

The usual scene unfolds after this, although there is no insulting, striking, spitting or slapping; just one little slap and that is it. Verse 18:28 is the last time that Caiaphas is mentioned - although he does seem to address Jesus while he is not on the stage:

18:19 The high priest therefore asked Jesus about his disciples and about his teaching.

Jesus has been led to Annas just before that, in 18:13, and is led to Caiaphas in 18:24 - it is all a riddle and (only) one thing is clear: the role of the high priest is reduced to nothing.

It is a riddle of riddles - why on earth is John making this great scene around Caiaphas? Caiaphas is said to have lived from 14 BCE till 46 CE, and John is writing at least half a century later (there's more on dating the gospels in the chapter on Judas and Thomas). Is this John's attempt to fixate his gospel in the first half of the first century CE, by handing out new information about and from Caiaphas? I have no idea at all, but the sudden attention for and role of Caiaphas is notable.

Back to the last few logia; John is the fourth to use logion 55:

(55a) Jesus said, "Whoever does not hate his father and his mother cannot become a disciple to me.
(55b) And whoever does not hate his brothers and sisters and take up his cross in my way will not be worthy of me."

*12:25 He who loves his life will lose it. **He who hates his life in this world will keep it to eternal life**. 26 **If anyone serves me, let him follow me**. Where I am, there my servant will also be. **If anyone serves me, the Father will honor him**.*

'Father and mother' are turned into 'life in this world', and 'becoming a disciple' equated to 'keeping eternal life'. Logion 55b is split across the first and third sentence of verse 26 with 'hating brothers and sisters' substituted for 'serving Jesus', and being worthy of Jesus swapped for 'Father will honor'. Granted, it's out of the box - yet not so out of the box as the next:

(24a) His disciples said to him, "Show us the place where you are,

since it is necessary for us to seek it."
(24b) He said to them, "Whoever has ears, let him hear.
(24c) There is light within a man of light, and he lights up the whole world.
(24d) If he does not shine, he is darkness."
(59) Jesus said, "Take heed of the living one while you are alive, lest you die and seek to see him and be unable to do so."
(50a) Jesus said, "If they say to you, 'Where did you come from?', say to them, 'We came from the light, the place where the light came into being on its own accord and established itself and became manifest through their image.'
(50b) If they say to you, 'Is it you?', say, 'We are its children, we are the elect of the living father.'
(50c) If they ask you, 'What is the sign of your father in you?', say to them, 'It is movement and repose.'"

*12:34 The multitude answered him, "We have heard out of the law that the Christ remains forever. How do you say, 'The Son of Man must be lifted up?' Who is this Son of Man?" 35 Jesus therefore said to them, "**Yet a little while the light is with you.** Walk **while you have the light, that darkness doesn't overtake you**. He who walks in the darkness doesn't know where he is going. 36 While you have the light, believe in the light, **that you may become children of light**." Jesus said these things, and he departed and hid himself from them.*

Verse 34 is inspired by either 24a or 50a or both, questioning the presence and future of Jesus' whereabouts. Verse 35 is a conflation of 24c, 24d and 59, and verse 36 is driven by 50b.
Farfetched? Possibly, but it is a beautiful play on Thomas' themes. John's gospel is full of 'light' and 'dark': Mark has 4 and 3 verses with those words, Luke 15 and 8, Matthew 15 and 10, John has 25 and 9. I won't count anything for these, it is just too difficult to claim anything; verse 12:35 is a variation on 8:12, (only) such is for sure

Remarkably, in John Jesus explicitly triggers the possession of Judas:

13:26 ***Jesus therefore answered, "It is he to whom I will give this*** ***piece of bread*** *when I have dipped it." So when he had dipped the piece of bread, he gave it to Judas, the son of Simon Iscariot. 27* ***After the piece of bread, then Satan entered into him****. Then Jesus said to him, "What you do, do quickly."*

I'll comment on that in the next chapter, among others. Chapter 15 suggests that we have a variation on Matthew's use of logion 40:

(40) Jesus said, "A grapevine has been planted outside of the father, but being unsound, it will be pulled up by its roots and destroyed."

15:1 "I am the true vine, and my Father is the farmer.

There are 61 verses in the Tanakh with the word vine in it, which is hardly surprising given the count of the word vineyard. It is not unthinkable that John would compare Jesus to a vine, and it is very feasible that he would use the Father in the same verse when doing so.
The remainder of John is logia-free although he mixes a lot of Thomas in a wonderfully poetic way over and over again - although it is evident that by now John has as much right to Thomasine context as Thomas does.
John ends with a last remark:

21: 24 ***This is the disciple who testifies about these things, and*** ***wrote these things. We know that his witness is true****. 25 There are also many other things which Jesus did, which if they would all be written, I suppose that even the world itself wouldn't have room for the books that would be written.*

In an effort to appear as a reliable witness, the writer testifies about himself from the "we perspective", stating that his testimony is true. His ego has been playing up throughout the gospel, referring to himself as Jesus' beloved disciple, but this is highly amusing. Five times he refers to himself as the disciple whom Jesus loved, and in all honesty I think that he has every right to be loved by the Church Jesus: without John, I really wonder what would have become of Christianity.

What is the final logia score? It was 67 at the start of John, I've counted 3 new ones: 77, 59 and 111 - the total amount of logia copied from Thomas by the gospel-writers is 70, out of the theoretical maximum of 114: 61%.

With all gospel-writers discussed, it is time for one last chapter: it is on Judas, and Thomas

Judas and Thomas

The character of Judas perhaps is the most dynamic one of all the gospels, and undergoes a truly grand transformation. I'll start with the spoiler and state that Judas starts betraying Jesus with a kiss for apparently no reason, then becomes possessed by Satan before doing so and demands money for his deed, then the amount of money gets quantified and Judas shows remorse - the utmost form of remorse, yet ends up with being deliberately possessed by Satan as a result of a direct action of Jesus and betraying Jesus without a kiss and without being financially rewarded for it and also without showing remorse.

That does sound confusing, doesn't it? Four phrases separated by commas in that too long sentence, four gospel-writers: it is clear how this is going to unfold

Mark 3:16 Simon (to whom he gave the name Peter); 17 James the son of Zebedee; and John, the brother of James, (whom he called Boanerges, which means, Sons of Thunder); 18 Andrew; Philip; Bartholomew; Matthew; Thomas; James, the son of Alphaeus; Thaddaeus; Simon the Zealot; 19 and Judas Iscariot, who also betrayed him. Then he came into a house.

Mark names the disciples for the very first time and starts off with Simon, elaborating on his other name Peter and reserving one entire sentence and verse for him; then the next 10 disciples including Thomas are named in two verses and Judas has his own sentence and verse just like Simon. Why does Judas betray Jesus?

*Mark 14:10 Judas Iscariot, who was one of the twelve, went away to the chief priests, that he might deliver him to them. 11 They, when they heard it, were glad, and **promised to give him money**. He sought how he might conveniently deliver him.*

Money - but that's not his motive, certainly not a quantifiable one in Mark's case. Mark leaves a lot of loose ends, probably most if not all unintentional, and this may be one of them: the chief priests promise Judas money in return, but Judas doesn't ask for it; he betrays Jesus out of the blue. He doesn't think of money when going to the priests, he doesn't bring it up before talking to them, and the money is entirely the initiative of the priests. There is no enmity between Jesus and Judas, no scenes, no nothing - there certainly isn't the motive of money for betraying him.

In Luke there is a major shift in Judas:

*Luke 22:3 Satan entered into **Judas, who was also called Iscariot, who was counted with the twelve**. 4 He went away, and talked with the chief priests and captains about how he might deliver him to them. 5 **They were glad, and agreed to give him money**. 6 **He consented**, and sought an opportunity to deliver him to them in the absence of the multitude.*

Where Mark leaves it unclear whether the money that Judas received was his own initiative met by the priests, in Luke it appears to be a mutual agreement, a bargain, so Judas must have brought it up or at least accepted the offer, it seems - but it is still unclear if followed to the letter. Did they agree among themselves to give Judas money without him asking for it? That is very well possible. Does 'they' refer to the collection of chief priests including Judas? That can only mean that they all were glad, including Judas.

Luke neither provides Judas with a motive nor does he quantify the amount, although he does make it explicit that Judas accepts the money: Judas 'consented'. He does however provide him with an excuse: Judas is possessed by Satan. Mark leaving out that Judas was possessed? Ah, just a finical detail - Matthew leaves it all out as well, undoubtedly to support Mark's unfortunate omission I suppose: if all three had mentioned it then that would have been highly conspicuous, providing reasonable suspicion that the possession of Judas was made up afterwards. This way the damage is somewhat controlled, although it naturally is very extraordinary that someone within the inner circle of Jesus was possessed without anyone doing or saying anything about it - as well as Mark omitting that minor detail.

How would this add to the narrative, the possession by Satan of Judas? One of its effects is clear; it holds Judas a lot less accountable for his actions. Only three times Judas is mentioned in Luke: his introduction '[...]Judas Iscariot, who also became a traitor.', these verses right here, and the two consecutive verses of his betrayal: every single action of and by Judas in the gospel of Luke is (highly likely wholly) inspired by Satan, done under the influence of Satan. What's more, Judas doesn't actually kiss Jesus:

*Luke 22:47 While he was still speaking, a crowd appeared. He who was called Judas, one of the twelve, was leading them. **He came near to Jesus to kiss him**. 48 But Jesus said to him, "Judas, do you betray the Son of Man with a kiss?"*

That little play ends right there, no further action from Judas: there is no actual kiss; it is almost as if the kiss got swapped for the possession by Satan. In Luke, Judas doesn't kiss Jesus - period. It might seem that he does, you might think that he does, but that's just the programming in your head talking to you: Judas doesn't kiss Jesus in Luke.

Odd as it may seem, the significance and meaning of this will become clear in a bit, in this very chapter

It is in Matthew that Judas' primary motive, money, gets quantified - and the fresh Satanic possession is dropped:

*Matthew 26:14 Then one of the twelve, who was called Judas Iscariot, went to the chief priests 15 and said, "**What are you willing to give me if I deliver him to you**?" So they weighed out for him thirty pieces of silver. 16 From that time he sought opportunity to betray him.*

There we have it, a clear financial motive - Judas not only brings it up, he starts with it: no more room for interpretation, it is clear beyond a doubt that Judas' motive was money. Whether that was his only motive remains unclear but it clearly is his primary one. The thirty silver pieces serve scripture fulfilment.

Judas is no longer possessed by Satan, but plays his predestined role: Jesus seems content with Judas betraying him, even calling him friend when the scene takes place:

*Matthew 26:49 Immediately he came to Jesus, and said, "Greetings, Rabbi!" and kissed him. 50 **Jesus said to him, "Friend**, why are you here?" **Then they came and laid hands on Jesus, and took him**.*

'Friend': is that a Matthean attempt to reinforce the pointer to Psalms 41:9? That will be discussed in only a few pages from now. Time to address the potter and the thirty silver pieces, the comments will be brief:

*Matthew 27:3 **Then Judas**, who betrayed him, when he saw that Jesus was condemned, felt remorse, and **brought back the thirty pieces of silver** to the chief priests and elders, 4 saying, "**I have sinned in that I betrayed innocent blood**." But they said, "What is that to us? You see to it." 5 He threw down the pieces of silver in the sanctuary and departed. **Then he went away and hanged himself**. 6 The chief priests took the pieces of silver and said, "It's not lawful to put them into the treasury, since it is the price of blood." 7 **They took counsel, and bought the potter's field with them to bury strangers in**. 8 Therefore **that field has been called "The Field of Blood" to this day**. 9 Then that which was spoken through **Jeremiah the prophet was fulfilled, saying, "They took the thirty pieces of silver, the price of him upon whom a price had been set, whom some of the children of Israel priced, 10 and they gave them for the potter's field, as the Lord commanded me**."*

At the end Judas gets remorseful and returns the money to the priests, and hangs himself. The priests take the money and buy "a potter's field to bury strangers in" and according to Matthew that fulfils Jeremiah:

*(Jeremiah 19:1 Thus said Yahweh, "Go, and **buy a potter's earthen container**, and take some of the elders of the people, and of the elders of the priests;*
(...)
*6 Therefore, behold, the days come," says Yahweh, "**that this place will no more be called 'Topheth'**, nor 'The Valley of the son of Hinnom', but '**The valley of Slaughter**'.*
(...)
*10 "Then you shall break the container in the sight of the men who go with you, 11 and shall tell them, 'Yahweh of Armies says: "Even so I **will break this people and this city, as one breaks a potter's vessel**, that can't be made whole again. **They will bury in Topheth, until there is no place to bury**. 12 This is what I will do to this place," says Yahweh, "and to its inhabitants, even making this city as Topheth.)*

A translation mishap, I suppose. There is a potter's container here, which gets broken in front of the audience: 'kings of Judah, and inhabitants of Jerusalem' (Jeremiah 19:3). God will break them like the potter's vessel, and they will be buried in the freshly renamed 'valley of Slaughter'. Where does Matthew's quote point to?

(Zechariah 11:13 Yahweh said to me, "Throw it to the potter, the handsome price that I was valued at by them!" I took the thirty pieces of silver, and threw them to the potter, in Yahweh's house.)

Matthew confuses prophecy again. His verse 9 points to Zechariah, verses 7 and 8 point to Jeremiah. Whatever, it is beyond a reasonable doubt that Matthew invented the thirty silver pieces to fulfil prophecy, just as he made up the entire scene around it

This Judas, clearly out for money, called friend by Jesus while he betrays him, showing remorse and hanging himself is very, very different from the Judas of Mark, and even from the Judas of Luke. The kiss is back: it almost does seem like the possession and the kiss are mutually incompatible.

That is not all: John introduces enmity between Jesus and Judas. Since Mark, Mary has anointed Jesus' head (save for Luke)

Mark 14:4 4 But there were some who were indignant among themselves, saying, "Why has this ointment been wasted?

(In Luke it's just a woman who anoints his feet, and the disciples are even absent)

Matthew 26:8 But when his disciples saw this, they were indignant, saying, "Why this waste?

John 12:3 Therefore Mary took a pound of ointment of pure nard, very precious, and anointed Jesus' feet and wiped his feet with her hair. The house was filled with the fragrance of the ointment. 4 **Then Judas Iscariot, Simon's son, one of his disciples, who would betray him, said, 5 "Why wasn't this ointment sold for three hundred denarii, and given to the poor***?" 6 Now he said this, not because he cared for the poor, but because he was a thief, and having the money box, used to steal what was put into it. 7* **But Jesus said, "Leave her alone***. She has kept this for the day of my burial. 8 For you always have the poor with you, but you don't always have me."*

John follows Luke and has Mary anoint the feet, not the head. And suddenly lets Judas play the role of indignant all by himself - not the disciples as Mark and Matthew state. Judas gets told off by Jesus and is portrayed as a thief - a deepening of Judas' character for sure. How wonderful it all is, having the freedom to rewrite history whenever you feel like it!
But John has much more in mind. Jesus has known - and disclosed - since Mark that he'd be betrayed by a friend, but this time he doesn't use the word 'betray':

John 6:70 Jesus answered them, "Didn't I choose you, the twelve, **and one of you is a devil***?" 71 Now he spoke of Judas, the son of*

Simon Iscariot, for it was he who would betray him, being one of the twelve.

John 13:2 During supper, the devil having already put into the heart of Judas Iscariot, Simon's son, to betray him,

John 13:26 Jesus therefore answered, "It is he to whom I will give this piece of bread when I have dipped it." So when he had dipped the piece of bread, he gave it to Judas, the son of Simon Iscariot. 27 After the piece of bread, then Satan entered into him. Then Jesus said to him, "What you do, do quickly."

Jesus knows that Judas is going to be possessed - the word 'devil' is no accident. To make unmistakably clear that Jesus only triggers the possession in stead of causing it, John mentions that the devil is already in the heart of Judas, before Jesus gives him the bread. Next is the scene where Jesus is taken

John 18:3 Judas then, having taken a detachment of soldiers and officers from the chief priests and the Pharisees, came there with lanterns, torches, and weapons. 4 Jesus therefore, knowing all the things that were happening to him, went out, and said to them, "Who are you looking for?" 5 They answered him, "Jesus of Nazareth." Jesus said to them, "I am he." Judas also, who betrayed him, was standing with them. 6 When therefore he said to them, "I am he," they went backward, and fell to the ground. 7 Again therefore he asked them, "Who are you looking for?" They said, "Jesus of Nazareth." 8 Jesus answered, "I told you that I am he. If therefore you seek me, let these go their way," 9 that the word might be fulfilled which he spoke, "Of those whom you have given me, I have lost none."

Judas doesn't even kiss Jesus anymore! He is just a poor puppet of Satan - or is it God? Judas doesn't go to the priests to bargain nor does he receive any money, and as such is deprived of the stage to perform his act of remorse on.

Jesus directly triggers the possession of Judas by giving him the bread, but doesn't cause it: Judas already had Satan in his heart, likely because he's a bad person - evidence of which was provided by John adding the detail that he is a thief.

From motiveless and kissing traitor Judas becomes possessed and ceases the kissing, then Matthew swaps the possession for the kiss, suddenly has him regret his act and utterly remorsefully hang himself, after which John again ceases the kissing and reintroduces the possession, doesn't have Judas regret anything, removes the motive of money and Judas lives happily ever after. Quite possibly Judas even has witnessed Jesus' return: Luke and Matthew (and Mark in his long ending added later) are careful to explicitly mention 'eleven' there, John doesn't seem to bother about the numbers of disciples. Three times Jesus shows himself after the crucifixion, and every time Judas is neither explicitly present nor explicitly absent

How very, very awkward indeed. Why? It is evident that Judas betraying Jesus doesn't come from Thomas and it isn't prophecy but scripture from Psalms, so I don't see a reason for this exceptional sandbox effect. The Judas of John is just bland, especially the final betrayal scene (and that is the last we see of Judas) appears a remote action, distant, passive - completely impersonal. Why take it to that extreme? The only thing that remains of Judas in John is the act of betraying and the being possessed - nothing else.

I have no explanation for it, but the transformation of the character, motive and actions is so great that it deserves equal attention

Thomas is the other one who undergoes great change - albeit only in one gospel:

John 11:16 Thomas therefore, who is called Didymus, said to his fellow disciples, "Let's go also, that we may die with him."

Thomas gets mentioned more than once in a single gospel for the first time: Mark, Luke and Matthew use his name only once, in order to introduce him next to the other disciples. John has his name in seven verses and even goes much further than that, Thomas gets singled out and identified: the Twin. The first and only time that the four gospel-writers refer to him as anything other than just 'Thomas', it is a clear reference to "our" Thomas, which I will explain shortly.

John's attitude toward Thomas isn't a neutral one, in fact it's quite biased:

John 14:5 Thomas said to him, "Lord, we don't know where you are going. How can we know the way?"

Thomas is portrayed as not the brightest tool in the shed there, although Philip and Judas (the other one) will follow up with similar questions. The next scene is one that we all know because that has been rubbed in hard, very hard, in order to exemplify the core explanation of the Church for everything; 'take it all on faith and faith alone':

*John 20:24 But **Thomas, one of the twelve, called Didymus, wasn't with them when Jesus came**. 25 The other disciples therefore said to him, "We have seen the Lord!" But he said to them, "**Unless I see in his hands the print of the nails, put my finger into the print of the nails, and put my hand into his side, I will not believe**." 26 After eight days again his disciples were inside and Thomas was with them. Jesus came, the doors being locked, and stood in the middle, and said, "Peace be to you." 27 **Then he said to Thomas, "Reach here your finger, and see my hands. Reach here your hand, and put it into my side. Don't be unbelieving, but believing**." 28 **Thomas answered him, "My Lord and my God**!" 29 Jesus said to him, "**Because you have seen me, you have believed. Blessed are those who have not seen, and have believed**."*

Doubting Thomas - we have been taught to pity him, despise him perhaps, haven't we? This is a second-rank disciple at the very best, and John puts him down once more, with feeling:

John 21:1 After these things, Jesus revealed himself again to the disciples at the sea of Tiberias. He revealed himself this way. 2 Simon Peter, Thomas called Didymus, Nathanael of Cana in Galilee, and the sons of Zebedee, and two others of his disciples were together
(...)
15 So when they had eaten their breakfast, Jesus said to Simon Peter, "Simon, son of Jonah, do you love me more than these?" He said to him, "Yes, Lord; you know that I have affection for you." He said to him, "Feed my lambs." 16 He said to him again a second time, "Simon, son of Jonah, do you love me?" He said to him, "Yes, Lord; you know that I have affection for you." He said to him, "Tend my sheep." 17 He said to him the third time, "Simon, son of Jonah, do you have affection for me?" Peter was grieved because he asked him the third time, "Do you have affection for me?" He said to him, "Lord, you know everything. You know that I have affection for you." Jesus said to him, "Feed my sheep.

Peter gets the promotion. If you want to make something clear, repeat it. If you want it to be remembered forever, repeat it twice. Peter's rooster will never be forgotten, and this is meant to be equally memorable. Thomas is present on this occasion and gets completely ignored, while having to play the role of the silent witness, a perfect stage prop - he was there so Jesus could in theory have picked him, but naturally didn't: Peter is the winner, Thomas is the loser, case closed - that simple is how it should all be viewed. Before the beginning of John, Thomas was just a name and a disciple, as anonymous as most, getting only that one obligatory mention per gospel when Jesus appoints his disciples. At the end of John, Thomas is quite a character: his full name is Thomas also called Didymos and he's ignorant, distrusting, lacking faith - especially for a disciple - and he sits somewhere at the bottom of the food chain.
Is Thomas better off than Judas is in Mark? Much better, that just

was a loathsome person, a backstabbing traitor, a truly disgusting person.

Is Thomas better off than Judas is in Luke? That's a tough one; with the kiss gone in Luke there's only the Satanic possession and the money - but Judas does consent to the money, whether he brought it up by himself or not, even though he is possessed at that moment. The Judas of Luke certainly isn't better off than Thomas, although he couldn't have helped being possessed and did nothing wrong while he was not possessed.

Is Thomas better off than Judas in Matthew? No, that Judas is a villain. Remorse? Shame and guilt, nothing else - or perhaps it was sincere. Getting someone killed for 30 silver pieces, about a month worth in wage? Shameless - and he wasn't even possessed! The Judas of Mark is worse because he showed no remorse, but this one is next. Thomas is certainly better off than the Judas of Matthew.

Is Thomas better off than the Judas in John? Now that is a tough one for sure. No money, no kiss, but he is a thief, and John deliberately discloses that little fact just one chapter before his possession kicks in. Compared to Luke, does being a thief outweigh consenting to money for betraying someone? It is a lot less bad, I think: the Judas of John is the least despicable of all, perhaps we can agree on that.

But is the Judas of John better off than the Thomas of John? Thieving Judas versus doubting Thomas, what will it be? When it comes to being a Christian, a thief I think: a bit of confessing, no more thieving, and your slate is clean - although his record can't be expunged. But lacking faith? In the presence of Jesus? Doubting your fellow disciples, even Jesus himself? That's a life sentence, truly

John putting Thomas on stage in the quantity and quality that he does comes more than close to discrediting the Jesus of Thomas by attacking his author "Didymos Judas Thomas", this can't be mistaken for anything else. Explicitly mentioning "Didymos" three times is no coincidence, and it is highly remarkable that Thomas gets more than one mere mention of only his name while standing in line for the presentation of the disciples to the public. Yet elaborate stories like these, on top of that? This a similarly unveiled attack at the author of the text of Thomas as that same text accuses the Pharisees - there is no doubt about that.

If Thomas is being discredited by John here, that means there must be a need to do so, and that need must arise from something. The need must be contemporary to John, and likely to have arisen or crossed the boundary from irrelevant (enough) to relevant (enough), perhaps with an eye on the near future as well.
That something is highly likely to be either support for Thomas from within the Church or even resistance to the Church from Thomas supporters within the Church. That need couldn't have been about quality of that support or resistance but solely about quantity: nothing Thomas said is refuted, his persona is only made unbelievable, incredible - it is a pure ad hominem, meant to damage the image of the author.
When we take a look at dates, that means that around 90-110 CE (the currently believed dating for John's gospel) there was a large enough volume of Thomas supporters within the Church for John to write this gospel. Given the spread of the Thomas verses in John, it is not a mere afterthought but part of his total task. Luke and Matthew are believed to have been written around 80-90 CE, and Mark around 65-73 CE - all dates on the four gospels are from 'Dating the Bible' on Wikipedia, April 8th 2019.
When was the text of Thomas written? That is easy to guess of course, with Mark written in 65 CE at the earliest and the crucifixion pinpointed to around 31 CE with the help of Luke: 40 CE at the very earliest, but more likely to be around 45-55 CE. The gospel-writers must have made sure to place the events of Jesus well before the first appearance of Thomas, of course.
So, some 45 to 55 years after the likely appearance of Thomas, apparently there was such a massive support for Thomas that the Church felt the urgency to address him in one of their gospels, and taint his name.
If that is his name, that is

These are the secret sayings which the living Jesus spoke and which Didymos Judas Thomas wrote down.

These are the cryptic saying that the spiritually alive Jesus spoke and which Judas (the twin) wrote down in Greek and Syriac

The emphasis in italic is my interpretation of that translation. Judas? It says Didymos Judas Thomas - you mean Thomas? No, I think this is a hint at the language copies by the author. Didymos is Greek for twin, Thomas is Aramaic or Classical Syriac for twin - Judas is the only name in there. So it is a text spoken by Jesus that Judas wrote down as twin copies: one in Greek and one in Classical Syriac. The author's name might be Judas the twin, or simply Judas. My interpretation is as such indeed, that the text that we have was published in two languages, and that its author made himself known as Judas; so it probably became known as the words of the Jesus of Judas. That is, at least to the people who were bilingual enough to distinguish the two different words for twin and 'get it'; which in all likelihood was a considerably smaller group than those who would simply read Didymos Judas Thomas and stick with the last word

Judas the traitor, Judas the backstabber, Judas the destroyer of Jesus - for almost two millennia his name has been associated with everything that is despised and no parents in their sane mind name their baby Judas. But that is the public image of Judas, and the last image that the last gospel-writer depicts is incredibly more nuanced: basically, John's Judas was just a bit of a thief and nothing else - you can't hold someone accountable for his deeds while under Satanic possession.
Just as the Church felt and gave in to the need to address the author of the text of Thomas in John, did the Church similarly feel and give in to the need to address the author of the text of Thomas in the three other gospels?
I am deliberately ignoring the whole Iscariot scheme, as long as it's

unknown what 'Iscariot' means or was meant to mean, it is completely content-free and most certainly context-free: Judas Iscariot is just Judas, although not even that is a constant. Luke once calls him 'Judas, who was also called Iscariot' as if it were two single names in stead of one double name. John stresses the fact that he is the son of the previously unknown Simon Iscariot, and John does so four times - what is the purpose of those seemingly trivial details? Does John intend to add warmth and humanity to Judas by pointing to his father, whose first name very coincidentally is identical to that of the best disciple in the world, likely to evoke a positive association? Or is 'Simon Iscariot' merely a more useful pointer to that which 'Judas Iscariot' was intended to refer to? Does Matthew (having Jesus call Judas 'Friend' right after the kissing) perhaps provide a pointer? Was Psalms 41:9 really intended to show that Jesus was betrayed by a 'friend'? It seems such a feeble quote:

(Psalms 41:9 Yes, my own familiar friend, in whom I trusted, who ate bread with me, has lifted up his heel against me.)

John clearly doesn't like Matthew's ideas. He destroys Matthew's alleged Nazarene prophecy by sowing doubt about Jesus being from Galilee. Notwithstanding Matthew's attempt to mitigate the highly illogical baptism of Jesus by implying scripture, John simply doesn't have Jesus baptised at all.
What is John's take on this significant part of the last supper?

*John 13:26 Jesus therefore answered, "It is he to whom I will give this **piece of bread when I have dipped it**." So when **he had dipped the piece of bread**, he gave it to Judas, the son of Simon Iscariot. 27 After the **piece of bread**, then Satan entered into him. Then Jesus said to him, "What you do, do quickly." 28 Now nobody at the table knew why he said this to him. 29 For some thought, because Judas had the money box, that Jesus said to him, "Buy what things we need for the feast," or that he should give something to the poor. 30 **Therefore having received that morsel**, he went out immediately. It* *was night.*

John mentions 'piece of bread' three times, and includes the dipping of it on two occasions. Remarkable - the story could have easily been just as follows: 'Jesus therefore answered, "It is he to whom I will give this piece of bread when I have dipped it." So when he gave it to Judas, the son of Simon Iscariot, (then) Satan entered into him'.

Is John trying to tell us something? On the way out, the piece of bread is brought up again - while using a synonym, 'morsel'. Highly remarkable, highly remarkable indeed.

The original story is told by Mark; what is his depiction of this event?

*Mark 14:18 As they sat and were eating, Jesus said, "Most certainly I tell you, **one of you will betray me-he who eats with me**." 19 They began to be sorrowful, and to ask him one by one, "Surely not I?" And another said, "Surely not I?" 20 He answered them, "It is one of the twelve, **he who dips with me in the dish**.*

Mark shares the eating together and the dipping - the bread is broken two verses later.

As accustomed, Luke sometimes treats major Church events as a careless afterthought. His entire story on Jesus telling the disciples that he's going to be betrayed, hinting at who it will be and how that can be recognised by the bread and the dipping, and then the disciples wondering who it is; all of that is condensed by Luke to:

Luke 22:21 But behold, the hand of him who betrays me is with me on the table.

Luke just doesn't want anything to do with it, period. He left out the kissing as well...

Matthew?

Matthew 26:22 They were exceedingly sorrowful, and each began to *ask him, "It isn't me, is it, Lord?" 23 He answered, "**He who dipped his hand with me in the dish will betray me**. 24 The Son of Man goes even as it is written of him, but woe to that man through whom the Son of Man is betrayed! It would be better for that man if he had not been born." 25 **Judas, who betrayed him, answered, "It isn't me, is it, Rabbi?" He said to him, "You said it**." 26 As they were eating, Jesus took bread, gave thanks for it, and broke it. He gave to the disciples and said, "Take, eat; this is my body."*

Matthew also mentions both the eating together, the bread (implicitly, only 3 verses later is it mentioned), and the dipping (of the hand, alas, but still). And cunningly has Judas "say" that it is him who will betray Jesus, exactly identical to the answer that Jesus gives when asked whether he is king of the Jews - but let's not get sidetracked.

The complete scene has the elements of eating together, and dipping bread - and John explicitly refers to it as a 'morsel'. There is quite a lot of dipping going on in the Tanakh: tunics, hyssop, fingers, living birds even - mostly in blood, and all serve rituals. There is only one scene where food is dipped:

*(Ruth 2:14 **At meal time Boaz said to her, "Come here, and eat some bread, and dip your morsel in the vinegar.**" She sat beside the reapers, and they passed her parched grain. She ate, was satisfied, and left some of it.)*

The context of the book of Ruth with regards to this very scene is about Jews-by-choice, basically. Ruth is a Moabite, a foreigner, a stranger, a heathen, yet is very warmly received by Boaz in the scene above; the only scene in the entire Tanakh where the words 'bread' and 'dip' are in the same verse - likewise for the words 'morsel' and 'dip'. Put extremely concise, Ruth teaches that foreigners who convert to Judaism can become good Jews and that foreign wives can become exemplary followers of Jewish law. Ruth will end up being the great-grandmother of (the) David, so it is likely to have been a familiar scene. Boaz isn't just a wealthy landowner, he is very kind and lets Ruth collect grain from his fields for free, while instructing his servants to keep an eye on her.

Its significance in the gospels? It is used to depict Judas as an outsider, an outlander, a foreigner, a heathen, who nonetheless was wholeheartedly welcomed by Jesus, as a friend: hence the word in Matthew's version, not because that would refer to Psalms:

*(Psalms 41:9 Yes, **my own familiar friend**, in whom I trusted, who ate bread with me, **has lifted up his heel against me**.)*

The lifting up the heel is a metaphor and basically could mean anything - this is the only verse in the entire Tanakh where heels are lifted. But betrayal? The connotation is obviously negative, the image it directly presents to me is what nowadays would be called "doing a runner" - jumping ship, abandoning a situation. When you are running away from me I can see your heel; seeing the sole of your foot could occur on many other occasions, when you're lying on your back, crossing one leg over the other, and so on. It is farfetched that abandoning someone would mean betrayal, just as farfetched that the eating together of the bread - with the dipping being explicitly present in each gospel describing it, even twice in John's - would refer to this psalm, where there is no dipping going on. And of course it is a Matthean prophecy, but that should not come as a surprise: it is so common by now that Matthew makes up scripture or fulfilled prophecies that it's only telling us that there's something significant going on, and that Matthew most likely is trying to justify something that in all likelihood is not true.

If all the dipping and eating of the bread together doesn't point to betrayal, but would imply that Judas is an outsider, a heathen, a foreigner - who gets treated very kindly by a man of might: the message likely is that he should be considered all of the above - then where is the reference to the betrayal? There must be scripture underlying that, such is for sure.

It is in the kissing:

*(Samuel 20:9 **Joab said to Amasa, "Is it well with you, my brother?"***

Joab took Amasa by the beard with his right hand **to kiss him**. *10 But Amasa took no heed to **the sword that was in Joab's hand. So he struck him with it** in the body, and shed out his bowels to the ground, **and didn't strike him again**; and he died. Joab and Abishai his brother pursued Sheba the son of Bichri.)*

Now that is quite a scene - isn't it? Impressive, extreme, vile; so utterly ugly that it is almost beautiful, in a sense - beautifully ugly. Joab certainly is not a nobody, he is a son of the sister of David. When Joab's brother gets killed in a fair fight, Joab murders his killer while pretending to want a quiet chat with him, against the wish of David. Against the wish of David, Joab kills David's son Absalom: Absalom gets stuck with his head in a tree, and is hanging there defenceless; Joab thrusts three darts in his heart, just like that. When David replaces Joab as commander of his troops with Amasa, Joab kills him - this is that scene right here. When David is to be followed up by his son and promised king Solomon, Joab sides with his eldest brother in stead. Joab is the prototype of the betrayer, and a vicious and vile killer at that.
And that is the pointer to Judas, when he kisses Jesus: he personifies Joab, the traitor of traitors. Vicious, vile and ruthless. There are 36 verses in the Tanakh where a kiss is mentioned, and usually there is weeping and embracing going along with it, next to blessing. There is only one violent scene with a kiss in it, and this is it: the utmost despicable act of Joab, traitor of all traitors.

Mark has both pointers (the friendly pointer to Ruth and the extremely unfriendly pointer to Joab) and so does Matthew. Luke has none and John only has the (remarkably elaborate) pointer to Ruth, although Luke does mention the intention of kissing but doesn't act it out. I am truly puzzled what to do with the unfulfilled act of kissing in Luke - it once more raises the question about actually which league Luke was playing in: he most certainly was addressing the Thomas believers, given his overwhelming focus on the literal Thomas material. In the light of that it makes sense that he doesn't want to label Thomas a heathen foreigner seeking to voluntarily join the new religion like Ruth did; and Luke certainly wouldn't want to label Thomas a traitor in front of his audience. My guess is that Luke did the best he could; not having Judas actually kiss Jesus was enough for him to "prove" that Judas wasn't a traitor - he perhaps wasn't as brave and bold as John who simply dropped the entire kissing scene completely. Yet that same brave and bold John didn't dare to drop the baptism scene, and did exactly with the baptism of Jesus what Luke did with the kiss of Judas: sketch the scenery, enact the scene, but just don't let it actually happen - and no one will ever notice

Back to Matthew who brought us here, unveiling the true scene behind the starting event of the last supper: is his 'Friend' exclamation by Jesus meant to be sincere or sarcastic? It couldn't possibly be sarcastic, even though the Jesus of Matthew is so full of darkness, compared to the others

*Matthew 26:49 Immediately he came to Jesus, and said, "**Greetings, Rabbi!" and kissed him**. 50 **Jesus said to him, "Friend**, why are you here?" Then they came and laid hands on Jesus, and took him.*

Matthew must be intending to somehow mitigate the role of Judas with this verse, it is almost a happy scene with the inappropriate, almost adolescent salute of Judas - is Jesus pretending to be Boaz here, friendly as always? And is Judas personifying the shy Ruth with his greeting? Is the Jesus of Matthew saying "It's alright my friend", in stead of "I knew it, it was written in Psalms all along, my 'friend'"? I can only guess and will dig no further

My findings are clear, and I think that they are more than plausible: the starting scene of the last supper, with its dipping of bread (or hand), refers to Boaz and Ruth eating together and dipping bread. Its significance to the gospels is that, completely identical to Boaz and Ruth, Jesus is kindly and wholeheartedly welcoming the foreign and heathen Judas who is voluntarily seeking to join a new religion, and Jesus stresses that very fact right before he announces that

Judas will betray him.

Judas kissing Jesus is a direct reference to Joab kissing Amasa, and its significance to the gospels is to portray and depict Judas as the most vicious, vile, ruthless, treacherous traitor of traitors.

Judas betraying Jesus isn't predicted or prophesied anywhere, and the explicit mention of 'Friend' by Matthew, even directly after Judas has kissed him, highly likely only serves as a pointer to the dining scene. Matthew reaffirms that - even then! - Jesus is still kindly and wholeheartedly welcoming Judas; and that, exactly that, is what breaks Judas' heart when he sees Jesus condemned, and it has him throw the money in front of the priests and hang himself. Why all this fuss about Judas?

Judas is meant to personify the author of the text of Thomas in all four gospels, just as Thomas is meant to personify the author of the text of Thomas - only in the gospel of John. The author's "full name" was Didymos Judas Thomas, and would have become known to Aramaic speaking people as Judas (the twin), and to Greek speaking people as (Didymos) Thomas.

The text of Thomas likely spread first among people speaking Aramaic, (decades) after which it also became known among people speaking Greek. For some reason, the most likely being fierce (enough) resistance, the role of Judas was gradually downplayed by the Church.

Where Mark portrayes him as a heathen foreigner (using the dipping of the bread) as well as a traitor (by having Judas kiss Jesus), Luke has none of those two events and merely suggests the kissing without actually letting it happen. To downplay the role of Judas even further because Luke's task was to address the Thomas supporters among the Christians, he even invents Judas being possessed by Satan. Matthew entirely sticks to Mark but mitigates Judas betraying Jesus by having Jesus refer to the dipping of the bread scene right after Judas kisses him, reinforcing the image that he still welcomes Judas as a friend. John mitigates it all even further by also having Judas possessed, and then putting so much emphasis on the dipping as well as the bread that the entire scene almost collapses under its weight, and tops it off by going even further than Luke did: the word 'kiss' doesn't even exist in the gospel of John

The Thomas of John is proof that the Church doesn't shy away from discrediting the author of the text of Thomas and is more than willing to invest more than a few verses on that. Then why wouldn't they do so 30-40 years earlier? They'd have to be extremely carefully with doing so, because it would give away that the text of Thomas existed before the first gospel was written - and that they very well knew it, and considered it a great enough threat to address it.
And that could mean only one thing.
And so it does

I'll admit that Judas being supposed to be addressed as the author of the text of Thomas might not be my strongest case; nonetheless it is beyond a doubt that the character of Judas went on a rollercoaster ride, yet still ended up tainted for life - a fate that he shares with only one other actor from the gospels: Thomas, also known as Didymos

Penultimate: dialogue and debate, truths and opinions

A text is content; it is perfectly happy by itself, and of itself. All the context it needs is contained within its content; anything we add, we do so solely at our own risk. An interpretation of a text can never be valued higher than the text itself; if one were to do so, he would be obliged to extend the same courtesy to everyone else, and any dialogue would quickly turn into a debate, where majority - or is that mob - rule would determine the indecisive outcome. If interpretation were commonly accepted as a means to value a text, there would be neither heresy nor orthodoxy; viewing something as heresy would simply be contested with a wrong interpretation of a text, labelling the interpreter as heretic because his determination of the text as heresy reflects back solely on his interpretation and thus himself.

Let's consider a sample text. It is rather short, and contains only the word 'black':

Black.

That is the entire text: one word. Next unfolds a scene between two persons, A and B:

A: "I love this text, it is unlike anything else. It is so succinct, riddling, and it so clearly expresses the yang of everything, the dark side: black".

B: "Hahah, do you really think so? The author is a cunning man, playing with your perceptions. Of course he wrote 'black', just to mislead you. It is beyond the slightest doubt that he means something else with it - not just something else, but quite the opposite: 'white'. He purposely uses the word 'black', not to put the focus on 'black', but on its counterpart: 'white'.

A: "Oh come on, you must be joking. Had he wanted to write 'white', he easily could have: it is his own text! It says 'black', so 'black' it is - and nothing else". B: "You just don't understand the deeper meaning behind this word, the entire text: an acquaintance of mine made the same error. Now why would he have constructed such a simple notion, with the focus of the entire text being on this one word? It would be very mundane to write 'white' if one indeed were to mean 'white', and there would be no point to be made, no deeper mystery behind it - it wouldn't convey a message like it does. People who are in the know perceive the beauty of this baffling wonder, exactly like Magritte made the painting of the pipe, describing it in text with 'Ceci n'est pas un pipe' - you don't hear anyone claim that Magritte actually meant to say that the pipe isn't a pipe, do you?!"

And so on - the hostile debate could go on for many pages. There is another example just like that, with a similar unfolding but a different reasoning:

A: "I love this text, it is unlike anything else. It is so succinct, riddling, and it so clearly expresses the yang of everything, the dark side: black".
B: "The text you have is a fake, a fraud. Unfortunately, it still exists although it should have been destroyed long ago. Some label it as a scribal error but it is obvious that it has been purposely changed into 'black' from 'white' in order to serve the scribe's goal. The great historian Palavrus famously lost his temper when commenting on it: 'An atrocity, simply a crime against mankind' he labelled it. And it is, really, a brutal edit by a devious scribe, intentionally misleading people with his vile tampering with the text".
A: "Really? Then the sun perhaps also is a fraud, pretending that it is a source of energy providing us with light, while in fact it is a black hole merely giving us the impression that it is a sun, right? You have not a shred of evidence for your pathetic claims other than that some idiot called Palavrus dared to voice his false claim centuries ago - the very prototype of a vile attempt, solely intended to mislead people"

And so on - see what I'm doing here? A conversation quickly turns to debate, skipping the stage of dialogue. A loses his temper because B states his opinion as truth, overruling the common truth that is visible to both; there now are two truths, and the least obvious one is elevated to The Truth - and the one adhering the common, most obvious truth is labelled as ignorant, a fool. B implies that he himself is right about the truth, and that A is wrong - and that is impossible to digest.

It should never be about who is right and who is wrong - we all view the world from within our own worlds and are always right because we all have our own truths: whatever you believe becomes true to you, as simple as that. Truth must not be confused with reality of course: you can firmly believe you can fly, and as long as you don't put that to the test you will be just fine.

Truths are nothing more than mutual agreements made by individuals in groups; from the beginning of times it was just as true for the average human that the earth was flat as it now holds true that it is round, yet the earth still doesn't care what we think of it, and never will. If one had stated back then that the earth was round one would be ridiculed, laughed at, maybe even hurt or worse. Whenever you are in a church, don't be surprised that it is absolutely true that there will be a Judgment Day and an afterlife, provided by God and likely facilitated by Jesus. Don't be surprised when you are at an atheist convention and it is absolutely true that there is none of those things.

These two truths can coexist and both hold true (as long as the twain don't meet under regular circumstances), simply because we can't put them to the test - we don't know for sure what reality is like, unlike the reality of the earth. We believe these truths in large enough numbers and that's the only reason how and why - and where - they become truths and stay true, as long as you're in the right group. You will be laughed at and ridiculed when you're the only atheist in a church, and maybe you'll even get pushed around a bit. You will be laughed at and ridiculed when you're the only Christian at an atheist convention, and maybe you'll even get pushed around a bit.

Truths are made by people - without people truths wouldn't exist. We people are addicted to truths, in general; we force each other to adhere to truths, pick either black or white; if one dares to stand in the grey area in between we accuse that person of being indecisive, a turncoat, someone who cannot make up his or her mind. Truths divide all, and only unite those who share the same version of it.

The less knowledge you have the easier it is to stay out of that grey area: for instance the earth isn't perfectly round but it's elliptic; the diameter at the equator is 43 kilometres larger than the pole-to-pole diameter. Does that matter? That is entirely and solely influenced by your involvement - if you are concerned with planetary movement involving the earth then it is an extremely significant detail

On this earth 150,000 people die every day; over one hundred people die every single minute. Does anyone care about that? No. Yet we do care if a few dozen die in a plane crash or a bombing, a few hundred or thousand in an earthquake or tsunami - insignificant, trivial numbers compared to the one million people that die every week. Why do we care? Firstly because we know, secondly because it's one of our truths that we should care - and that's all there is to it. It is not a truth that we are not supposed to care about those deaths, and it certainly isn't a truth that we are supposed to not care - there simply isn't a common truth about it at all.

If you did not know about that certain tsunami, that's okay - but the minute you do, you're expected to form and voice an opinion about it, and pick either side of the truth on that very subject; and you'd be better off stating that you don't care rather than saying that you don't know whether you do care or don't

Truths are not about content, they are about context. Dialogue is about content, debate is about context. How different could those two conversations have been:

A: "I love this text, it is unlike anything else. It is so succinct, riddling, and it so clearly expresses the yang of everything, the dark side: black".

B: "It does say 'black', such is true and beyond a doubt. But I'm rather fond of the opinion that the author is a cunning man, playing with your perceptions - in fact, I'm convinced that such is the case: it has become true to me. He wrote 'black' just to mislead you. It think he means something else with it - not just something else, but quite the opposite: 'white'. He purposely uses the word 'black', not to put the focus on 'black', but on its counterpart: 'white'.

A: "That's a quite unconventional point of view, but an interesting idea. Where did you get that from, and why would he have done such a thing?"

B: "It's just a brain bug of mine, really. There's a deeper meaning behind this word, the entire text: why would he have constructed such a simple notion, with the focus of the entire text being on this one word? It would be very mundane to write 'white' if one indeed were to mean 'white', and there would be no point to be made, no deeper mystery behind it - it wouldn't convey a message. I think this is exactly like Magritte who made the painting of the pipe, describing it in text with 'Ceci n'est pas un pipe'"

Mutual understanding and agreement. Acknowledgement of what the other person says. A clear distinction between truths and opinions - and a complete absence of "anger words". What is the result? Not division, but union: the idea of B now coexists with the idea of A. Dialogue, not debate

As simple as that? Basically, yes.
Then why don't we all do that and live in harmony, with the worst outcome of a conversation being that we agree to disagree? Because most don't perceive that our truths are opinions, and that we have no idea whether they're reality - we never took the time to check either notion. When our truths get threatened we start to doubt them ourselves, and we feel offended by that doubt that we inflict upon ourselves because we are not supposed to be doubting;

one of our truths is that we have to stick to our truths, lest we are labelled indecisive, a turncoat. The result is that we get angry because we perceive ourselves to have become doubtful, and that anger gets directed towards the apparent cause: the place whence the last external action took place.

Putting a finger on a sore spot, is what that is: I put my finger on your sore spot, and you feel the pain. You associate the pain with me, and direct your reactions to me. But it is your pain, and it is directly linked to your sore spot - it's all yours, and entirely yours alone. I'm not causing your pain, your own sore spot is.

Yes I touched your sore spot, but whether that was done intentionally or on purpose is, primarily, irrelevant. The reality is not that I cause your pain, although most people perceive exactly that to be the truth; the reality is that your spot causes your pain, and that I directed attention to your spot. You associate your last internal emotion with the last external action, and react accordingly; my touch, your pain: I caused you pain.

"I hate it when you say that! It reminds me of my little brother who died way too early, and that is a tragic event that hurts me deeply, always bringing immediate tears to my eyes".

"I hate you! Look at how you're hurting me, can't you see I'm crying?!".

Two truths, each equally true - of course. One leaves room for dialogue, one opens the door to debate. Both describe reality, but one of them does so with a lot more detail: does that matter? Only to those involved: those who already are, and those who want to become so

What remains is the matter of right or wrong. Another one of our unfortunately unchallenged truths is that the world is (to be) divided into right and wrong: right is good and wrong is bad, good feels good and bad feels bad - such is our programming. A related truth is that hurting someone intentionally is bad, and hurting someone accidentally is good - if we stick to only those two absolute qualifications. We never questioned that truth either, but we are programmed accordingly: if it is obvious to me that you intentionally hurt me then I (am allowed, or even supposed to) get angry and blame you for that hurt. If it is obvious to me that you accidentally hurt me then I say "It's okay, you didn't mean to"; the original result and pain remains unchanged, but it is a truth that I am now not entitled to become angry at you or blame you. Does becoming angry at you, or not, diminish the original pain? Not at all, that pain has been inflicted already, prior to the question of anger being justified or not - and blaming follows that same road of reasoning. Blaming you will not influence the pain that has been already inflicted, in the past; blaming you will only influence my future actions.

Then what is the use of settling the matter of intentionality, what is its goal, its purpose, its effect? Its only purpose seems to manifest itself when we reflect on the event, when we call it back to memory: when we touch that sore spot, that wound, that trauma - τραύμα is the Greek word for wound. When we put our own finger on our own sore spot, we call the image back to life that we stored in our brain; we don't recall the event nor bring that back to life, we just interact with ourselves, in ourselves; nothing of that affects reality outside of ourselves - it only affects our own truths. When the label of intentionality is affixed to the image recalled, we feel entitled to derive more hurt and anger from that image, that solidified memory, than when it isn't.

When we touch our own wounds and evaluate our pain, the primary sole effect of judging about and deciding on intentionality is whether or not to inflict more pain upon ourselves.

When we derive that extra hurt and anger from our pain, we immediately feel it, and it becomes real to us. We subconsciously evaluate the process we just went through, decide that we followed the right road of reasoning and thus did the right thing, and justify to ourselves that the outcome is also right: and we then add that new truth to our truths.

None of that affects anyone outside us, anything outside our brain: it all happens in our brain and nowhere else. The extra hurt and anger only exists in our brain and gets stored inside ourselves, and nowhere else - at that very point when we think about actions that lie in the past. And which action doesn't?

There is (only) one perfectly sane reason for the use of determining intentionality, but that only applies to the future, not the present nor the past. If someone did something on purpose then the chances are much higher that it might occur another time than when it was done accidentally. There is a lesson to be learned in both cases, the need for which arises out of the natural need of self-protection, and the two extreme outcomes of that learned lesson vary from being on extreme alert to being completely not alert - for a repetition of the event, in the future

Feel free to feel hurt by anything; that is everyone's "right" and the pain is real - in your mind, but that doesn't make it less real for you. However, it is your responsibility to handle the truths that come into being after the pain has been inflicted: are those truths yours, or others', or both? Most of the time, the truths that we have are our truths, not others' - when we drill down to the finest level of detail. The more casually and superficially we observe a truth, the greater the chance that it is also a truth of someone else, or even a common truth. Yet the truths that we struggle with often, if not always, get nitpicked by us down to the atomic level and beyond - we consider every single smallest detail of it.

The more detailed something is observed, the higher the chance of mismatching truths - that is a reality for all. As demonstrated earlier, the higher your involvement in something, the more important details become; and that is why you are so incredibly more likely to disagree about something that you care about, than about something you don't care about

A convinced atheist can be the best of friends with a deeply religious person, they can even live together and love one another - as long as they don't want to impose their truths onto one another that are not part of their common truths. They will disagree about everything when they discuss religion because their involvement in religion is very high, and as such the level of detail will be very high - they really care about religion. The deeply religious person also cares for religion, but both care about it.

The chance that people will disagree is exactly proportional to the level of their involvement in something

It is my truth that the gospel-writers copied Thomas, and given my level of involvement at this very moment of writing this, it is safe to label it as a Truth for me. Is it real, a Reality? Only in my brain, at best - but I most certainly wouldn't label it as such, as it is just my opinion and nothing more, or less.

Will I feel hurt if you don't share that opinion, my truth on this subject? No, not at all, but I might feel hurt when you laugh at me or ridicule me, because you'll then likely be touching a sore spot of mine - which is something else entirely and won't affect my truth on this.

Dialogue might affect my truth on this, shaping it into a common truth perhaps - I would really appreciate that, and I wholeheartedly welcome it.

Will you feel hurt because of my opinion, my truth? That can only occur when it's not your truth, and when it threatens that truth and touches a sore spot

Conclusion

After some 85,000 gospel-writers' words, a few things are crystal-clear. Some others are still obscure, and the rest is in between. And some are fiction, some are facts, and some are in between.
The following facts are crystal-clear:

There is a distinctly visible process of evolvement and growth between the first and the last gospel-writer with regards to content and context of Thomas material; usually subtle differences and improvements are made by each gospel-writer upon creating their own version of it.
The first gospel-writer usually suffers the pioneer's fate, adding elaborations and explanations to the usually very concise text of Thomas. Sometimes extra content is added that relates to scripture, making the result even larger and longer.
The next or last gospel-writer usually fixes errors that were introduced, and will move around a few words.
The content of Luke shows the greatest resemblance to the material of Thomas by far, and Matthew has a very strong preference for inserting admonitions to his proverbial theme of "weeping and gnashing of teeth"

All parables in the text of Thomas follow a strict five element structure: every element is explicitly named. The parable has a subject, and a distinguishing property which forms the begin state of the parable. There is an action and condition which, if fulfilled, will transform the begin state of the subject to an end state - and that end state will generate a spin-off, a result.
The action is the absolute essence of the parables of Thomas: the falling on good soil in the parable of the sower; the falling on tilled soil in the parable of the mustard seed; the sending of servants in the parable of the vineyard.
Every Thomas parable has allegory and makes rich use of (in)animate objects: those objects play an important role and are never there just as stage props. The net is cast into the sea and

drawn up full of fish and acts along until the end; the sword is thrust into a wall and reveals the secret; the fruit patiently awaits its collection, albeit in vain

The Thomas parables in the gospels didn't survive the act of copying: of only one out of thirteen did all five elements remain intact.
There are parables in the gospels that are not in Thomas, just a bit more than those that are. All parables not in the text of Thomas don't have such a strict structure, only two out of fifteen do: what most have in common is that they are mundane stories that compare good to bad.
The vast majority of the gospel-writers' narratives are lengthy stories filled with humans interacting and dialoguing with other humans, and they are devoid of allegory. Very few objects are deployed, and none of those objects serve any purpose: the vineyard of the labourers might as well have been a scrap yard, the coins of the 'ten coins' just pebbles, the lamps of the virgins just lunch bags - none contribute anything to the story

The next deals with the unclear, and is neither fiction nor fact - but a legitimate question without an answer. Given opportunity, motive and means, who is likely to have copied whom?

Did Thomas copy the parables from the gospel-writers or vice versa? These are the only known two sources containing them so it must be either-or.
It seems almost impossible for Thomas to have copied the gospel-writers. With even John having some material in common with Thomas it would mean that Thomas would have had to go through all 85,000 gospel-writers' words in order to have the complete material at his disposal. The first century CE did not have an ample supply of readily available complete bibles as we have today, and prolonged access to such material would have been difficult.
What would Thomas' goal be, what would his motive be? He is certainly not presenting his Jesus as a religious person and his

"movement", if any, consists solely of self-orientation and introspection. That can be monetised today, as the various self-help sections in bookstores and libraries prove, but wasn't a known market back then, although there had been various "schools of thought" since 500 BCE. What would his point be in copying the Church Jesus if he didn't apply that to a religion himself? He doesn't have anything on Jesus' death nor any link to any prophecy - there's not a shred of a Messiah in his story. If he intended to profit from the popularity of Jesus, then why is his Jesus so completely different?

Did Thomas have the means to copy the gospel-writers? Looking at only his parables, how feasible is it that he managed to consider all twenty-eight parables and stories and select the thirteen that he would have? Could he have turned them all into his own parables according to his strict five element structure of explicitly named subject, begin state, action, end state and result? And removing all the moralistic messages and the central theme of "beware of Judgment Day; repent or else"?

Spotting, for instance, that the parable of the mustard seed would become a true Thomas parable if a proper action and condition were added to it, maybe something like "falling on tilled soil"? Spotting that the parable of the vineyard consisted of two parts and that it would be a perfect idea to separate the corner stone sentences and turn the two into a parable and a separate logion, and have that logion immediately follow the parable? Why wouldn't he just have thrown it away or at least moved it to some inconspicuous place?

If he had copied thirteen of his sixteen parables from the gospel-writers, wouldn't he have deemed it fit to make up a few extra ones so it would be less obvious that he did base almost all of his parables on the gospels?

Would Thomas have had the incredible form of organisation, management and knowledge to put together logia that were spread across multiple chapters or even gospels, yet could be used together because they shared a common theme? For instance combining the two masters with the old and new wine, which are separated by 10 chapters in both Luke and Matthew? Or piecing together the women (not) nursing children with the woman praising the womb that bore Jesus, 12 chapters apart in Luke? And how about taking logion 39a from Luke 11:52, the only place in the gospels where the key(s) of knowledge appears, and combining that with logion 39c from Matthew 10:16, the only place where the serpents and doves are mentioned?

It is perfectly feasible that the gospel-writers copied Thomas:
It is evident and beyond a doubt that the words of Thomas came to the attention of the Church and there are dozens of Church books from the first centuries CE testifying to that. A bit over 5,000 words, it was easy to digest and very small compared to the gospels that the gospel-writers evidently and beyond a doubt did process in order to write their own gospel.
What would their motive be? It is evident that the church very much disliked the words of Thomas, labelling them as heresy, and dozens of Church books written spread that message in the first centuries CE. Was the Church intent on refuting the words of Thomas even at the time of John being written? Undeniably so. It is also a testimony to the size of the impact of the words of Thomas; if one makes it on the heresy list of the Church one must be enough of a nuisance.
Did the gospel-writers have the means to copy Thomas? Selectively quoting those parts they could use, or copy word for word yet slightly change words, or combine both strategies? Splitting logia and using different parts in different places to serve different purposes? It is beyond a doubt that it could have happened that way - whether it did or didn't is something else entirely

Thomas and the gospel-writers don't only share parables, they also share themes: making the two one, children entering the kingdom. And they also share the criticism of Judaic customs such as fasting, giving alms and praying - with a few significant differences.
The following are undisputable facts:
Where Thomas rejects praying, fasting and giving alms as a whole,

and accuses only the Pharisees of misleading the people and knowingly hiding the truth from them, the gospel-writers combine both themes and accuse the Pharisees of being hypocrites and using praying, fasting and giving alms to pretend that they are righteous. The gospel-writers embrace the acts of praying, fasting and giving alms in general.

The children who enter the kingdom is a central theme in Thomas and it doesn't get clarified at all how and why that would be the case. The gospel-writers ever so slowly elaborate on it until Matthew suddenly comes up with the argument of alleged inherent humility for being the reason why children would enter the kingdom; then John completes and ends the theme with his 'born anew'.

Making the two one is another crucial and central theme in Thomas, and it doesn't become quite clear what he means by that; he even speaks of one becoming two. The gospel-writers have good context there: a pointer to Genesis and God making the one two, and Mark suggests that he did so in order for those two to become one again in matrimony. Matthew - again it's Matthew - takes that a whole lot further when merely repeating Mark's words, and puts words in God's mouth that clearly and unequivocally belong to the writer of Genesis alone; then John introduces becoming one to Christ and God

So what could be deduced from those facts? Some other facts for starters: Thomas doesn't explain a single parable, doesn't explain or clarify at all how and why children would enter the kingdom, doesn't explain or clarify at all how the two would become one; the gospel-writers explain a lot of parables, explain why the children would enter the kingdom, explain why and even how the two could become one.

Based upon those recapitulated facts, what could be reasoned? Plausibility concerning the way in which one would be most likely to be successful when copying other people's work and claiming it as his own.

How plausible is it that Thomas would take parables from the gospels, explained as they are, and twist and turn them into his own - while making them even more cryptic than they were? That would decrease their level of legibility and intelligibility, and certainly not increase their likely acceptance. How credible is it that on top of that Thomas would not copy the explanation parts in part or in whole, nor change them, but drop all of them entirely? It would be guaranteed that such would lead to a highly mystic and cryptic piece of text that is guaranteed to meet with much resistance: Jesus certainly didn't speak those parables, Jesus surely didn't speak parables that were that cryptic, Jesus certainly didn't never (sic) explain even a single parable - it would severely weaken and conceivably even cripple Thomas' case. The very least Thomas could and should have done is undermine the explanation of the gospel-writers.

How plausible is it that Thomas would take the theme of children entering the kingdom from the gospels and elaborate on it as much as he did? Without addressing the disciples or anyone else as "child(ren)" at all? Without explaining why children would enter the kingdom? That would weaken his case considerably - Jesus didn't say all that about children entering the kingdom, Jesus told why children will enter the kingdom, Jesus explained exactly how we can enter the kingdom as children. The very least Thomas could and should have done is undermine the explanation of the gospel-writers.

How plausible is it that Thomas would take the theme of making the two one from the gospels - if he had recognised the few lines of text as such - and turned it into the very grand theme that it is in his text? Without explaining how the two would become one? That would confuse everyone who knew the gospels: Jesus never said all that, Jesus only said that God made the one two so that they can be made one again through marriage, and that you become one with God and Jesus and all other believers if you just believe in Jesus. The very least Thomas could and should have done is undermine the explanation of the gospel-writers.

Looking at it from the other side, the gospel-writers copying Thomas - regardless of the question whether there ever was a living

Jesus alive or not. How plausible is it that the gospel-writers would copy almost all of the parables of Thomas, twist and turn them into their own, making most of them less cryptic by splitting them or adding more detail, extra storylines even?

How plausible is it that they would slap on just a bit more of their own parables in order to obfuscate the fact that the others originated from Thomas? How credible is it that they would add a much needed explanation to them given their cryptic nature, thereby even further fixating their grasp on them? That would really strengthen their case in every aspect, to take away any room for interpretation of the parables - and it would greatly limit the need for people to go elsewhere; only few ask questions when most if not all answers are already given.

How plausible is it that the gospel-writers would take the theme of children entering the kingdom from Thomas and desperately try to breathe life into it given the total lack of clarity in Thomas? That they for instance would try to address the disciples or anyone else as "child(ren)", familiar as they were with referring to grown ups as children given the 668 occurrences of the phrase 'children of Israel' in the Tanakh which obviously refers to the people of Israel, the Jews. That they would try to explain why children would enter the kingdom? That would strengthen their case considerably, presumed that that case still is to claim that their Jesus is the real Jesus, not the Jesus of Thomas - with an explanation and even instruction about how one could enter the kingdom like a child, they would provide an answer where Thomas only evokes questions.

How plausible is it that the gospel-writers would take the theme of making the two one from Thomas - easily recognisable as a very grand theme in his text and impossible to neglect? And explain not only how the two would become one, but also how and why the one became two? That would confuse everyone who knew Thomas: they would provide an answer where Thomas merely evokes questions

Following are facts about the names of some actors in the gospels. Where ever they are not facts, the word 'likely' is used

Jesus of Nazareth? The last name was likely misread and derived from the prophecy of Samson's conception and birth, who was to be a Nazirite (meaning: consecrated, separated); Samson's birth was foretold to his barren and childless mother by an angel: 'the child shall be a Nazirite to God from the womb. He shall begin to save Israel out of the hand of the Philistines'. Not a true prophecy but a prediction, yet not about Jesus - and already fulfilled by Samson himself.

That prophecy was likely conflated with a properly read, yet also already fulfilled, prophecy from Isaiah: God spoke to Ahaz the son of Jotham: 'Behold, the virgin will conceive, and bear a son, and shall call his name Immanuel.'

Immanuel? Jesus, not Immanuel, was the name of the main character in the text of Thomas - not a real person, for all we know, but well known for his detest of the entire concept of religion.
So in order to be able to adopt the text of Thomas that Isaiah prophecy likely was adapted: the gospel-writers have an angel appear to Mary (in Luke's gospel) and Joseph (in Matthew's gospel) instructing to name the baby Jesus (in Luke's gospel) and Immanuel (in Matthew's gospel, upon which Joseph names the baby Jesus)

John the Baptist? Just a name in that same text of Thomas, mentioned only once. From the very beginning John is portrayed by the gospel-writers as the incarnation of Elijah; in fact there are more verses about John and Elijah than about John doing his (extremely non-descript) baptism thing. Like Jesus, John is a name that appears nowhere in the Tanakh. And like Jesus, an angel instructs his parent(s) to give him a different name than one would expect.
John not only is the most important prophet of Christianity but also the only one, and the sole prophet in the entire history of Judaism as well as Christianity to be actually alive during the coming of a Messiah. However, John conveniently gets quickly killed by Herod Antipas - likely to fulfil a "prophecy" about Elijah himself that was

interpreted incorrectly - so that Elijah can play his utterly silent role in the Transfiguration, in order to fulfil a true Malachi prophecy about the Messiah being preceded by Elijah

Judas? The actual name of the author ("Didymos Judas Thomas") of the text of Thomas, a riddle only intelligible to those who were well versed in Greek (where Didymos means twin) as well as (Aramaic or) Classical Syriac (where Thomas means twin): twin copies of the text of Thomas likely originally existed, one in Greek and one in Classical Syriac. The words were lost for almost 2,000 years, yet now they likely will never die.
Judas is scapegoated right from the beginning by Mark and betrays Jesus with a kiss. Luke omits the kiss but has him be possessed by Satan, and Matthew leaves out that last apparently minor detail just like Mark did but adds that Judas haggles his price to be 30 silver pieces (likely only in order to incorrectly interpret two other prophecies) and after his deed shows remorse, giving back the money and hanging himself. John mentions none of Matthew's inventions but shows that Judas is a thief; he has Jesus explicitly trigger Judas' possession and leaves out the reward, the kiss - basically everything that has been attributed to Judas by all during the creation of the gospels. From a kissing traitor possibly only driven by financial greed, Judas becomes an innocent puppet in the hands of God yet will always be remembered as Judas the traitor, tainted for life

Thomas? The name by which the author of the text of Thomas likely came to be known to most, likely only decades after it first appeared - and still the name by which it is known now.
Thomas is mentioned only once in each gospel of Mark, Luke and Matthew when the disciples are presented, yet suddenly gets thrown into the spotlights by John who names him "Thomas called Didymos", thereby directly pointing to the text of Thomas. John's lengthy script for Thomas consists of him acting out misunderstanding, ignorance and unbelief, and in John's final act Thomas gets put on the stage with the result and likely only intent

of being utterly ignored, silently witnessing how Jesus transfers his power to Simon Peter. From a completely anonymous and inactive disciple Thomas becomes an unwilling stage prop, the prototype of the nonbeliever: doubting Thomas, tainted for life

Simon Peter? Yet another name in that very same text of Thomas again. One of only three persons deemed worthy to tell Jesus whom he is like, and likely casted for his leading role in the gospels because he answered "You are like a righteous angel"

Finally, I would like to stress some peculiarities. It is crystal-clear that Mark wrote Church history and left his fellow gospel-writers with a legacy - a forced heirship that they couldn't refuse.
Mark declared all foods clean, Matthew changed that to not having to wash your hands before eating.
Mark said that God instructed man to make the two one, Matthew put those words in God's mouth so it actually seems as if God did do what Mark claimed.
Mark had Jesus baptised, which didn't make sense because baptism was for repentance of sins and Jesus naturally had never sinned. Matthew reluctantly has Jesus baptised, John simply refuses to do so.
Mark creates the starting scene of the last supper with Jesus referring to Judas dipping his bread with Jesus, in order to refer to scripture and thus depict Judas as a heathen foreigner willing to join the new religion, kindly and wholeheartedly welcomed by Jesus. Luke completely refuses to support that idea, Matthew stresses it even after Jesus has been kissed by Judas, John more than fully embraces that idea.
Mark creates the kissing scene when Judas betrays Jesus, in order to refer to scripture and thus depict Judas as the most vicious, vile, ruthless, treacherous traitor of all traitors. Luke refuses to support that idea and copies the scene without the actual kiss, Matthew turns it into a friendly scene, and John completely refuses to support the idea.
Judas, as well as Thomas, is supposed to personify the author of the

text of Thomas, Didymos Judas Thomas. From the very start of the gospels, it was known that the text of Thomas existed, and its author fiercely discredited

So much for that. After more than 125,000 words I will rest my case. More or even all prophecies could be explored in detail, given the extreme flexibility witnessed in the interpretation of those I just happened to stumble upon during the study of the logia of Thomas in the gospels - but I have seen more than enough. More or even all books of the New Testament could be studied in order to try to shed more light on the evolution of the material from Thomas - but it would only be yet more hearsay and make belief (sic): that is one of the central messages of the Church throughout the gospels; simply hear and accept the word.

To be honest and quite frank, at times it was disheartening and unpleasant to go through every single word of the gospel-writers. Raised as a Roman Catholic I was far from unfamiliar with Jesus, the Church and their (contradicting) messages, but I've never had a look at scripture that was this close, broad and extensive. I actually feel quite relieved to be writing these final words, closing the book on an idea that popped up as a vague notion ten years ago; ever since I started looking into it I have become increasingly occupied with it and the end sprint has been exhausting

My penultimate, the prelude to this conclusion, has a very particular goal. That goal most certainly is not that everyone can go around hurting people because that would only be touching their wounds which would be entirely their problem to address in splendid isolation - that is most definitely not the case.

The goal is to strive for dialogue, and look for common truths.

I find it very hard to imagine that there's not anything in Jesus that doesn't appeal to most if not all. The forgiving Jesus of the Church, the Jesus who listens, the Jesus who loves. The inquisitive Jesus of Thomas, the Jesus who tells us that we're from the light, the Jesus who tells us to shine neither will they say, 'Look, here!' or, 'Look, there!' for behold, God's Kingdom is within you."

You see the mote in your brother's eye, but you do not see the beam in your own eye.
When you cast the beam out of your own eye, then you will see clearly to cast the mote from your brother's eye

Jesus said, "Love your brother like your soul, guard him like the pupil of your eye."